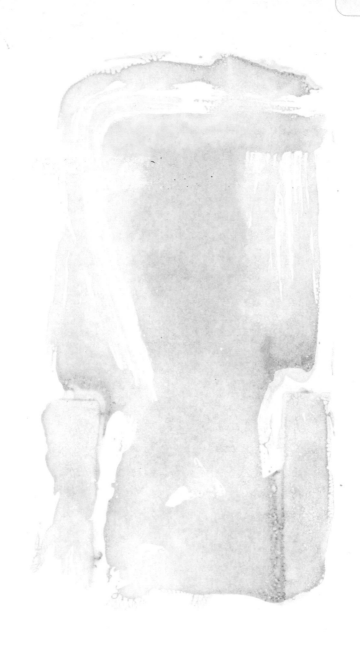

A
Reader's
Guide to
Contemporary
History

A
Reader's
Guide to
Contemporary
History

Edited by
Bernard Krikler
and Walter Laqueur

Quadrangle Books
Chicago

A READER'S GUIDE TO CONTEMPORARY HISTORY
Copyright © 1972 by Bernard Krikler and Walter Laqueur
All rights reserved, including the right to
reproduce this book or portions thereof in any form.
For information, address: Quadrangle Books Inc.,
12 East Delaware Place, Chicago 60611.

FIRST AMERICAN EDITION

First published in England by
George Weidenfeld & Nicolson Ltd., London

Printed in England.

Library of Congress Catalog Card Number: 72-75849
International Standard Book Number: 0-8129-0255-6

Contents

Contributors

DENNIS AUSTIN is Professor of Government in the University of Manchester. His publications include *West Africa and the Commonwealth*, *Politics in Ghana 1946–60* and *Britain and South Africa*.

WILLIAM BRUGGER was formerly Materials Officer at the Contemporary China Institute. He is now Lecturer in Politics at the Flinders University of South Australia.

K. N. CHAUDHURI is Lecturer in the Economic History of Asia in the University of London. His publications include *The English East India Company* and *The Economic Development of India under the East India Company 1814–1858*.

VIOLET CONOLLY is the former head of the Soviet research desk at the Foreign Office. Her publications include *Beyond the Urals*.

ALISTAIR HENNESSY is Professor of History in the University of Warwick. His publications include *Modern Spain* and articles and contributions on a wide range of Latin-American topics.

RICHARD MAYNE has been an official of the ECSC High Authority and of the EEC Commission. He is a regular contributor to a number of publications and is the author of *The Community of Europe*, *The Recovery of Europe* and *Europe in 1945*.

RUTH MCVEY is Lecturer in Politics with reference to South East Asia at the School of Oriental and African Studies, University of London. She is author of *The Rise of Indonesian Communism* and of a number of articles and monographs on the contemporary history of South-east Asia.

W. N. MEDLICOTT is Stevenson Professor Emeritus of International History in the University of London. He is Senior Editor of *Documents on British Foreign Policy 1919–1939*, and his publications include *Contemporary England 1914–1964*, *British Foreign Policy since Versailles 1919–1963*, *Bismarck and Modern Germany* and *The Congress of Berlin and After*.

STUART SCHRAM is Professor of Politics with reference to China in the University of London and Head of the Contemporary China Institute. He is the author of *The Political Thought of Mao Tse-tung*, and of a biography of the Chinese leader.

HEINZ SCHURER is Librarian of the School of Slavonic and East European Studies, University of London. He has contributed articles to a number of journals.

LAWRENCE SILVERMAN is Lecturer in Politics in the University of Reading, where he teaches American government and politics.

WILLIAM TORDOFF is Reader in Government in the University of Manchester. He is author of *Ashanti Under the Prempehs* and *Government and Politics in Tanzania*.

M. E. YAPP is Lecturer in the History of the Near and Middle East at the School of Oriental and African Studies, University of London and Chairman of the Centre for Near and Middle Eastern Studies. He is the author of several articles on the contemporary history of the Middle East.

Preface

The aim of this volume, as the title suggests, is to assist the student and general reader interested in contemporary history. For some parts of the modern world so much material is available and it is expanding at such a rapid rate that the task of selection is all-important. For other regions the problem is one of scarcity and here too the student may find signposts useful.

We hope this volume will provide such guidance as well as stimulate further reading. Logic and convenience dictated a regional approach to avoid overlapping and to make for easy reference. In each case an expert was asked to write a bibliographical essay on his region, selecting and commenting on the books available (mainly in English) and indicating specific problems which face the reader. No artificial attempt was made to impose uniformity on the authors. Where there are marked differences from region to region, and where each has its own specific and complex problems, we felt that matters of emphasis and arrangement were best left to the individual contributor.

We hope the reader will find this arrangement both interesting and helpful.

BERNARD KRIKLER AND
WALTER LAQUEUR

Introduction

W. N. Medlicott

The fact that this book of bibliographical essays is entirely devoted to contemporary history is evidence of a popular demand and response which is relatively new. In England at any rate the demand does not go back much beyond 1914, when books such as R. W. Seton-Watson's *Southern Slav Question* (1911) and E. D. Morel's *Morocco in Diplomacy* (1912) began to alert an uneasy generation about the sinister possibilities of current international politics. Since then the crises of our turbulent and ever changing world have led to a constant curiosity as to when, how, where, and why things have happened, a curiosity shared by both historians and the public. But it is only the continuity of interest that is new: the writing of contemporary history has been a familiar art since the days of Thucydides.[1]

It is, of course, an unsatisfactory term. We are clear about one thing: 'contemporary' does not mean 'contemporaneous'. But otherwise, what are its limits? It is sometimes said to mean the events of our own lifetimes, but the life span of, say, the late Dr G. P. Gooch, the doyen of 'contemporary' historians when he died in 1968 at the age of ninety-four, was very different from that of a young historian writing his first book at the age of twenty-four. In France it has long been the practice to apply the term to the period since the revolution of 1789, and that date has also indeed some significance for North America (following the birth of the United States) and for Europe generally. English historians in the inter-war

---

[1] The nineteenth century produced outstanding examples such as Albert Sorel's *Histoire Diplomatique de la Guerre Franco-Allemande* (2 vols., Paris, 1875).

1

years usually regarded the year 1914 as the obvious turning point, marking the end of a real or imagined era of peace and prosperity. Others, including Professor Hans Rothfels, argue that contemporary history starts in 1917, when our planet became one world with the Russian Revolution and American intervention in Europe.[2] It could be objected to this that the political isolationism practised by both countries in differing measures during the twenties and thirties postponed their real assumption of the star roles on the world stage until 1941, and some would accordingly regard this as the more significant date. It is evident that as time moves on the initial date tends to be advanced; 1945 now marks the beginning of the latest distinctive phase of recent history and this is in the main the one covered in this work.[3]

While no general agreement has been reached on precise dates for the period which is 'contemporary' for historians, it is generally felt to have some quality distinguishing it from earlier periods. Professor Geoffrey Barraclough, writing in 1964, even maintained that the current period of contemporary history, which he dated from around 1890, is the beginning of an entirely new era in history, marked off from the conventional three-fold division of history into ancient, medieval, and modern.[4] If this is so, then 'contemporary history' becomes even less satisfactory as a title, for it is rather confusingly being made to differentiate the recent phase from the past both in time and in character. It would clearly be better to limit the use of the term to the former, and find another label for the post-modern epoch of history, if such exists.

We can agree as to the greater rapidity of developments and the spectacular increase in man's power of destruction and creation in many spheres in the twentieth century. But whether there is a real break in historical continuity in these

[2] Hans Rothfels, *Zeitgeschichtliche Betrachtungen* (Göttingen, 1959), pp. 10–11, 58, 149.

[3] *Contemporary History in Europe*, ed. D. C. Watt (London, 1969), reprinting papers by 23 contributors, is a very useful survey of writings on recent history down to 1945 in twelve European countries and the USA.

[4] G. Barraclough, *An Introduction to Contemporary History* (London, revised ed., 1966), pp. 12–18: a very stimulating, controversial, and comprehensive essay.

cases – apart from the frequent transition from an evolutionary to a revolutionary tempo – is more doubtful. Each new generation repudiates the past to some extent. Children are bored with the virtues and standards of their parents, and indeed one of the problems of contemporary historians is the fact that while some people are keenly interested in the recent past, others want to hear as little about it as possible. As one young man put the point in 1899, 'Each generation exults in the immediate possession of life, and regards with indifference, scarcely tinged by pride or pity, the records and monuments of those that are no more'.[5] So there is a danger that those who are keenly interested in contemporary developments may exaggerate their novelty. 'The living are often too ready to deny the dead the right to live.'[6]

On the whole it is questionable whether the events of the twentieth century – in the suggested period from 1890 to 1945 – are sufficiently unique to justify talk of a new era in history. Certainly there were wars, rumours of war, the rise and fall of empires, economic upheavals. But war is no novelty. The successful repudiation of European control, often with European connivance, is a long historical process of which the first landmarks were the break-up of the four great colonial empires of France, Britain, Spain, and Portugal between 1763 and 1824. The second British empire did not go the way of the first because the inevitability of peaceful separation was recognised in time, but the more amicable fading out of imperial authority associated with the concept of 'dominion home rule' began with the British North America Act of 1867 and not the India Independence Act of 1947. Nor was Europe so continuously predominant in the world before the twentieth century as many commentators imply. The West was not able to break through the Islamic barrier to the east before the late eighteenth century; nor did it force open the door in the Far East until the mid-nineteenth century. The role of the United States as a world power since 1917 is certainly without precedent, but the same cannot be said of Russia, which was an active world power from Warsaw to Vladivostok and a

5 W. S. Churchill, *The River War* (London, 1899), i, 11.
6 Heinrich von Srbik, *Aus Österreichs Vergangenheit* (Salzburg, 1959), p. 270.

3

challenge to its neighbours throughout the nineteenth century.

We can however undoubtedly find one or two developments in the period *after* 1945 which have no real analogies in the past and might possibly justify talk of a new historical era. They are essentially technological. Space travel is one, and even the rocketry techniques on which it is based are a very recent scientific development. Thermonuclear weapons after 1945 soon developed a destructive power which was quantitatively so much greater than earlier systems as to constitute a unique *qualitative* difference; this lay essentially in the high probability of total destruction in war with the new weapon, whereas under all earlier systems a forlorn hope had always existed for men of desperate courage.[7] One may doubt on the other hand whether the emergent independent states of Africa and Asia supply anything really new in world politics, for there had after all been independent states or tribes in both continents before the relatively short era of colonial rule. Their preference for non-alignment and for 'third-force' diplomacy suggests that they are no more likely to dominate international politics than the earlier emergent sub-continent, Latin America. Possibly the international monetary system and the ramifications of economic aid on an international basis which emerged from the Bretton Woods conference and later confabulations constitute a genuine innovation, both in its technical grasp and vast complexity; the inflationary over-heating of many national economies seems likely to continue indefinitely, deprived of the safety valve of major war. Pollution and the population-explosion are also new anxieties.

But altogether it is probably unprofitable to question ourselves too closely about the uniqueness or otherwise of our era; its extent is an academic conundrum which may entertain posterity. The nature of contemporary history and the characteristic difficulties of studying it are, however, worth closer examination.

It is concerned essentially with events which form the

[7] Some of the more sophisticated qualifications of this proposition are examined at length in Raymond Aron, *Peace and War, a Theory of International Relations* (London, 1966), pp. 611–51.

direct basis for decisions on problems of public importance at the present day or in the immediate future, as distinct from those which provide only a *general* historical background, or have no concern with modern problems at all. When the late President John F. Kennedy decided in October 1962 to challenge Mr Krushchev over the missile bases in Cuba he must have based his decision as to how the Russians would react on what he or his advisers had learned about Soviet behaviour patterns and Mr Krushchev's personality during recent years. And since all governments must base their decisions on whatever relevant information is available to them we can say that they are continually putting contemporary history to practical use. The evidence however tends in such cases to lose its direct relevance rather rapidly as we go back in time. Valid judgments must usually be confined to living persons. Soviet reactions even under Stalin might have been by no means the same as those of Mr Krushchev's day (apart from the fact that the crisis would probably not have arisen at all under Stalin). And an exhaustive knowledge of Russian modes of behaviour under Peter the Great and the rest of the Romanovs would have been of no help at all in the actual circumstances of October 1962.

It can be argued, incidentally, that only in cases of this sort does the study of history ever serve a direct practical purpose. The point of crisis will evidently have passed long before historians begin to write books about it. In such delicate international confrontations, which usually take an unduly personalised form, there is a clash between the politicians who dread damaging publicity and the demands of the nervous public, agitated or excited by the possibilities. But as soon as the moment of extreme tension has passed the press turns to other things, and the historian who decides to write lengthily about the issues will usually be left with incomplete data and a diminishing public appeal. So while his interest and the fitful curiosity of the public may have a common origin, these soon diverge; his hope of royalties or academic preferment, the need to occupy his mind, or possibly a political or ideological axe to be ground, will keep him at work, and he will press for systematic information about which the public no longer cares very ardently.

This divergence between popular and professional interest accounts for most of the controversies which have arisen over the writing of contemporary history, and which deal essentially with the problem of access to official material and the historian's capacity for dealing with it in a truly scholarly manner. This involves in the first place the much debated question of bias. Is not the historian likely to be too much influenced by party feeling and national hatreds and animosities to write with even a fair measure of objectivity about recent times? Can the reader read without seeing the words through a distorting haze of passion? There seems, in fact, little cause for alarm in either case. The two questions did, nevertheless, cause grave concern to professional historians in England (although not it would seem elsewhere) between the wars. R. W. Seton-Watson thought it useful to make 'A Plea for the Study of Contemporary History' the subject of his Creighton Lecture in 1928.[8] It was not a plea for the writing of recent history (which as he pointed out had had eminent practitioners since Herodotus[9]) but for its acceptance as academically respectable. It was still being argued in some quarters that while an older historian might venture on to this dangerous ground after schooling his emotions in a prolonged study of medieval texts, the best training for a younger one would be in periods too remote to threaten in any way his blood pressure. One young Oxford historian remarked in 1921 that it was not considered good form for any scholar of less than sixty years standing to write on any period that was either familiar or interesting, and the resulting narrations had, he said, 'the dreary impartiality of the Recording Angel, without that completeness which is the sole attraction of his style'.[10]

There is always a danger that the historian (or indeed any scholar in any field) will approach his subject with his mind

[8] *History*, April 1929, pp. 1–18.

[9] 'Herodotus, Xenophon, Thucydides, Tacitus, or, in later times, Matthew Paris, Froissart, Villani, Guicciardini, Machiavelli, De Thou, Clarendon, Burnet are but a few names selected at random, but not, I think, unfairly' (p. 4).

[10] Philip Guedalla, *Men of Letters* (London, 1927), pp. 2–3.

preconditioned by general assumptions or inflamed by earlier controversies, but this state of affairs is not confined to recent history. Few Englishmen can do justice to the Spanish colonising mission, nearly four hundred years after the Spanish Armada. A Mayor of Chicago was still fighting King George III in 1930. The main influence in bringing respectability to the study of recent history has been the change of approach since the 1920s to historical studies generally. The belief, accepted so readily by Acton and his generation, that the writing of 'final' history will become possible with the opening of all essential archives, has long been abandoned. Well aware of the relativity of truth and the insidious treachery of the unconscious bias and the unconscious mind, English historians can scarcely regard the possible deficiencies of the contemporary historian as exceptional. In this mood of self-abasement G. M. Trevelyan could only suggest in 1946 that although we cannot avoid bias we can write reputable biographies of our contemporaries if we do not write *against* our bias.[11]

It is now readily accepted that historical writing to be profitable must be controversial. The long-standing myths about national character and the individual reputations and policies of long-dead statesmen endure unchallenged as grassroot assumptions only as long as no one is sufficiently interested or bold to argue about them. Historians' reputations, moreover, soar when they are locked in debate with fellow specialists; it appears that the flow of books on such well-advertised themes as the English civil war, the American civil war, French revolutionary repercussions, Bismarck's virtuosity, and the profitability of the Norman Conquest is inexhaustible. By a kind of Parkinson's law the supply of print keeps pace with the demand. So there is no need to regard a flow of books on such wildly controversial topics of recent history as Munich, Korea, Suez, Vietnam and the like as differing from today's established historical practice. Indeed, preconceptions, unexamined assumptions, are perhaps less likely to prevail among writers on living controversies who

11 G. M. Trevelyan, 'Bias in History', *History*, March 1947, pp. 3–4.

are continually reminded that there are two (or more) sides to every question.

Rather more complex is the problem of coping with the *evidence* for recent history. It is abundant (for almost any topic that one can choose), but usually incomplete. So it is too for earlier periods of history: but in those cases the evidence has often disappeared for ever, whereas vast masses of official documents, private letters, business records, and the personal recollections of living persons relating to recent history are known to exist but are not for the time being available. This is a tantalising situation for the contemporary historian, who can in fact find plenty to write about in the information already available, but is inclined to spend time in agitating for the further opening of the archives. The result is a running fight between historians and governments, and for a number of reasons governments usually win this battle to defend their archives against what they regard as premature examination.

One reason for this is that public interest, as already remarked, is fitful; it is catered for during the course of the more publicised crises by an immediate flow of information which is usually sufficient to satisfy the avidity of Parliament and the press; it quickly turns to other issues. This flow of contemporary official information is, and indeed has to be, extensive, even in totalitarian states, and even in war-time. It is impossible, for example, to conduct a wartime food or clothes rationing system without published regulations which are of great interest to the economic-intelligence agencies of enemy countries. Again, apart from material relating to political crises, there is a constant publication of government reports and blue books on social, educational, and similar problems which is indispensable material to the historian: we know, for example, how much those good contemporary historians, Friedrich Engels and Karl Marx, depended on such sources as the first English blue books on factory conditions of the 1840s and the annual reports of the Commissioners of HM Inland Revenue. In putting out all this information governments are seeking primarily to supply what is necessary for the conduct of affairs, but they also aim to satisfy the immediate interest of the public, and when this leads to systematic programmes of publication these may even be ahead of the demand. This is perhaps true of, for example, the twenty-eight volumes on the civil history of the United Kingdom in the second world war, which cannot be said to have had much popular success.

Official resistance to what is regarded as premature publication is also justified by practical arguments. Vital information must not be given to foreign rivals in delicate economic or diplomatic transactions; officials must be assured that they can speak and act with complete frankness throughout their careers. A government official, after his first years of apprenticeship, will have at least thirty years of possibly high office and would naturally prefer that his confidential official acts and writings should not be broadcast to the world during that time. If they are, then the uninhibited frankness of his minutes and correspondence will speedily end. The British nineteenth-century blue books give an excellent example of how over-generous publicity can defeat its own purpose. Although some foreign secretaries, notably Canning, used the blue book as a bold weapon of publicity, others became increasingly irked by a popular demand which they found it difficult to resist. Accordingly, although documents were apparently never forged, they might be abbreviated or omitted altogether; more important was the fact that dispatches were normally written for publication in as innocuous a form as possible, while the more vital and personal messages might be conveyed in private letters. After 1885 both political parties seem to have tacitly agreed not to make embarrassing demands for diplomatic papers when in opposition.[12]

Although the more reticent phase of foreign policy which followed helped to establish the myth that secret diplomacy had caused the 1914 war there was no return to nineteenth-century blue book practice in the inter-war years. A certain number appeared, but it was recognised that the nineteenth-century blue books were an unusual development which engendered questionable editorial methods, with distressing counterparts on the continent. However, a great deal was pub-

---

[12] H. Temperley and L. M. Penson, *A Century of Diplomatic Blue Books 1815–1914* (Cambridge, 1938), pp. vii–viii, xi–xii.

lished in other forms. The compulsory registration of treaties with the League of Nations ensured publicity for formal agreements. Open diplomacy at its worst, as exemplified by the outpourings of the dictators, forced their rivals into counterpublicity. Secrecy was also reduced by the success of the Italian and later Soviet espionage services in winkling out many British, French, and American governmental secrets. The appetites of students of contemporary history were satisfied for some time by the publication of a series of volumes dealing with British foreign policy from 1898 to 1914, along with similar French and German publications.[13] In general it could be said that, while revealing a good deal, the British government had successfully maintained its right to say what should or should not be revealed. The British Foreign Office archives were still available to students only on what was broadly a fifty-year basis, that is, they were open during the later 1930s only to the end of 1885.

In the new post-war era after 1945 there was again ample publication of basic official material for the recent great war and for the pre-war years, including a series of Foreign Office documents which was expected to reach over fifty volumes when completed.[14] On the other hand the fifty-year rule continued until the middle sixties, and there was again no systematic publication of near-contemporary documents comparable with the golden age of blue-book production. Although there was some grumbling on this point the critics concentrated their attack on the fifty-year rule, and did succeed in securing a cabinet decision shortening the period to thirty years in 1966. In spite of some misgivings in official circles at this partial retreat, the thirty-year period of closure that remained still left the last word as to publication about sensitive current issues with the government of the day. It is true however that the British thirty-year period is shorter than that of almost all other governments except the United States, which has a twenty-five year period (thirty-five for foreigners).

---

[13] G. P. Gooch and H. Temperley, *British Documents on the Origins of the War 1898–1914* (London, HMSO, 1926–1938).

[14] E. L. Woodward, Rohan Butler, W. N. Medlicott and others, *Documents on British Foreign Policy, 1919–1939* (London, HMSO, 1947, continuing).

Whether the British and American governments benefit on balance by their frankness is a moot point. In a highly controversial diplomatic issue such as the Anglo-French-Soviet negotiations of the summer of 1939 the British doubts and hesitations can be headlined, those of the Soviet leaders concealed.

The most useful function of the true contemporary historian (one writing, that is, on the events of the last twenty-five or thirty years) is to provide the first orderly and objective analysis of the confused masses of information immediately released by public events. His function is thus an extension of that of the mass-information media such as the press and radio, which provide similar interim reports for the public. The Chatham House *Survey of International Affairs* (in more or less annual volumes since 1924) is a valuable example of careful pioneering work on these lines: it makes no claim to offer new information from unpublished sources. The other important class of book in this field is the one that does present new information, either in the form of straightforward memoirs (such as Lord Avon's *Full Circle*, 1960) or accounts of phases of crisis based on some measure of confidential information from the participants (such as A. M. Schlesinger, *A Thousand Days*, 1965, or Theodore H. White, *The Making of the President 1964*, 1965). Both classes of work, however, serve the same basic purpose of sorting out and preserving the essential facts from the overwhelming masses of perishable evidence that confronts us.

Meanwhile the task of reducing this material to manageable proportions is paralleled by officials in all governments who systematically work through the official papers and decide what is worthy of permanent preservation. The nightmarish bulk of these papers before 'weeding' means that the historian should be grateful to the official, although there remains a permanent doubt as to whether in the process some vital pieces may not have been sent to the incinerator. It is certainly not the case, as many historians fondly imagine, that after thirty years everything now in the British official archives will be found in the Public Record Office. Much of the material in governmental archives is trivial, repetitious, or purely ephemeral in interest, and only those documents are preserved which are likely to be needed for future official use. Some are preserved but are kept permanently from public scrutiny. In the end only one per cent of all documents used in British government departments goes to the Public Record Office.

But while the officials are selecting (and possibly destroying) the vital evidence, the contemporary historian should above all be seizing the opportunity for contact with living witnesses and for testing and expanding their knowledge of great events. In this way he can himself clarify and sometimes add to knowledge and create fresh documentary material. As the late Gavin B. Henderson wrote in 1941, 'We can meet and discuss matters, any day we like, with men who were at Dunkirk. Would not the true medievalist give up his whole life's research for the sake of one interview with one Saxon who fought beside Harold at Hastings?'[15] Such opportunities provide the unique fascination of this aspect of history for scholars, and some compensation for setbacks, for he must never forget that public interest in contemporary history is partial and intermittent and has a disconcerting habit of vanishing in a great wave of boredom with some aspects of the recent past. It has indeed to be recognised that while the writing of contemporary history is a worthwhile occupation for the best historians, the public incentives to write are not so inevitable as is sometimes assumed. No doubt the public will get, in the end, the contemporary history it deserves.

[15] G. B. Henderson, 'A Plea for the Study of Contemporary History', *History*, June 1941, p. 53.

1

Western Europe

Richard Mayne

Introduction

Since 1945, if not earlier, Western Europe has no longer been the main focus of international affairs. On the surface, at least, it has been comparatively peaceful. Disagreements among and within its constituent countries have been dwarfed by tensions and conflicts elsewhere – in Eastern Europe, in the Middle East, in Latin America, in South-East Asia. Economically and politically, it has been overshadowed by the growth of non-European giants – the United States, the Soviet Union, the People's Republic of China. Even in the arts, its old predominance has been disputed; and what is true of the arts is also true of science and technology.

Yet despite this relative decline, Western Europe has continued to attract unceasing attention from journalists and scholars, compounding the inherent problems of contemporary history with an over-abundance of documentation. By now, students of the period not only lack perspective: they also risk not seeing the wood for the learned labels on the trees. Any guide to the literature on post-war Western Europe, therefore, must cut a bold swathe through the underbrush, at the risk of seeming partial or cavalier.

For the sake of convenience, the subject can be divided in one of three ways – geographical, chronological, or topical. The geographical approach is that which most commended itself in the past, when the differences between European countries seemed more important than their similarities: then, it was natural to consider in turn the problems of Britain, of France, of Germany, and so on, rather than the common problems that face them all. Even today, this approach remains necessary; and one section of the present bibliography reflects that need. The chronological approach is likewise still useful, since whatever the conceptual framework into which the facts are fitted, one aspect of history will always be linear – the unending succession of days, months, and years. But in an area so thickly overgrown with narrative, analysis, speculation, and advocacy, the most helpful breakdown of the subject seems likely to be a classification by topics – provided that this is flexible enough to admit elements of the other two.

Four main problem areas, in particular, have been studied by historians of post-war Western Europe. The first concerns the second world war, its effects, and the effort to recover from it. The second is the tension between Eastern and Western Europe, its military consequences, and attempts at *détente,* disengagement, and disarmament. The third is the complex of relations between Western Europe and the United States of America. The fourth, perhaps the most forbiddingly well-documented, is the halting progress towards Western European unity. All four, clearly enough, are interrelated. East-West tension was itself partly a result of the second world war; so was the new relationship between Western Europe and America; so was the impulse towards European unity. The gradual uniting of Western Europe has had repercussions on both the Soviet Union and the United States; they in their turn have affected both the recovery and the unification of Western Europe. But if all four themes are thus intertwined, each remains provisionally valid; and each can be divided, moreover, into subsidiary topics that succeed each other during the course of time.

The second world war as such is excluded by the terms of reference of the present study; but its effects and its sequels include population shifts, political realignments, the break-up of the colonial empires, and the deliberate pursuit of reconstruction and economic growth. East-West tension, likewise, covers not only the division of Europe and the beginnings of the 'Cold War', but also the formation of defensive alliances and the successive attempts at *rapprochement.* Western

14

Europe's relationship with the United States, similarly, has undergone a number of transitions, from the early days of the Marshall Plan and OEEC (later OECD) to efforts at 'Atlantic partnership' and a growing consciousness of the 'technological gap' and the 'American challenge'. Finally, the progress towards Western European unity has passed through various phases, including the foundation of the Council of Europe, the establishment of the successive European Communities, and the gradual evolution of Great Britain's attitude to the whole venture.

These, then, are the main topics to which the present survey is a guide. Each has engendered controversy, amply reflected in the literature. They are not, however, exhaustive. In addition to the four main themes, a number of others have been studied at some length – ranging from single episodes like the 1956 Suez crisis to more general topics such as Communism and the French Left. In some cases, these have been classified under national headings; in others, at the sacrifice of logic but in the interests of clarity, they have been left in categories of their own.

General: Bibliographies, Sources, and Surveys

At a European level, one readily accessible bibliography is that by L. L. Paklons (*European Bibliography*, Bruges, 1964). This, however, has two disadvantages: first, it is mainly concerned with European unification, and secondly, it is somewhat out of date. More recent general bibliographies can be found in some of the non-specialist works mentioned below. Also helpful are the British Museum *Catalogue of Printed Books* and *Subject Index* and the similar compilations of the Library of Congress; but more helpful still are the services of librarians – not only in the various universities, but also in the Royal Institute of International Affairs at Chatham House and in the British Library of Political and Economic Science at the London School of Economics. Finally, there is something to be said for special collections such as the Wiener Library and the library of the European

Community Information Service, as well as for consulting specialist bookshops.

Official documents of all kinds need little introduction. British blue books and white papers are available from the Stationery Office, which issues an annual catalogue; similar facilities exist in most other European countries. Sometimes equally useful, and in English, are United States publications such as the Department of State *Bulletin* and the state papers published at intervals as *Foreign Relations of the United States*. Of almost equal interest are the documents of the various legislative and other assemblies – *Hansard*, Congressional reports and *Records*, and the debates and reports of such bodies as the European Parliament, the Consultative Assembly of the Council of Europe, and the Assembly of Western European Union. The latter is particularly informative on matters of defence, as are some publications of the Secretariat-General of the North Atlantic Treaty Organization. On economic matters, the Organization for Economic Co-operation and Development (OECD, formerly OEEC), produces the most enlightening general material, although mention should also be made of the specialised agencies of the United Nations, including the Economic Commission for Europe (ECE); while the European Communities are a mine of detailed data and statistics concerning mainly the Common Market countries. *Basic Statistics of the Community*, published annually by the Communities' Statistical Office, indeed covers most of the rest of Western Europe, as well as the USA, Japan, and the USSR.

Alongside these official documents, much is to be learned from other source material, such as the annual *Statesman's Yearbook, International Yearbook and Statesman's Who's Who, International Organization,* and *Europa Yearbook.* Less summary are *The Annual Register of World Events* and the *Surveys* and *Documents* published by the Royal Institute of International Affairs at Chatham House. Chatham House also issues two periodicals: the quarterly *International Affairs,* even more useful for its bibliographical help than for its articles and its sometimes testy book-reviews; and *The*

World Today, a monthly without book-reviews but packed with up-to-date and authoritative articles. *Foreign Affairs*, the American counterpart of *International Affairs*, is particularly notable as the vehicle for articles signed, if not always written, by the world's leading statesmen: it is thus not only an invaluable guide to current affairs, but also very often a document in its own right.

The international press in general, of course, is equally indispensable. *Keesing's Contemporary Archives* provides useful summaries. The annual *Index* of *The Times* is similarly helpful; but of all existing newspapers perhaps *Le Monde* is the most exhaustive. Close runners-up, in addition to *The Times*, include *The New York Times*, *The Financial Times*, the *Frankfurter Allgemeine Zeitung*, and the weekly *Economist*, together with its *Foreign Report*. Among other useful periodicals are *Government and Opposition*, the *Journal of Contemporary History*, and such more specialised publications as the *Political Science Quarterly*.

General surveys and works of reference include the brief *Atlas of European Affairs*, edited by Norman J. G. Pounds and Robert C. Kingsbury (London, 1964), and the voluminous and discursive *Western Europe: A Handbook*, edited by John Calmann (London, 1967). This latter includes not only country-by-country surveys, but also specialist essays on politics, economics, the arts, and European unification. In the field of comparative government, two American books stand out: Fritz Nova's *Contemporary European Governments* (Baltimore, 1963), and Robert G. Neumann's *European Government* (4th edition, New York, 1968); while a recent survey by Stephen Holt, *Six European States* (London, 1970), is a compilation of yearbook-style data limited to the Common Market Six. Wider-ranging, but with essays of very diverse quality, is *A New Europe?* edited by Stephen R. Graubard (Boston, Mass., 1964); on more specialist subjects, there is much of value in *European Political Parties*, edited by Stanley Henig and John Pinder (London, 1969) and in the huge if now dated compilation edited by J. Frederic Dewhurst and others, *Europe's Needs and Resources* (New York, 1961), the bulk of whose very comprehensive statistics refer to the mid-fifties. A more recent study of consumer patterns, living standards, and popular attitudes is the Reader's Digest *Survey of Europe Today* (London, 1970), whose findings may usefully be compared with its predecessor *Products and People* (London, 1963).

Outstanding among general historical works that have a bearing on Western Europe since 1945 are Geoffrey Barraclough's *An Introduction to Contemporary History* (London, 1964), David Thomson's *Europe Since Napoleon* (revised edition, London, 1966), and the classic Ludwig Dehio's *The Precarious Balance* (New York, 1962). Volume VI of the *Cambridge Economic History of Europe,* edited by H. J. Habakkuk and M. M. Postan (Cambridge, 1965) is also relevant in places.

The most vivid overall history of Western Europe since 1945 is perhaps Richard Mayne's *The Recovery of Europe* (London, 1970), a large part of which is devoted to European unification. More orthodox in this respect are Walter Laqueur's *Europe Since Hitler* (London, 1970) and the slighter *Western Europe since 1945,* by D. W. Urwin (London, 1968). Slighter still is Maurice Crouzet's illustrated *The European Renaissance Since 1945* (London, 1970), which suffers from some inaccuracies. Older works that are still useful are H. Stuart Hughes's *Contemporary Europe: A History* (Englewood Cliffs, NJ, 1961) and R. C. Mowat's *Ruin and Resurgence 1939–1965* (London, 1966). More summary, and written in the light of 'the European Idea', are Jacques Freymond's *Western Europe Since the War* (New York/London, 1964), and John Lukacs's *Decline and Rise of Europe* (New York, 1965).

The period is peculiarly rich in memoirs by statesmen and civil servants. In alphabetical order, the most useful are as follows. Dean Acheson has touched on Western European problems in two books – the gossipy *Sketches from Life* (New York, 1961), and the exhaustive *Present at the Creation* (London, 1970), which greatly amplifies but does not much alter its predecessor's account. In a very different, far drier style, Konrad Adenauer's *Memoirs* document the German end of the same post-war policies: so far only two of the four volumes have appeared in English (London, 1966 and 1968). Equally dry are the recollections of C. R. Attlee, *As It Happened* (London, 1954) and *A Prime Minister Remembers,* recorded by Francis Williams (London, 1961). George Ball's *The Discipline of Power,* a forceful exposition of 'Atlantic Partnership', contains much livelier indiscretions, although primarily a work of advocacy. In *Moscow Mission 1946–1949* (London, 1950), Walter Bedell Smith gives one man's view of the developing 'Cold War'; in two books of reminiscences, *Speaking Frankly* (New York, 1947) and the more flaccid *All in One Lifetime* (London, 1960), James F. Byrnes recalls a more optimistic period and gives his version of his quarrel with Harry S. Truman. Winston Churchill's *The Second World War* (London, 1948–54) bears somewhat on post-war events, as do his post-war speeches, collected by R. S. Churchill in *The Sinews of Peace* (London, 1948). More strictly relevant, and just as individual, are the post-war memoirs of Hugh Dalton, *High Tide and After* (London, 1962). Still more individual, not to say idiosyncratic, is *Memoirs of Hope* (London, 1971), the translation of Charles de Gaulle's fragmentary *Mémoires d'Espoir.* More entertaining, if less monumental, is *Quai d'Orsay 1945–1951* (London, 1958), by Jacques Dumaine, one-time Head of Protocol at the French Foreign Office. Lord Avon, the former Anthony Eden, has contributed his own viewpoint to history in the two post-war volumes of his own memoirs, *Full Circle* (London, 1960) and *The Reckoning* (London, 1965); on such subjects as Suez, his account should be treated with caution. This is particularly so in view of the comparative frankness of Dwight D. Eisenhower, in *Mandate for Change* (New York, 1963) and *Waging Peace* (London, 1966). A further useful American source is the *Memoirs of Cordell Hull* (New York/London, 1948); as are the stylish *Memoirs 1925–1950* (London, 1968) of George F. Kennan. No less stylish is *Tides of Fortune 1945–1955* (London, 1969), by Harold Macmillan, and the subsequent *Riding the Storm 1956–1959* (London, 1971). Credible if not always creditable sidelights on a great man and great events are offered by Lord Moran's *Churchill: The Struggle for Survival* (London, 1966); further sidelights on history, some from a rather misleading direction, can be found in Robert Murphy's *Diplomat Among Warriors* (London, 1964). In *The Continuing Battle* (abridged, London, 1971), Paul-Henri Spaak sheds light on Belgium, European unification, and NATO, including some revealing documents. *Retour à Zero,* by Paul Stehlin (Paris, 1968) is a French military man's view of the same years and some of the same events. For a diplomatist's account of the early post-war years and some of the work of Ernest Bevin, Lord Strang's slight *Home and Abroad* (London, 1956) is useful. Harry S. Truman, finally, deals at length with European devastation and recovery, and with the problems of divided Germany and Berlin, in the two volumes of his own jaunty memoirs, *Year of Decisions* and *Years of Trial and Hope* (London, 1956).

As a supplement to formal memoirs, further colour is supplied by the reports and reminiscences of journalists. Chronologically the first in this period is Edmund Wilson's *Europe Without Baedeker* (London, 1948), a shocked account of the immediate aftermath of war. Howard K. Smith, in *The State of Europe* (London, 1950) provides a systematic survey of the European countries, East and West, with an eye-witness version of events in Czechoslovakia. *Fire in the Ashes: Europe in mid-century* (New York, 1953) is a much more impressionistic and 'literary' report by the future historian of US presidential elections, Theodore H. White. John Gunther, in *Inside Europe Today* (London, 1961), offers a brisk panorama in the style of his other 'Inside' books; Don Cook, in *Floodtide in Europe* (New York, 1965), ranges over some twenty years' reporting to supply occasional small revelations and a highly-charged narrative of Europe's recovery and re-orientation. The most recent of such works is Anthony Sampson's *The New Europeans* (London, 1968), a lively, quirkish, and personal report on how continental Europe in 1967–8 struck the author of *Anatomy of Britain* (London, 1962), *Anatomy of Britain Today* (London, 1965), and *The New Anatomy of Britain* (London, 1971).

The Effects of War and Recovery

Although the cessation of hostilities lies outside the present terms of reference, some key works on the subject remain relevant. The first is H. R. Trevor-Roper's pioneering study, *The Last Days of Hitler* (revised edition, London, 1962); a second is Arthur Bryant's *Triumph in the West 1943–1946*, based on the Alanbrooke diaries (new edition, London, 1965); a third, Chester Wilmot's controversial genealogy of East-West rivalry, *The Struggle for Europe* (new edition, London, 1959). Also relevant, although more 'popular' in its approach, is Cornelius Ryan's account of the fall of Berlin, *The Last Battle* (London, 1966).

On the peace conferences and early post-war relations between the wartime leaders, two indispensable sources are Joseph Stalin's *Correspondence with Churchill, Attlee, Roosevelt and Truman* (London, 1952), and the official reports of the Potsdam Conference, issued both by the UK Foreign Office (*Protocol of the Proceedings of the Berlin Conference*, London, 1947) and by the US Government (*The Conference of Berlin 1945*, Washington, 1960). Herbert Feis has made three illuminating studies of these subjects: *Churchill, Roosevelt, Stalin: the War They Waged and the Peace They Sought* (Princeton, NJ, 1957); *Between War and Peace: The Potsdam Conference* (London, 1960); and *The Atomic Bomb and the End of World War II* (London, 1966). In *Atomic Diplomacy: Hiroshima and Potsdam* (London, 1966), Gar Alperovitz argues that the destruction of Hiroshima was intended as a warning to the USSR.

On the early post-war period and the division of Europe, the most helpful general works are *The Realignment of Europe,* edited by A. and V. M. Toynbee (London, 1955); *The Hard and Bitter Peace,* an uncompromising statement of the 'Western' view by G. F. Hudson (London, 1966); and *Entre guerres et paix,* by the former French Foreign Office official Jean Laloy (Paris, 1966).

The post-war plight of Europe, and efforts to remedy it, can be studied in depth in *UNRRA: The History of the United Nations Relief and Rehabilitation Administration,* by George Woodbridge and others (three volumes, New York, 1950). Particular aspects are dealt with in F. K. Hoehler's *Europe's Homeless Millions* (New York, 1945); the ECE report on *The European Housing Problem* (Geneva, 1949); Malcolm J. Proudfoot's *European Refugees 1939–52* (London, 1957); and three studies by J. B. Schechtman: *European Population Transfers 1939–1945* (New York, 1946), *Postwar Population Transfers in Europe 1945–1955* (Philadelphia, 1962), and *The Refugee in the World: Displacement and Integration* (New York, 1963). Robert Kee's *Refugee World* (London, 1961), although covering a later period, is a vivid evocation of 'displaced persons' ' lives.

The end of European colonialism, which for some countries was a direct consequence of the war, and for others followed shortly thereafter, is the subject of three general studies: G. Carter's *Independence for Africa* (New York, 1960); S. C. Easton's *The Twilight of European Colonialism* (London, 1961); and the same writer's later and more general *The Rise and Fall of Western Colonialism* (London, 1964). The special problem of Algeria figures below, in the section on France; but here may be mentioned H. Goldberg's *French Colonialism: Progress or Poverty* (New York, 1959). Also of interest are C. E. Carrington's *The Liquidation of the British Empire* (London, 1961); R. Lemarchand's *Political Awakening in the Belgian Congo* (Berkeley, Calif., 1964); A. P. Merriam's *Congo: Background of Conflict* (Evanston, 1961); L. H. Palmier's *Indonesia and the Dutch* (New York, 1962); and *The Emancipation of French Indochina* (New York, 1961). J. Duffy's *Portugal in Africa* (New York, 1962) is a reminder that colonialism lingers on.

Western Europe's economic recovery from the war – as distinct from the Marshall Plan, to be considered below – is touched on in several more general works, notably Angus Maddison's *Economic Growth in the West* (New York / London, 1964), Charles P. Kindleberger's *Economic Growth in France and Britain 1851–1950* (Cambridge, Mass., 1964), and Andrew Shonfield's more analytic study of *Modern Capitalism* (London, 1965). A good if now rather dated textbook is Paul Alpert's *Twentieth-Century Economic History of Europe* (New York, 1951). E. F. Penrose's *Economic Planning for the Peace* (Princeton, NJ, 1953) bears witness to the preoccupations of the early fifties, as does the

ECE report, *Growth and Stagnation in the European Economy* (Geneva, 1954). In *Economic 'Miracles'* (London, 1964), Jossleyn Hennessy, Vera Lutz, and Giuseppe Scimone examine economic growth in Germany, France, and Italy respectively, with a highly sceptical eye on planning. More general economic histories of post-war Western Europe are M. M. Postan's *An Economic History of Western Europe 1945–1964* (London, 1967) and Charles P. Kindleberger's *Europe's Postwar Growth: the Role of Labour Supply* (Cambridge, Mass., 1967), the former less systematic and the latter less specialised than their titles might suggest. On purely agricultural developments, P. Lamartine Yates's *Food, Land, and Manpower in Western Europe* (London, 1960) is useful; as is David Granick's classic study of the business world, *The European Executive* (New York, 1962).

On monetary matters, *Banking in Western Europe*, edited by R. S. Sayers (Oxford, 1962), surveys the banking institutions of eleven countries, not including the UK, which is dealt with in his *Banking in the British Commonwealth* (Oxford, 1953). A useful companion volume is *Eight European Central Banks*, published under the auspices of the Bank for International Settlements, and covering Belgium, France, Germany, Italy, the Netherlands, Sweden, Switzerland, and the UK (London, 1963). R. N. Gardner's *Sterling-Dollar Diplomacy* (Oxford, 1956) is invaluable, particularly for the period of the US loan to Britain. The Euro-Dollar market has been studied at length by Paul Einzig in *The Euro-Dollar System* (London, 1964), *Foreign Dollar Loans in Europe* (London, 1965), and *The Euro-Bond Market* (London, 1969), which is a revised version of its predecessor. Also helpful is E. Wayne Clendenning's *The Euro-Dollar* (London, 1970). Less conservative, to say the least, are the analyses and recommendations of Robert Triffin, notably in *Europe and the Money Muddle* (New Haven, Conn., 1957) and *The World Money Maze* (New Haven, Conn., 1967). A good general introduction is Fred Hirsch's *Money International* (London, 1967); an interesting symposium of conflicting views is *Monetary Reform and the Price of Gold*, edited by Randall Hinshaw (Baltimore, 1967). *The Gold War* (London, 1970),

23

by Ian Davidson and Gordon L. Weil, brings the controversy further up to date.

East-West Tension, Defence and Disengagement

The 'Cold War' is perhaps best studied in a broader context and longer perspective; but a number of books have been devoted to it even under its own prejudicial title. Its origins are treated by Martin Herz in *Beginnings of the Cold War* (Bloomington, Ind., 1966) and by Kenneth Ingram's early *History of the Cold War* (London, 1955). A more recent, generally reliable narrative is that by André Fontaine of *Le Monde*, originally published in Paris in 1965 and 1967, and translated as *History of the Cold War* (two volumes, London, 1969–70). *The Cold War: a Re-appraisal*, edited by Evan Luard (London, 1964), is a thoughtful collection of essays rather than a thorough revaluation. More ambitious is Louis J. Halle's *The Cold War as History* (London, 1967), as rewarding as it is occasionally wayward. For a brief, orthodox, and Western-angled account, see David Rees's *The Age of Containment* (London, 1967). The precise opposite is D. F. Fleming's *The Cold War and its Origins 1917–1960* (two volumes, London, 1961), a vast, very eclectically documented, but sometimes stimulating assault on Western self-righteousness. David Horowitz's *From Yalta to Vietnam* (revised edition, London, 1967) betrays the equal self-righteousness of a fierce critic of the West.

The Left in Europe Since 1789, by David Caute (London, 1966), is a popular and illustrated but rather idiosyncratic history. Supplementing it are two symposia: *Communism in Western Europe,* by M. Einaudi and others (Ithaca, New York, 1951); and *Communism in Europe,* edited by William Griffiths (Cambridge, Mass., 1964). *The European Right,* edited by Hans Rogger and Eugen Weber, is a similar if less homogeneous survey of the opposite end of the political spectrum (London, 1965). Nearer the centre, the Christian Democrat movement has been studied by M. P. Fogarty in *Christian Democracy in Western Europe* (London, 1957) and by M. Einaudi and F. Goguel in *Christian Democracy in Italy and France* (Notre Dame, Ind., 1952).

For defence, in addition to official publications, the technical data published annually by the London-based Institute for Strategic Studies in *The Military Balance* can be regarded as indispensable. More general and popular studies include Drew Middleton's *The Defence of Western Europe* (New York, 1952), and F. W. Mulley's *The Politics of Western Defence* (London, 1962). *Arms and Stability in Europe* (New York/London, 1963) is an authoritative study by Alastair Buchan and Philip Windsor. On NATO and Europe, a pioneering study still of interest is Ben T. Moore's *NATO and the Future of Europe* (New York, 1958); M. Margaret Ball's *NATO and the European Unity Movement* (New York, 1959) is also useful. More recent and technical are Alastair Buchan's *NATO in the 1960s* (London/New York, 1965) and Brigadier K. Hunt's *NATO Without France* (London, 1966).

On détente, disengagement and arms control, Michael Howard's *Disengagement in Europe* (London, 1958) is a good introductory survey, with arguments of its own. Coral Bell's *Negotiating From Strength* (London, 1962) is more considered. Two books by Willy Brandt, *The Ordeal of Coexistence* (London, 1963) and *A Peace Policy for Europe* (London, 1969), expound the German Chancellor's cautious *Ostpolitik;* Zbigniew Brzezinski's *Alternative to Partition* (New York, 1965) makes somewhat different suggestions perhaps less consonant with Western European unity. On arms control, *The Spread of Nuclear Weapons,* by John Maddox and Leonard Beaton (London, 1962), is still useful, although somewhat superseded by Beaton's *Must the Bomb Spread?* (London, 1966) and *The Politics of Arms Control* (New York, 1969).

Western Europe and the United States

Some general studies may serve as an introduction to this broad problem area: G. F. Kennan's *American Diplomacy 1900–1950* (London, 1952); George Lichtheim's *Europe and America* (London, 1963); *The United States and the Western*

Community (Haverford, Penn., 1957), edited by H. Field Haviland, Jr; *Political Community and the North Atlantic Area* (Princeton, NJ, 1957), by Karl W. Deutsch and others; and *France, Germany, and the Western Alliance*, by Karl W. Deutsch and L. J. Edinger (New York, 1966).

On the Marshall Aid period, the two most useful American reports are that by the President's Committee on Foreign Aid, *European Recovery and American Aid* (Washington, 1947), and that by the Select Committee on Foreign Aid, *Final Report on Foreign Aid* (Washington, 1948). For statistical summaries, the best early sources are the US Department of Commerce's *Foreign Aid by the United States Government 1940–1951* (Supplement to the *Survey of Current Business*, Washington, 1952), and *American Foreign Assistance*, by William Adams Brown, Jr, and Redvers Opie (Washington, 1953). The bureaucratic background in Washington is rather excitedly sketched by Joseph Marion Jones in *Fifteen Weeks* (paperback edition, New York, 1964); the political views of the head of the ECA, Paul Hoffmann, can be found in his *Peace Can Be Won* (New York, 1951). The most readable general history of the Marshall Plan is Harry Bayard Price's *The Marshall Plan and its Meaning* (Ithaca, New York, 1955); a more contemporary account is Howard S. Ellis's *The Economics of Freedom* (New York, 1950); and William Diebold, Jr, deals skilfully with more technical questions in *Trade and Payments in Western Europe* (New York, 1952). For a biography of George C. Marshall, see R. Payne's *General Marshall* (London, 1952). On the European side, in addition to the OEEC sources already mentioned, Ernst van der Beugel's *From Marshall Aid to Atlantic Partnership* (Amsterdam/London/New York, 1966) supplies not only the narrative implied by its title, but also eye-witness accounts of the early workings of OEEC. On the successor organisation OECD, the only full-scale academic work is Henry G. Aubrey's *Atlantic Economic Co-operation* (London, 1967).

'Atlantic Partnership', the phrase popularised by President J. F. Kennedy, is expounded by the American journalist Joseph Kraft in *The Grand Design* (New York, 1962), which has the merit and drawback of infection by the Kennedy magic. The deeper implications of the policy, especially in the economic field, are ably set out by Pierre Uri in *Partnership for Progress* (New York, 1963); its political aspects, from a German viewpoint, by Kurt Birrenbach in *The Future of the Atlantic Community* (New York/London, 1963); while defence questions are touched upon by François Duchêne in *Beyond Alliance,* a pamphlet prepared for the Atlantic Institute (Paris, 1963). *The Grand Design* (London, 1965) is a slightly later repetition of the same themes by the controversial German politician, Franz-Josef Strauss.

Critics and sceptics have also considered these questions, the most notable being Henry Kissinger in *The Necessity for Choice* (paperback edition, New York, 1962) and *The Troubled Partnership* (paperback edition, New York, 1965). In *Atlantic Crisis* (New York, 1964) Robert Kleiman skilfully reconstructs the rift in transatlantic relations caused by the Skybolt missile controversy and the veto on Britain's first attempt to join the Common Market. Drew Middleton's *Crisis in the West* (London, 1965) carries the same story a little further. Ronald Steel's *The End of Alliance* (London, 1964) draws pessimistic conclusions; so does Harold van Buren Cleveland's *The Atlantic Idea and its European Rivals* (New York, 1966).

The so-called 'American challenge' – the fear that Europe may become dominated by US business firms – found its prehistorian in Edward A. McCreary, with *The Americanization of Europe* (New York, 1964); it was also dealt with by Christopher Layton, in *Trans-Atlantic Investments* (Paris, 1966), before the now classic study by Jean-Jacques Servan-Schreiber, *Le Défi américain* (Paris, 1967; English edition, *The American Challenge,* London, 1968; paperback, 1969). *Europe versus America?* by Ernest Mandel (London, 1970), is an approach to these problems and their political implications by a member of the 'New Left'.

The 'technological gap' is an aspect of this general theme that some have treated separately. Laurence Reed's *Europe in a Shrinking World* (London, 1967) is highly readable; *Science and Technology in Europe,* edited by Eric Moonman, is a rather scattered collection of authoritative essays

(London, 1968). The most exhaustive treatment so far, however, is Christopher Layton's *European Advanced Technology: A programme for Integration* (London, 1969). A much briefer statement of the same general argument is Franz-Josef Strauss's *Challenge and Response* (London, 1969).

The Unification of Western Europe

On the 'European Idea', the best short introduction is still Bernard Voyenne's *Petite histoire de l'idée européenne* (new edition, Paris, 1965). More exhaustive is J. B. Duroselle's *L'Idée européenne dans l'histoire* (Paris, 1965); less so, but concerned also with present-day matters, is Lord Gladwyn's *The European Idea* (paperback edition, London, 1967). In *European Unity in Thought and Action* (Oxford, 1963), Geoffrey Barraclough subjects the continuity of the 'European Idea' to close and critical examination. Rene Albrecht-Carrié, in *The Unity of Europe* (London, 1966), deals more in detail with its later phases; W. O. Henderson, in *The Genesis of the Common Market* (London, 1962), is particularly interesting on the nineteenth century. For the early twentieth, the best guide is Henri Brugmans' *L'Idée européenne 1918–1965* (Bruges, 1965). In *An Idea Conquers the World* (London, 1953), Count Richard Coudenhove-Kalergi tells the story of his own 'Pan-Europe' movement. A more reflective and brief study of the nature of European society is Denis de Rougemont's *The Meaning of Europe* (London, 1965).

On the post-war moves towards Western European unity – although with sidelights on their pre-history – there is Richard Mayne's *The Community of Europe* (London, 1962). The United States' role in these moves is investigated by Max Beloff in *The United States and the Unity of Europe* (London, 1963). Monnet is the centrepiece of M. and S. Bromberger's gossipy and not always reliable *Jean Monnet and the United States of Europe* (New York, 1969); but Monnet's own thoughts are better documented in *Les Etats-Unis d'Europe ont Commencé* (Paris, 1955), an early compilation from his speeches, and in the *Statements and Declarations 1955–67 of the Action Committee for the United States of Europe*

(London, 1969). The views of an early British 'European' are preserved in R. W. G. Mackay's posthumous *Towards a United States of Europe* (London, 1961).

The best overall survey of the various European organisations is *European Unity*, by Michael Palmer and others (London, 1968) – in part a revised version of the earlier study by Political and Economic Planning, *European Organizations* (London, 1959). Two further works still of interest are A. H. Robertson's *European Institutions* (revised edition, London, 1966) and Kenneth Lindsay's *European Assemblies* (London, 1960). Useful general histories include Arnold J. Zurcher's not always meticulous *The Struggle to Unite Europe 1940–1958* (New York, 1958); Jean Lecerf's *Histoire de l'unité européenne* (Paris, 1965); F. Roy Willis's *France, Germany, and the New Europe 1945–1967* (London, 1969); and M. Curtis's *Western European Integration* (New York, 1965).

On the Council of Europe, in addition to the debates and reports already mentioned, the most useful general works are V. D. Hurd's *The Council of Europe* (New York, 1958) and the Council's own *Ten Years of European Co-operation* (Strasbourg, 1958). For the earlier atmosphere, the European Movement's *The European Movement and the Council of Europe* (London, 1949) is still worth consulting. A more specialist work, by an American political scientist, is Ernst B. Haas's *Consensus Formation in the Council of Europe* (Berkeley, Calif., 1960). A. H. Robertson's *The Council of Europe* (second edition, London, 1962) is a helpful and detailed background study.

On the European Coal and Steel Community, an early introductory work is Henry L. Mason's *The European Coal and Steel Community* (The Hague, 1955); but the most comprehensive studies are William Diebold Jr's *The Schuman Plan* (New York, 1959), Louis Lister's more technical *Europe's Coal and Steel Community* (New York, 1960), and Ernst B. Haas's *The Uniting of Europe* (revised edition, Stanford, Calif., 1968), which treats the ECSC as a case-study in the political 'spillover' effects of economic integration. H. A. Schmitt's *The Path to European Union* (Baton Rouge, La., 1962) is more restricted in range, but brief and reliable.

European Integration, edited by C. Grove Haines (Baltimore, 1957) is a vivid symposium on the general lessons of the ECSC; Norman J. Pounds' and William N. Parker's *Coal and Steel in Western Europe* (Bloomington, Ind., 1957) supplies the (solid) technical background.

The abortive European Defence Community figures chiefly in the periodical literature, in general works and in a few studies not available in English. The most accessible single book on the subject is *France Defeats EDC* by Daniel Lerner and Raymond Aron (New York, 1957).

Euratom, the European Atomic Energy Community, is also sparsely documented in English, except in its own publications. There are two early American studies still of some interest: Klaus E. Knorr's *Euratom and American Policy* (Princeton, NJ, 1956), and Ben T. Moore's *Euratom: the American Interest in the European Atomic Energy Community* (New York, 1958). Otherwise, the most helpful work on the political, legal, and institutional sides is *Euratom, Analyses et Commentaires* (Brussels, 1958), by Jacques Errera and others.

The Common Market or European Economic Community, on the other hand, is the subject of innumerable studies. One of the most authoritative introductions is *United Europe: Challenge and Opportunity* (Cambridge, Mass./ Oxford, 1962), by Walter Hallstein, the EEC Commission's first President. Robert Lemaignen, another member of the first EEC Commission, has published engaging and illuminating memoirs of its early days in *L'Europe au berceau: souvenirs d'un technocrate* (Paris, 1964); while Jean-François Deniau, formerly an official and later a member of the Commission, has contributed a good theoretical study of it in *The Common Market* (third edition, London, 1962). Introductory manuals on the EEC, written wholly or partly by staff members, include *International Manual on the European Economic Community*, edited by H. K. Junckerstorff (St Louis, Mo., 1963); *A Handbook on the European Economic Community*, edited by Gordon L. Weil (Washington/New York/London, 1965); and *Community Europe*, by Roger Broad and Robert Jarrett (London, 1967). Reliable studies by journalists include Pierre Drouin's *L'Europe du Marché commun* (Paris, 1963);

Paul Fabra's *Y a-t-il un marché commun?* (Paris, 1965); and Stuart de la Mahotière's *Towards One Europe* (London, 1970).

On the theory and practice of European economic integration, a first sceptical essay was Michael T. Florinsky's *Integrated Europe?* (New York, 1955). It was followed by the rather less severe *Economic Theory and Western European Integration* (London, 1958), by Tibor Scitovsky. More interesting, because written in the light of the Common Market's practical experience, are Stephen Holt's *The Common Market: the Conflict of Theory and Practice* (London, 1967), and D. Swann's *The Economics of the Common Market* (London, revised, 1972). *Economic Integration in Europe*, edited by Geoffrey Denton (London, 1969), is a fairly specialised symposium; *The Political Dynamics of European Economic Integration*, by Leon N. Lindberg, is an American political scientist's admirable examination of the Common Market's workings in three key fields.

More specialised aspects of the EEC have attracted separate attention. The legal innovations of the system have been studied as early as the days of the Coal and Steel Community, in D. G. Valentine's *The Court of Justice of the European Coal and Steel Community* (The Hague, 1954). More recent work includes *Common Market Law*, by Alan Campbell and Dennis Thompson (London, 1962); *The Court of the European Communities*, by Werner Feld (The Hague, 1964); Stuart A. Scheingold's *The Rule of Law in European Integration* (New Haven, Conn., 1965); and Edward Wall's *Europe: Unification and Law* (London, 1969). On economic policy, a good brief introduction is Geoffrey Denton's *Planning in the EEC* (London, 1967); so is *Concentration or Competition: A European Dilemma?* (London, 1967) by D. Swann and D. L. McLachlan, joint authors of the more elaborate *Competition Policy in the European Communities* (London, 1967). On agriculture, a standard introduction is *Food, Farming and the Common Market*, by M. Butterwick and C. J. Rolfe (Oxford, 1968); Adrien Zeller's *L'Imbroglio agricole du marché commun* (Paris, 1970) is a well-documented attack on the EEC's agricultural policy by a member of the Commis-

31

sion's staff; useful background is supplied by S. H. Franklin's sociological study of *The European Peasantry* (London, 1969), and by the discursive survey of social change inside and outside agriculture edited by R. H. Beck, *The Changing Structure of Europe* (Minneapolis, 1970); also relevant is Sergio Barzanti's *The Underdeveloped Areas within the Common Market* (Princeton, NJ, 1965). On transport, see Brian T. Bayliss's *European Transport* (London, 1965), and the briefer, more stimulating *The Transport Policy of the European Communities* (London, 1969). On trade unions, the key works are those of R. Colin Beever: *European Unity and the Trade Union Movement* (Leyden, 1961), and *Trade Unions and Free Labour Movement* (London, 1969). In a cognate area, a useful study is Brian Criddle's *Socialists and European Integration* (London, 1969). On the Community institutions, a good brief guide is Richard Mayne's *The Institutions of the European Community* (London, 1968); on the staff, David Coombes's short *Towards a European Civil Service* (London, 1968) and his more elaborate *Politics and Bureaucracy in the European Community* (London, 1970).

On the Common Market and the rest of the world, an excellent partisan introduction is Max Kohnstamm's *The European Community and its Role in the World* (Columbia, Mo., 1964). On world trade issues, James Jay Allen's *The European Common Market and the GATT* (Washington, 1960) and Isaiah Frank's *The European Common Market: An Analysis of Commercial Policy* (New York, 1961) both reflect mainly American preoccupations, which are more explicitly dealt with in F. S. C. Northrop's *European Union and United States Foreign Policy* (New York, 1954), in *The European Economic Community and the United States*, by Robert R. Bowie and Theodore Geiger (Washington, 1961), in Randall Hinshaw's *The European Community and American Trade* (New York, 1964), in Don D. Humphrey's *The United States and the Common Market* (New York, 1962 /London, 1965), and in George M. Taber's *John F. Kennedy and a United Europe* (Bruges, 1969). The Community's policy and attitudes vis-à-vis developing countries are dealt with summarily in Sir William Gorell Barnes's brief *Europe and the Developing World* (London, 1967) and its African policy in P. C. C. Okibo's *Africa and the Common Market* (London, 1967). *India and the European Economic Community*, by Dharma Kumar (Bombay, 1966) is a penetrating study by an Indian economist; Sidney Dell's *Trade Blocs and Common Markets* (London, 1963), a critical cross-questioning by an expert from the United Nations.

The Common Market's political difficulties and possible political future are surveyed in John Pinder's polemical *Europe Against De Gaulle* (London, 1963). The political ideas of the former French President are summarised and attacked by Lord Gladwyn in *De Gaulle's Europe* (London, 1969); his quarrel with the Common Market in 1965 is described in John Newhouse's *Collision in Brussels* (London, 1968) and in Miriam Camps's *European Unification in the Sixties* (New York, 1966). The aftermath of the 1965 crisis is also dealt with in Altiero Spinelli's *The Eurocrats* (Baltimore, 1966). Miriam Camps's *What Kind of Europe* (London, 1965) is partly a brief study of the preceding months' history, partly a speculative look ahead; similarly marked by then current preoccupations is David P. Calleo's *Europe's Future* (New York, 1965). T. D. Cabot's *The Common Market: Economic Foundation for a United States of Europe?* (New York, 1959) raises the political question explicitly, as does Roy Pryce's short *The Political Future of the European Community* (London, 1962). In *Towards Political Union* (London, 1964), the Political Commission of the European Parliament offers a series of documents on the abortive 'Fouchet Plan' for political cooperation among the Common Market six; in *Europe After De Gaulle* (London, 1969), Roy Pryce and John Pinder propose a federal alternative. This and other 'scenarios' for Europe's future organisation are considered in *Europe's Futures, Europe's Choices,* edited by Alastair Buchan (London, 1969).

Great Britain's relations with the European Communities are almost as well documented in English as the Communities themselves. A useful handbook to the literature is Carol Ann Cosgrove's *A Reader's Guide to Britain and the European Communities* (London, 1970). The best single history is

Miriam Camps's *Britain and the European Community 1959–1963* (London, 1963); its story is continued in *Britain Faces Europe*, by Robert L. Pfaltzgraff, Jr (Philadelphia, 1969). For a slightly earlier period, see the Royal Institute of International Affairs booklet, *Britain in Western Europe* (London, 1956); for the period of the Coal and Steel Community, H. J. Heiser's *British Policy with regard to the Unification Efforts on the European Continent* (Leyden, 1959); for the controversies surrounding the Free Trade Area proposal and its sequel, Emile Benoit's *Europe at Sixes and Sevens* (New York, 1963). For the breakdown of the 1961–63 negotiations, a racy journalistic account is Nora Beloff's *The General Says No* (London, 1963); a more considered study of this and especially later episodes is John Newhouse's *De Gaulle and the Anglo-Saxons* (London, 1970). On the 1967 attempt to join the Common Market, the best documentation is supplied by *The Second Try: Labour and the EEC* (London, 1968), edited by Uwe Kitzinger. Other useful general studies and collections are: Evan Luard's *Britain and Europe* (London, 1961); Alexander Lamfalussy's comparison of growth rates and economies, *The United Kingdom and the Six* (London, 1963); Uwe Kitzinger's essay collection, *Britain, Europe, and Beyond* (Leyden, 1964); *Britain and the Common Market 1967*, edited from a BBC talks and discussion series by Anthony Moncrieff (London, 1967); *Economics: Britain and the EEC*, edited by M. A. G. van Meerhaeghe (London, 1969); and H. J. Huizinga's barbed and amusing reminiscences, *Confessions of a European in England* (London, 1958). Among the advocates of British membership of the European Communities, the most notable are: Anthony Nutting, in *Europe Will Not Wait* (London, 1960); Uwe Kitzinger, in *The Challenge of the Common Market* (Oxford, 1961); John Pinder, in *Britain and the Common Market* (London, 1961); Michael Shanks and John Lambert, in *Britain and the New Europe* (London, 1962); John Mander, in *Great Britain or Little England?* (London, 1963); Drew Middleton, in *The Supreme Choice* (London, 1963); Edward Beddington-Behrens, in *Is There Any Choice? Britain Must Join Europe* (London, 1966); John Lambert, in *Britain in a Federal Europe* (London, 1968); Pierre Uri, in his symposium *From Commonwealth to Common Market* (London, 1968); and J. L. Zaring, a member of the US CIA writing in his own name, in *Design for Europe* (Baltimore, 1969). Works of a more hostile or critical character include E. Strauss's *Common Sense About the Common Market* (London, 1958) and *European Reckoning* (London, 1962); W. Horsfall Carter's *Speaking European* (London, 1966); Piers Dixon's *Double Diploma* (London, 1968), a biography of Sir Pierson Dixon by his son which includes critical comments on the 1961–63 negotiations; Douglas Jay's *After the Common Market* (London, 1968), a well argued but narrowly conceived statement of the economic case against Britain's joining the Common Market; and *The Atlantic Commonwealth* by George E. G. Catlin, an advocate of Atlantic alternatives (London, 1969). On the technical problems of British membership, Edgard Pisani and others discuss agriculture, monetary policy, technology, and institutions in reports prepared for the Action Committee for the United States of Europe and published as *Problems of British Entry Into the EEC* (London, 1969). Agriculture is also examined by T. K. Warley in *Agriculture: the Cost of Joining the Common Market* (London, 1967); the pound sterling, by Susan Strange in *The Sterling Problem and the Six* (London, 1967); and fiscal policy, in *Taxes in the EEC and Britain: the Problem of Harmonization* (London, 1968). Finally, *The Free Trade Area Proposals,* edited by G. D. N. Worswick (Oxford, 1960), examines the Free Trade Area project, and *The Seven,* by F. V. Meyer (London, 1960), the European Free Trade Association.

Individual Countries and Miscellaneous

Austria

Two popular surveys describe Austria's post-war recovery: R. Hiscocks's *The Rebirth of Austria* (London, 1953), and G. Shepherd's *The Austrian Odyssey* (London, 1957). *Four-Power Control in Germany and Austria 1945–1946,* edited by Arnold Toynbee, covers the immediate postwar years.

Benelux and the Benelux Countries

In *Negotiations for Benelux* (Princeton, NJ, 1957), the British economist James Meade describes the steps that led to the nascent economic union of Belgium, the Netherlands, and Luxembourg. Margot Lyon's *Belgium* (London, 1971) is an excellent introduction; Frank E. Huggett's *Modern Belgium* (London, 1969) a fairly up-to-date survey. *Mr Europe*, by J. H. Huizinga (London, 1961). Books on the Netherlands are few in English: one notable contribution to post-war history is Henry L. Mason's *The Purge of the Dutch Quislings* (London, 1956). On Luxembourg, there is A. H. Cooper-Prichard's *History of the Grand Duchy of Luxembourg* (Luxembourg, 1950).

France

Two general histories, in particular, contain useful sections on the postwar period: Alfred Cobban's *History of Modern France, Vol. III, 1871–1962* (paperback edition, London, 1965) and David Thomson's *Democracy in France Since 1870* (fifth edition, London, 1969). On the immediate post-war period, Dorothy M. Pickles's *French Politics: the First Years of the Fourth Republic* (New York/London, 1953) is outstanding. Also useful is Alexander Werth's *France 1940–1945* (Boston/London, 1956); on the Liberation in particular, see Peter Novick's *The Resistance versus Vichy* (London, 1968). Gordon Wright's *The Reshaping of French Democracy* (London, 1950) is more general. On the Fourth Republic, a good standard work is Jacques Fauvet's *La IVième république* (Paris, 1959); far more detailed, however, is Philip M. Williams's *Crisis and Compromise: Politics in the Fourth Republic* (London, 1964). For 'inside stories', the best source is Georgette Elgey's *La République des illusions* (Paris, 1965), together with her *La République des contradictions* (Paris, 1968). On foreign policy, see Alfred Grosser, *La IVième république et sa politique extérieure* (Paris, 1961). On Mendès-France, there are two rather unacademic works: Alexander Werth's *The Strange History of Pierre Mendès-France* (London, 1957) and Pierre Rouanet's partisan *Mendès-France au pouvoir* (Paris, 1965).

On De Gaulle and the Fifth Republic, there are many works. The most notable biographies are those of Edward Ashcroft, *De Gaulle* (London, 1952); Paul-Marie de la Gorce, *De Gaulle entre deux mondes* (Paris, 1964); Alexander Werth, *De Gaulle: A Political Biography* (third edition, London, 1969); Aidan Crawley, *De Gaulle* (London, 1969); and Jean Lacouture, *De Gaulle* (London, 1970). On the Fifth Republic itself, see Philip M. Williams's and M. Harrison's *De Gaulle's Republic* (London, 1960) and Dorothy Pickles's *The Fifth French Republic* (third edition, London, 1965). Paul Reynaud's *La politique étrangère du Gaullisme* (Paris, 1964) is an enjoyably ferocious attack. On the OAS, etc, see John Steward Ambler's *The French Army in Politics* (Columbus, Ohio, 1966). For a gossipy account of De Gaulle's assumption of power in 1958, see Merry and Serge Bromberger's *Les 13 complots du 13 mai* (Paris, 1959); for only slightly less gossipy information about the General, J.-R. Tournoux's *Pétain et de Gaulle* (Paris, 1964) and *La Tragédie du Général* (Paris, 1967).

On French politics in general, the best introduction is Pierre Avril's *Politics in France* (London, 1969). Particular aspects are studied by W. Bosworth's *Catholicism and Crisis in Modern France* (Princeton, NJ, 1962); R. Capelle's *The MRP and French Foreign Policy* (New York, 1963); C. Micaud's *Communism and the French Left* (London, 1963); David Caute's *Communism and the French Intellectuals* (London/New York, 1964); B. D. Graham's *The French Socialists and Tripartism 1944–1947* (London, 1965); *Nationalization in France and Italy*, by M. Einaudi and others (Ithaca, NY, 1955); and Malcolm MacLennan's *French Planning: Some Lessons for Britain* (London, 1963).

General surveys of France and journalists' books include: Herbert Luthy's *The State of France* (London, 1955; published as *France Against Herself* in New York, 1955); David Schoenbrun's *As France Goes* (London, 1957); *France: Change and Tradition*, by Stanley Hoffmann and others (London, 1963); Janet Flanner's alert *Paris Journal 1944–1965* (London, 1966); Crane Brinton's *The Americans and the French* (Cambridge, Mass., 1968); and John Ardagh's *The New France* (new edition, London, 1970). On the 1968 '*événements*', the best study is *French Revolution 1968*, by Patrick Seale and Maureen McConville (London, 1968).

On the Algerian problem, the best introduction is Dorothy Pickles's *Algeria and France* (London, 1963), closely followed by the more vivid and personal *The Algerian Problem*, by Edward Behr (London, 1961). Also useful are J. Gillespie's *Algeria: Rebellion and Revolution* (London, 1960); C. L. Sulzberger's *The Test: De Gaulle and Algeria* (London, 1962); and Germaine Tillion's *Algeria, The Realities* (London, 1958).

Germany

General introductory surveys include: *Germany*, by John Midgley (London, 1968); *West Germany*, by Michael Balfour (London, 1968); and *The German Federal Republic*, by Alfred Grosser (New York, 1964). On politics, see Elmer Plischke's *Contemporary Government of Germany* (London, 1964); D. A. Chalmer's *The Social Democratic Party of Germany* (New Haven, Conn., 1964); and Ralf Dahrendorf's *Society and Democracy in Germany* (London, 1964). A useful official handbook is *Germany Reports* (Wiesbaden, 1953).

Histories of modern Germany include M. Dill's *Germany: A Modern History* (Michigan, 1961); F. Meinecke's *The German Catastrophe* (Cambridge, Mass., 1950); *The Shaping of Postwar Germany*, by Edgar McInnis, Richard Hiscocks, and Robert Spencer (Toronto/London, 1960); and *The Death and Life of Germany*, by Eugene Davidson (London, 1959).

On the zoning of Germany, see Philip E. Mosely's *The Kremlin in World Politics* (paperback edition, New York, 1960); on immediate post-war suffering, Victor Gollancz's *In Darkest Germany* (London, 1947); on the beginnings of the Federal Republic, J. F. Golay's *The Founding of the Federal Republic of Germany* (Chicago, 1958) and P. H. Merkl's *The Origins of the Western German Republic* (New York, 1963).

The Nuremberg trials are fully reported in *Trials of the Major War Criminals before the International Military Tribunal* (forty-two volumes, Nuremberg, 1947–9) and *Trials of War Criminals before the Nuremberg Military Tribunals* (fifteen volumes, Washington, 1951–2). Eye-witness accounts include R. W. Cooper's *The Nuremberg Trials* (London, 1946), and G. M. Gilbert's *Nuremberg Diary* (New York, 1947). Other studies include *Political Justice* by O. Kirchheimer (Princeton, NJ, 1961), and *The Nuremberg Trials,* by J. J. Heydecker and J. Leeb (London, 1962). Also relevant are Whitney R. Harris's *Tyranny on Trial* (Dallas, Texas, 1954); Lord Hankey's *Politics, Trials, and Errors* (Oxford, 1950); and Gordon Young's *The Fall and Rise of Alfried Krupp* (London, 1960). William Manchester's heavily loaded *The Arms of Krupp* (paperback edition, 1970) also has sections on the Krupp trial.

On post-war military government of Germany, a general survey is given in *Four-Power Control in Germany and Austria 1945–1946,* edited by Arnold Toynbee (London, 1956). More detail can be found in F. S. V. Dennison's *Civil Affairs and Military Government: North-West Europe 1944– 1946* (New York, 1961). On the American zone, there are two graphic studies by Harold Zink – *American Military Government in Germany* (New York, 1947), and *The United States in Germany 1944–1955* (New York, 1957). A useful symposium is *Governing Post-War Germany,* by E. H. Litchfield and others (Ithaca, NY, 1953). General Clay's own account of his stewardship is provided in *Decision in Germany,* by Lucius D. Clay (London, 1950); Henry Morgenthau's short-lived recipe for the 'pastoralization' of Germany, in *Germany is our Problem* (New York, 1945). On the British zone, an interestingly personal account is that by Raymond Ebsworth, *Restoring Democracy in Germany: the British Contribution* (London/New York, 1960); further sidelights on British attitudes occur in D. C. Watt's *Britain Looks to Germany* (London, 1965) and Constantine Fitzgibbon's *Denazification* (London, 1969). Also relevant is *The Struggle for Democracy in Germany,* edited by G. A. Almond (Chapel Hill, NC, 1949).

On Germany's East-West problems, useful studies include: *Wartime Origins of the East-West Dilemma over Germany,* by John L. Snell (New Orleans, 1959); *Germany Between East and West,* by Wolfgang Stolper (Washington, 1960); *Germany*

Between Two Worlds, by G. Freund (New York, 1961); *The Struggle for Germany 1914–1945,* by Lionel Kochan (Edinburgh, 1963); and *Germany Between East and West: The Reunification Problem* (Englewood Cliffs, NJ, 1965).

On Berlin, Wolfgang Heidelmeyer and Guenter Hindrich have edited a useful collection of *Documents on Berlin 1943–1963* (second edition, Munich, 1963). Accounts of the subject include: E. Butler's *City Divided: Berlin 1955* (New York, 1955); W. P. Davison's *The Berlin Blockade* (Princeton, NJ, 1958); B. L. R. Smith's *The Governance of Berlin* (New York, 1959); *Berlin – Pivot of German Destiny,* translated and edited by Charles B. Robson (Chapel Hill, NC, 1960); Hans Speier's *Divided Berlin* (London, 1961); John Mander's *Berlin: Hostage for the West* (London, 1962); and Philip Windsor's *City on Leave: A History of Berlin 1945–62* (London/New York, 1963). Journalistic accounts of the same subject include William H. Conland's *Berlin: Beset and Bedevilled* (New York, 1963) and *The Berlin Wall,* by Pierre Galante and Jack Miller (London, 1965).

On German economic revival, the writings of its leading symbol, Ludwig Erhard, provide some insights: *Germany's Comeback in the World Market* (London, 1954); *Prosperity Through Competition* (second edition, London, 1959); and *The Economics of Success* (London, 1963). A helpful early study is Henry C. Wallich's *Mainsprings of German Revival* (New Haven, Conn., 1955); useful for background is Norman J. G. Pounds's *The Economic Pattern of Modern Germany* (London, 1963). For less austere tastes, William Henry Chamberlin provides a readable narrative in *The German Phoenix* (London, 1964); while more technical problems are explored in Patrick Boarman's *Germany's Economic Dilemma: Inflation and the Balance of Payments* (New Haven, Conn./London, 1964), and in Karl W. Roskamp's *Capital Formation in West Germany* (Detroit, 1965). Richard Hiscocks has examined *Germany Revived* (London, 1966); and Heinz Abosch has claimed to detect *The Menace of the Miracle* (London, 1962).

On German foreign policy, the first work of significance is *Germany Rejoins the Powers,* by K. W. Deutsch and L. J.

Edinger (Stanford, Calif., 1959). In *Germany and Europe* (London, 1964), Heinrich von Brentano outlines the Adenauer policy he helped to implement; in *Decision for Europe* (London, 1964), his successor Gerhard Schroeder does the same. In *Histoire du réarmement allemand depuis 1950* (Paris, 1965), Jules Moch traces with some bitterness the re-creation of a German national army.

Miscellaneous and colourful surveys of post-war Germany include: *The Survivors: A Report on the Jews in Germany Today,* by Norbert Muhlen (New York, 1962); K. Boelling's *Republic in Suspense* (London, 1964); Peter H. Merkl's *Germany Yesterday and Tomorrow* (New York, 1965); Hermann Eich's tortured *The Unloved Germans* (London, 1965); and *This Germany,* by Rudolf Walter Leonhardt (Greenwich, Conn., 1964; paperback edition, London, 1969).

Greece
The early post-war history of Greece is well recounted in Bickham Sweet-Escott's *Greece: A Political and Economic Survey 1939–1953* (London, 1955).

Iberian Peninsula
Useful reading includes W. C. Atkinson's *A History of Spain and Portugal* (London/Baltimore, 1960); Stanley G. Payne's *Falange: A History of Spanish Fascism* (Stanford, Calif., 1961/London, 1962); Benjamin Wilks's *Spain: The Gentle Anarchy* (New York/London, 1965); J. W. D. Trythall's *Franco: A Biography* (London, 1970); George Hills's *Spain* (London, 1970); and *Oldest Ally: A Portrait of Salazar's Portugal* (London/New York, 1961).

Iceland
John C. Griffiths's *Modern Iceland* (London, 1969) is unique in this field.

Italy
Introductory surveys include Muriel Grindrod's brief *Italy* (London, 1964); Margaret Carlyle's excellent if dated *Modern Italy* (London, 1957); and Ninetta Jucker's vivid *Italy*

(London, 1970). Histories include H. Stuart Hughes's *The United States and Italy* (Cambridge, Mass., 1953); Muriel Grindrod's *The Rebuilding of Italy* (London, 1955); Denis Mack Smith's *Italy: A Modern History* (Ann Arbor, 1959); G. Mammarella's *Italy After Fascism* (Montreal, 1964); and Norman Kogan's *A Political History of Postwar Italy* (London, 1966). Also on politics, Wayland (Hilton-)Young's *The Italian Left* (London, 1949) is still worth consulting, although work of a very different order is being done by Joseph La Palombara, notably in *Interest Groups in Italian Politics* (Princeton, NJ, 1964). On economic affairs, a classic study is George H. Hildebrand's *Growth and Structure in the Economy of Modern Italy* (Cambridge, Mass., 1965); the interaction of economics with politics is examined by Joseph La Palombara in *Italy: The Politics of Planning* (Princeton, NJ, 1966); and more technical problems are considered by Bruno Foa's *Monetary Reconstruction in Italy* (New York, 1949). The problems of the Mezzogiorno are dealt with in Margaret Carlyle's *The Awakening of Southern Italy* (London, 1962); in Gustav Schlachter's *The Italian South* (New York, 1965); and in J. Martarelli's *Economic Developments in Southern Italy 1950–1960* (Washington, 1966). M. V. Posner and S. J. Woolf have studied *Italian Public Enterprise* (London, 1967); P. H. Frankel *Mattei: Oil and Power Politics* (London, 1966); and Dow Votaw *The Six-Legged Dog: Mattei and ENI – a Study in Power* (Berkeley/Los Angeles, 1964). Three slighter books of some interest are: G. R. Gayre's *Italy in Transition* (London, 1946), an eye-witness account of some early post-war scenes; Wayland Young's *The Montesi Scandal* (London, 1957); and Melton S. Davis's account of the same subject, *All Rome Trembled* (London, 1957).

Scandinavia

General works include: *The Scandinavian States and Finland: A Political and Economic Survey*, by G. M. Gathorne-Hardy and others (London, 1951); *Scandinavian Democracy*, edited by J. Lauwerys (Copenhagen, 1958); J. Wuorinen's *Scandinavia* (Englewood Cliffs, NJ, 1965); Donald

S. Connery's *The Scandinavians* (London, 1966); and *Government and Politics in the Nordic Countries,* by N. Andren (Stockholm, n.d.). More specialised are: F. Wendt's *The Nordic Council and Co-operation in Scandinavia (*Copenhagen, 1959), and T. Greve's *Norway and NATO* (Oslo, 1959).

United Kingdom, etc.

Such is the wealth of material that selection here must be severe. Among general histories, the most useful are A. J. P. Taylor's *English History 1914–1945* (Oxford, 1965), which sheds light on the post-war situation; Henry Pelling's *Modern Britain 1885–1955* (paperback edition, London, 1969) and David Thomson's *England in the Twentieth Century 1914–1963* (London, 1964); E. E. Reynolds' and N. H. Brasher's *Britain in the Twentieth Century 1900–1964* (Cambridge, 1964); C. M. Woodhouse's *Postwar Britain* (London, 1966). On economic affairs, the compilations by G. D. N. Worswick and P. H. Ady, *The British Economy 1945–1950* (Oxford, 1952) and *The British Economy in the Nineteen-Fifties* (Oxford, 1962) are indispensable; also valuable are Andrew Shonfield's *British Economic Policy Since the War* (revised edition, London, 1959) and Samuel Brittan's *The Treasury Under the Tories 1951–1964* (London, 1964). Sidelights on an earlier period are cast by Janet Beveridge's *Beveridge and his Plan* (London, 1954) and by *The Age of Austerity,* edited by Michael Sissons and Philip French (London, 1963); on a later, by Anthony Sampson's *Macmillan: A Study in Ambiguity* (paperback edition, London, 1968). On foreign policy (excluding policy vis-à-vis the Common Market, dealt with above), the most notable general works are Max Beloff's *New Dimensions in Foreign Policy* (London, 1961), and F. S. Northedge's *British Foreign Policy: The Process of Readjustment 1945–1961* (London, 1962). Stimulating speculation is offered by David P. Calleo's *Britain's Future* (London, 1968). Finally, one particular episode, the Suez crisis of 1956, has attracted a literature of its own: Merry and Serge Bromberger's characteristic *Secrets of Suez* (paperback edition, London, 1957); L. D. Epstein's *British Politics in the Suez Crisis* (London, 1964); Terence Robertson's *Crisis* (London,

1965); *Suez Ten Years After*, edited from BBC programmes by Anthony Moncrieff (London, 1967); Anthony Nutting's reminiscences, *No End of a Lesson* (London, 1967); and Hugh Thomas's study, *The Suez Affair* (London, 1967).

On the Saar, a contemporary account is F. M. Russell's *The Saar: Battleground and Pawn* (Stanford, Calif., 1951), while the definitive *ex post facto* study is Jacques Freymond's *The Saar Conflict 1945-1955* (London/New York, 1960). On Alto Adige, Antony Alcock's *The History of the South Tyrol Question* (London, 1970) leaves no stone unturned.

Selected Addenda (all London, 1971, unless specified)
Recent memoirs, etc., include Willy Brandt's *In Exile*; George Brown's *In My Way*; R. A. Butler's *The Art of the Possible*; Helmut Schmidt's *The Balance of Power*; and Harold Wilson's *The Labour Government 1964-70*. *Contemporary Europe*, ed. M. S. Archer and S. Giner, is a sociological survey; *Europe Tomorrow*, ed. Richard Mayne (London, 1972), a set of targets. On East-West problems see Karl E. Birnbaum's *Peace in Europe* (London, 1970), Michael Palmer's *The Prospects for a European Security Conference*, and Philip Windsor's *Germany and the Management of Détente*. Michael Niblock's *The EEC: National Parliaments in Community Decision-making*, Stuart A. Scheingold's *The Law in Political Integration* (Cambridge, Mass., 1971), Christopher Layton's *Cross-Frontier Mergers in Europe* (Bath, 1971), Peter Coffey's and John R. Presley's *European Monetary Integration*, and the eponymous Report by Giovanni Magnifico and John Williamson (London, 1972), are all good. On Britain in Europe, see Elisabeth Barker's *Britain in a Divided Europe*, Susan Strange's *Sterling and British Policy*, Ian Davidson's *Britain and the Making of Europe*, and *The Economics of Europe*, ed. John Pinder. On France: Jean Charlot's *The Gaullist Phenomenon*, Daniel Singer's Marxist *Prelude to Revolution: France in May 1968*, and Philip M. William's and Martin Harrison's severe *Politics in De Gaulle's Republic*. On Germany, Terence Prittie's *Adenauer* (London, 1972). On Italy, Elizabeth Wiskemann's *Italy Since 1945* and F. Roy Willis's *Italy Chooses Europe*.

2

The United States of America

Lawrence Silverman

The student of contemporary American history has to contend with a vast mass of material. Apart from the classic works in American history, with which most students will already be familiar, there are many excellent books dealing with aspects of the subject, which overlap and to a large extent are interchangeable with similar studies. It is essential therefore to be selective in one's approach. In this respect particular attention should be paid to the latest publications which frequently offer a resumé of previous work done in the field.

The reading list suggested below tries both to offer a broad selection from an expanding literature and to emphasise works which provide background knowledge for the student, that is which relate specific problems to the wider American context.

At the outset the great classic of American studies, Alexis de Tocqueville's *Democracy in America,* ed. J. P. Meyer and Max Lerner, 2 vols (1835, 1840; New York, 1968, paperback) must be recommended. Though thought of as a new country, the United States has one of the oldest continually operative constitutions in the modern world. Despite the many changes which have taken place, since de Tocqueville wrote, in a society with a flair for innovation, many of de Tocqueville's insights into the nature of American democracy are still relevant today. Much of what is now written about America is still directly or indirectly a commentary on de Tocqueville's work.

The American Character

There has always been lively discussion by Americans and others of what may be regarded as de Tocqueville's major theme, the American character, never more so than in recent years. Two books from across the Atlantic make a good starting point for the exploration of this topic: D. W. Brogan's *The American Character* (New York, 1944); and Geoffrey Gorer, *The American People* (New York, 1948). A quite different perspective is presented in Simone de Beauvoir's *L'Amérique au jour le jour* (Paris, 1954), the author's diary of her brief stay in the United States in 1947. But though the American character has been a matter of continuing concern to foreigners, the subject has been far more extensively covered by natives. Two works that serve to put the more particular observations in a broader context of national character are: Margaret Mead, *And Keep Your Powder Dry* (New York, 1942); and Clyde Kluckhohn, *Mirror for Man* (New York, 1944, ch. 9 especially).

Social Character

More recent works on this subject tend to divide into two series, those placing emphasis mainly on social and economic aspects of contemporary life in America, and those placing greater emphasis on its intellectual characteristics. A seminal work in the first series is *The Lonely Crowd*, subtitled 'A Study of the Changing American Character', by David Riesman, with Nathan Glazer and Reuel Denney (New Haven, Conn., 1950), which applies the relatively new technique of sample interviewing to the analysis of character, and concludes that Americans have changed from being 'inner-directed' to being 'other-directed': that is from being guided by one's conscience to conforming with one's peers. The publication of this book stimulated further speculation and investigation along the same lines, as well as critical reactions. The debate can be followed some of the way in the anthology edited by Seymour Martin Lipset and Leo Lowenthal, *Culture and Social Character* (Glencoe, Ill., 1961). *The Organization Man* by William H. Whyte (New York, 1956) and S. M. Lipset's *The First New Nation* (New York, 1956) are also required reading.

During the same period other analysts have been more concerned with the effects of economic developments. This approach, though the authors' attitudes differ considerably, can be followed in: David M. Potter, *People of Plenty: Economic Abundance and the American Character* (Chicago, 1954); John Kenneth Galbraith, *The Affluent Society* (London, 1958); and Vance O. Packard, *The Status Seekers* (London, 1959), a more popular piece. More critical are two works by C. Wright Mills: *The Power Elite* (London, 1956); and *White Collar: the American Middle Classes* (London, 1952). On this topic there is no shortage of provocative works; the following are worthy of note: E. Digby Baltzell: *An American Business Aristocracy* (first published as *The Philadelphia Gentleman*, Glencoe Ill., 1958); and *The Protestant Establishment* (New York, 1964); A. A. Berle, Jr, *Power Without Property* (New York, 1958); Gabriel Kolko, *Wealth and Power in America* (New York, 1962); articles in Earl F. Cheit (ed.), *The Business Establishment* (New York, 1964); Richard Rovere in *The American Establishment* (New York, 1962); and other articles in the Lipset and Lowenthal anthology cited above.

For the historical background to the urbanisation of the United States see: Constance Green, *The Rise of Urban America* (London, 1966); G. E. Mowry, *The Urban Nation, 1920–1960* (London, 1967); and the adaptation by Wolf von Eckardt of Jean Gottmann's major study, *Megalopolis: the Urbanized North-Eastern Seaboard of the United States* (New York, 1967). A. J. Vidich and J. Bensman, *Small Town in Mass Society* (New York, 1960).

Finally three works of a more general nature: R. M. Williams, *American Society* (rev. ed., New York, 1966); Oscar Handlin, *The American People in the Twentieth Century* (Cambridge, Mass., 1954); and Carl N. Degler, *Out of Our Past: the Forces That Shaped Modern America* (New York, 1962).

American Ideas

The intellectual character of America, the 'governing ideas' of its society, are themes that have been developed also with much enthusiasm since Tocqueville's day. Some very interesting works have been written on this subject, and a few of them at least ought to be read to gain a basic understanding of contemporary America. It is appropriate to mention first a work by an historian who is himself part of the subject-matter, having greatly influenced American thought: *The American Mind: an Interpretation of American Thought and Character Since the 1880s* by Henry Steele Commager (New Haven, Conn., 1950). A monumental contribution to this field of study is Max Lerner's *America as a Civilization: Life and Thought in the United States Today* (London, 1958).

Dealing more with 'higher' thought and culture in America are two anthologies: Arthur M. Schlesinger and M. White (eds), *Paths of American Thought* (London, 1964); and Joseph J. Kwiat and Mary C. Turpie (eds), *Studies in American Culture: Dominant Ideas and Images* (Minneapolis, 1960), which is more variable in character and quality. For a more personal, but highly penetrating, evaluation of American culture see Jaques Barzun, *The House of Intellect* (London, 1959). Well worth examining also in this context is Richard Hofstadter's *Social Darwinism in American Thought* (Boston, 1965); and, as a follow-up, Morton White's *Social Thought in America: the Revolt against Formalism* (Boston, 1966). Concerning developments in a particularly influential area of American 'high culture' see: C. Roscoe and Gisela J. Hinkle, *The Development of Sociology: Its Nature and Growth in the United States* (New York, 1966); and Albert Somit and Joseph T. Tanenhaus (eds), *The Development of American Political Science: From Burgess to Behavioralism* (Boston, 1967). In connection with the former see also, C. Wright Mills, *Sociology and Pragmatism: the Higher Learning in America* (ed. Irving L. Horowitz, New York, 1966), which is amusing as well as thought-provoking about its subjects; and respecting what might be termed the 'lower learning' see an equally provocative earlier work, Robert S. Lynd's *Knowledge for What?: the Place of Social Science in American Culture* (New York, 1964). For critical analysis of the academic treatment of politics in America see: Bernard Crick, *The American Science of Politics* (London, 1959); and Charles A. McCoy and John D. Playford (eds), *Apolitical Politics: a Criticism of Behavioralism* (New York, 1968).

Still on 'higher things', an important aspect of contemporary American culture that should certainly not be overlooked is treated in Alan Heimert's *Religion and the American Mind* (Cambridge, Mass., 1966). On the 'lower' side of things, especially worth reading is Bernard Rosenberg and David M. White (eds), *Mass Culture: the Popular Arts in America* (Glencoe, Ill., 1963). And an interesting work that deals with aspects of American culture, falling between these two levels, is Loren Baritz, *City on a Hill: a History of Ideas and Myths in America* (London, 1964).

Shifting slightly from ideas to ideals, a particularly interesting and important recent work dealing with historical developments in this area is Daniel J. Boorstin's *The Image: or What Happened to the American Dream* (London, 1961). It is instructive to read this book against the background of earlier thinking, as exemplified in Herbert Croly, *The Promise of American Life* (1904. Indianapolis, 1965).

Professor Boorstin's book raises problems about the writing of American history, a subject that is itself important in the present context, since American historians have often written with a view to establishing some point about the intellectual basis of the America of their day. Two general works that can be consulted on this are: H. Wish, *The American Historian: a Social-Intellectual History of the Writing of the American Past* (London, 1960); and Lee Benson, *Turner and Beard: American Historical Writing Reconsidered* (Glencoe, Ill., 1960). Anyone wishing to follow this line of enquiry further must certainly read Frederick Jackson Turner's own contribution, *The Frontier in American History* (1920. New York, 1968), which emphasises the importance of economic opportunity in the development of American social and political ideas. A somewhat different view is taken by

Louis Hartz in *The Liberal Tradition in America: an Interpretation of American Political Thought since the Revolution* (New York, 1955); he places more emphasis on the absence of a feudal past, and the reception of Lockean ideas in the period before independence. The, for America, less orthodox conservative view is set out in Clinton L. Rossiter's *Seedtime of the Republic: the Origin of the American Tradition of Political Liberty* (New York, 1953). Another historian, Richard Hofstadter, has emphasised the continuity of intellectual development through successive eras since the Revolution, particularly in *The American Political Tradition and the Men Who Made It* (New York, 1948), which demonstrates the basic agreement among American statesmen with different ideas.

Apart from these books which seek to establish the derivation of the contemporary intellectual character of America in general terms, there are some valuable works dealing with more specific themes. One such is another book by Richard Hofstadter, *Anti-Intellectualism in American Life* (London, 1964), though that has something of the character of a tract for the times. Two particularly important earlier works that can still be read with much profit are: R. B. Perry, *Puritanism and Democracy* (New York, 1944); and Carl L. Becker, *Freedom and Responsibility in the American Way of Life* (New York, 1953; based on lectures delivered in 1944). (Obviously, 1944 was a year that concentrated the American mind more than usual!) Two more recent works worth considering here, though not in the same class, are: Hans Kohn, *American Nationalism* (New York, 1957); and Y. Arieli, *Individualism and Nationalism in American Ideology* (Cambridge, Mass., 1964).

American Democracy

Among books of this kind there are some particularly valuable recent works dealing more broadly with Tocqueville's general theme of democracy, some placing greater emphasis on democratic ideas, others concerned primarily with democratic institutions. First, another minor classic by a British author, Harold J. Laski, *The American Democracy: a Commentary and an Interpretation* (London, 1949), which remains well worth reading for insights into the American system of government. A good intellectual history relevant to the subject is, Ralph H. Gabriel, *The Course of American Democratic Thought* (2nd ed., New York, 1956). An important contemporary treatment of the theme, of interest to all who have concern for the present status of democracy, is Robert A. Dahl, *A Preface to Democratic Theory* (Chicago, 1956). This book raises serious questions about the meaning of democracy today, some of which have arisen in consequence of recent empirical researches. Some of these same questions are raised in a more institutional context in another important modern work, William H. Riker's *Democracy in the United States* (2nd ed., New York, 1965). Professor Dahl has carried his thoughts further in his more recent book, *Pluralist Democracy in the United States: Conflict and Consent* (Chicago, 1967). Other works well worth consulting, though with a narrower focus, are: Morris Janowitz and Dwaine Marvick, *Competitive Pressure and Democratic Consent* (Ann Arbor, Mich., 1956); V. O. Key, Jr, *Public Opinion and American Democracy* (New York, 1962); and Murray Clark Havens, *The Challenge to Democracy: Consensus and Extremism in American Politics* (Austin, 1965). Two anthologies give a spectrum of views on these themes: Leonard J. Fein (ed.), *American Democracy: Essays on Image and Realities* (New York, 1964); and Henry W. Ehrman (ed.), *Democracy in a Changing Society* (New York, 1965). Two most interesting, if idiosyncratic, critical essays in defence of American democracy are: Reinhold Niebuhr, *The Children of Light and the Children of Darkness,* subtitled 'A vindication of democracy and a critique of its traditional defenders' (New York, 1945), expressing the thoughts of the leading American theologian, and Walter Lippmann, *Essays in the Public Philosophy* (London, 1956), giving the views of America's most important political commentator of recent times. More thoroughly critical of the ways of democracy is *All Honor-*

able Men: Corruption and Compromise in American Life by Walter Goodman (London, 1964).

Current Political Tendencies

Turning to more explicitly political aspects of the subject, a good starting point is Robert E. Lane's study of the political attitudes and beliefs of fifteen American working men: *Political Ideology: Why the American Common Man Believes What He Does* (New York, 1962). This work has been criticised on technical grounds, but can be taken as indicative of widespread if unsophisticated modes of thought in America. A less characteristic mode of American political thought is presented by Clinton L. Rossiter in *Conservatism in America: the Thankless Persuasion* (2nd ed., New York, 1962), representing at least one man's American conservatism. For supplementation, read also Allen Guttman, *The Conservative Tradition in America* (London, 1968). The word 'conservative' took on a rather different meaning from that intended by Rossiter during the later fifties and the sixties. The semantic mutation can be followed part way by reading Senator Barry Goldwater's book, *The Conscience of a Conservative* (New York, 1960). It can be followed right through with John A. Broyles, *The John Birch Society: Anatomy of a Protest* (Boston, 1964). The ground is well charted in Daniel Bell (ed.), *The New American Right* (New York, 1955) and in *The Radical Right* (New York, 1963). Richard Hofstadter, a contributor to the Bell anthology, has other important things to say on this and related matters in *The Paranoid Style in American Politics* (London, 1966), a collection of some of his essays. For a conspectus of this area of the American political field, see Arnold Foster and Benjamin R. Epstein, *Danger on the Right* (New York, 1964), published under the auspices of the Anti-Defamation League of B'nai B'rith.

Looking at the other side of the picture, a good introduction to some American brands of radicalism is T. B. Bottomore's *Critics of Society: Radical Thought in North America* (London, 1967). Broader in scope, one of the best books dealing with the subject that has come out in recent years, though not one that would receive the assent of all scholars, is Christopher Lasch, *The New Radicalism in America (1889–1963): the Intellectual as a Social Type* (London, 1966). It is a book that should certainly be read by anyone with an interest in this aspect of contemporary American politics, especially as it is one of the few to set the immediate past in historical perspective. Many books on the Left in America, especially the New Left, tend to be rather journalistic and lacking in historical sense. One that is rather better than most for those who wish to sample the material is *A Prophetic Minority: the American New Left* by Jack Newfield (London, 1967). However, such books tend to go out of date in a few months. A good book in a more traditional vein is Howard W. Morgan (ed.), *American Socialism, 1900–1960* (New York, 1960). Another interesting book that places recent tendencies in some sort of historical perspective, though its contents are of variable quality, is S. M. Lipset (ed.), *Student Politics: Movements Past and Present* (New York, 1967). Dealing with a different, though not unrelated, theme that has had some prominence in the last year or so is *The Radical Liberal: New Man in American Politics* by Arnold S. Kaufman (New York, 1968). This illustrates some of the confusion that has arisen in the traditional American spectrum in consequence of recent developments, and helps to make a little clearer what some leading American politicians and publicists are talking about.

Finally, two works of broader coverage that make fascinating reading when taken together: Daniel Bell, *The End of Ideology: on the Exhaustion of Political Ideas in the Fifties* (New York, 1964); and George Thayer, *The Farther Shores of Politics: the American Political Fringe Today* (London, 1968). Despite what the latter describes, the former remains an important contribution to the discussion of recent political trends in America, and, indeed, throughout the West.

Southern Politics

So far, the works cited have referred to the United States

53

overall, rather than to any sub-division of it in particular. For the most part, this is the appropriate approach for the general reader and student, since what is true of the whole is largely true of the parts. The great exception to this is the South, which has its own literature. Three books, each a classic in its own way, deserve special mention. First in time and importance is John C. Calhoun's *Disquisition on Government* (1851. New York, 1953), perhaps the only example of original political philosophy in the classic form produced by America. Its philosophy was overtaken by the consequences of the Civil War; but it remains a most valuable means to understanding the South, even today. A more recent presentation of the Southern mentality is Wilbur J. Cash, *The Mind of the South* (New York, 1941) which, though also overtaken by events, continues to offer significant insights into its subject. The third of these books, though not much later in time than the second, is very much more 'modern' in its methods, which are those of much contemporary political analysis in the United States. This is V. O. Key's *Southern Politics in State and Nation* (New York, 1949).

The American Economy

Having surveyed the very broad 'sociocultural' and 'sociopolitical' fields, it is appropriate to turn to the narrower and perhaps more mundane, though no less important, area of the 'socio-economic'. As a link with the kinds of works already considered, a particularly valuable book is, Francis X. Sutton *et al., The American Business Creed* (Cambridge, Mass., 1956). Broader in scope, and more systematic (also more idiosyncratic) in its critical stance, is another work by John Kenneth Galbraith: *The New Industrial State* (London, 1967). This book, some of the main themes of which were the subject of Professor Galbraith's Reith Lectures, has important and controversial things to say about Western economies and societies generally; but it naturally focuses primarily on the United States. It made its author symbolic of an economic point of view that is intellectually and politically at odds with the 'prevailing orthodoxy' (or 'neo-

54

orthodoxy'), but which expresses a quite traditional Western, more particularly American, philosophy. It is undoubtedly akin to certain works of C. Wright Mills and other critical observers of contemporary America, cited above (pp. 47–50). As a counterweight, an up-to-date historical treatment of the American economy written from a contrary standpoint should be read, and a book that meets the requirement particularly well is, Louis M. Hacker, *The Course of American Economic Growth and Development* (New York, 1970). Also informative, though now rather dated, is Thomas C. Cochran, *The American Business System: a Historical Perspective, 1900– 1955* (Cambridge, Mass., 1957). A standard text that has been brought up to date is Clement L. Harriss, *The American Economy: Principles, Practices and Policies* (5th ed., Homewood, Ill., 1965). In more speculative vein, and for that reason more thought-provoking, is Arnold B. Barach's *USA and its Economic Future* (New York, 1964). An interesting official publication, put out by the Bureau of Labor Statistics, and a useful source of basic data, is *Economic Forces in the United States in Facts and Figures* (Washington, DC, GPO, successive eds).

Dealing with the industrial economy more specifically are: Richard E. Caves, *American Industry: Structure, Conduct and Performance* (2nd ed., Englewood Cliffs, NJ, 1967); and George J. Stigler, *The Organization of Industry* (Homewood, Ill., 1968). For a perspective on the other side of industry, see Florence Peterson's *American Labor Unions: What They Are and How They Work* (2nd ed., New York, 1963). And on external economic relations see, Oscar R. Strackbein, *American Enterprise and Foreign Trade* (Washington, 1965).

The American Polity

To comprehend the immediate environment of contemporary American public affairs it is necessary to dip into the vast literature dealing with the political system of the United States which is also the readiest source of structured information on current affairs. Here, the inevitable starting-point is the Constitution itself. A standard work by one of the foremost

C

scholars in the field is Edward S. Corwin's *Constitution of the United States, Annotated* (Washington, DC: GPO, rev. ed., 1964). Among other works by the same author that have become standards are: with Jack W. Peltason, *Understanding the Constitution* (New York, 4th ed., 1967); and *The 'Higher Law' Background of American Constitutional Law* (Ithaca, 1955). A work on the same topic by another leading scholar, and one that is directed especially towards British students, is Bernard Schwartz, *American Constitutional Law* (London, 1955). For exhaustive treatment of the Constitution, see the same author's *Commentary on the Constitution of the United States* (New York, 3 vols., 1963–5). Bernard Schwartz has also written an excellent historical treatment of the Constitution, *The Reins of Power* (London, 1964). Anyone interested in the subject must read the classic by Charles A. Beard, *An Economic Interpretation of the Constitution* (New York, 1913). And in connection with this work, see also: Robert E. Brown, *Charles Beard and the Constitution* (Princeton, 1956); and Forrest McDonald, *We the People: the Economic Origins of the Constitution* (Chicago, 1963). Another important avenue is explored in Carl J. Friedrich, *The Impact of American Constitutionalism Abroad* (Boston, 1967).

In studying American public affairs, it is most important always to bear in mind the federal nature of the Constitution. For an understanding of this, particularly useful is, Robert A. Goldwin (ed.), *A Nation of States: Essays on the American Federal System* (Chicago, 1963). A more sustained analysis with an historical perspective is William H. Riker's *Federalism: Origin, Operation, Significance* (Boston, 1964).

The importance of the 'living' constitution in American life is brought out by consideration of specific constitutional cases and decisions, and the role of the Supreme Court in public affairs. There are many good books dealing with both topics. Particularly helpful on cases and decisions are: Alpheus T. Mason and William M. Beaney, *American Constitutional Law* (4th ed., Englewood Cliffs, NJ, 1968); Robert E. Cushman, *Leading Constitutional Decisions* (New York, 1966); and Rocco J. Tresolini, *Constitutional Decisions in*

American Government (New York, 1965). On the part played by the Supreme Court, two books by Glendon A. Schubert provide more than a descriptive introduction: *Constitutional Politics: the Political Behavior of Supreme Court Justices and the Constitutional Policies That They Make (*New York, 1960); and *The Judicial Mind: the Attitudes and Ideologies of Supreme Court Justices (1946–1963)* (Evanston, Ill., 1965). Regarding the place of the Supreme Court in American government, an informative and analytical study is, Samuel J. Krislov, *The Supreme Court in the Political Process* (New York, 1965). On the most momentous constitutional decision of recent times, see Daniel M. Berman's *It is so Ordered: the Supreme Court Rules on School Desegregation* (New York, 1966).

The subject of the Supreme Court leads on to a wider consideration of American political institutions. By way of preliminary reading there is much to be said for taking up another classic written by a foreign observer (in this case, British) which many would rank second only to Tocqueville's great work for its enduring qualities. It is *The American Commonwealth* by James, Lord Bryce (2 vols., London, 1888). Its present-day replacements are university textbooks, any of which will do as well as any other in giving the reader an informative, but not often enlivening, account of the American system of government today. There are, however, some very good books dealing with particular parts and aspects of American government and politics.

The American Presidency

On the Presidency, a standard historical work is, Edward S. Corwin, *The President: Office and Powers* (4th ed., New York, 1957). Of more analytical works on the subject, three are outstanding: Louis W. Koenig, *The Chief Executive* (2nd ed., New York, 1968); Richard E. Neustadt, *Presidential Power* (New American Library ed., New York, 1964); and James M. Burns, *Presidential Government* (Boston, 1965). A great many Americans have written on this topic, however, and this is one area in particular in which the reader must make his own selection. There are also many works dealing with special aspects of the Presidency. Among them, particularly worth consulting are: Richard F. Fenno, *The President's Cabinet* (New York, 1959); Corinne Silverman, *The President's Economic Advisers* (Alabama, 1959); Louis W. Koenig, *The Invisible Presidency* (New York, 1960), dealing with the President's advisers; Elmer E. Cornwell, *Presidential Leadership of Public Opinion* (Bloomington, Indiana, 1965); Erwin C. Hargrove, *Presidential Leadership: Personality and Political Style* (New York, 1966), which is good on Presidential decision-making; Theodore C. Sorensen, *Decision-Making in the White House* (New York, 1964), relating particularly to Kennedy's Presidency; Ernest R. May, *The Ultimate Decision: the President as Commander in Chief* (New York, 1960); Edgar E. Robinson *et al.*, *Powers of the President in Foreign Affairs, 1945–1965* (San Francisco, 1966); Sidney Warren, *The President as World Leader* (Philadelphia, 1964); and John Malcolm Smith and Cornelius P. Cotter, *Powers of the President During Crises* (Washington, 1960).

There is also much good material relating to individual Presidents. On Harry S. Truman we have, first, his *Memoirs* (2 vols., New York, 1968). An interesting recent biography is, Alfred Steinberg, *The Man from Missouri: the Life and Times of Harry S. Truman* (New York, 1962); and on his period of office, see also, Cabell Phillips, *The Truman Presidency* (New York, 1966). On two outstanding moments during the period, see: Irwin Ross, *The Loneliest Campaign: the Truman Victory of 1948* (New York, 1968); and John W. Spanier, *The Truman-MacArthur Controversy and the Korean War* (New York, 1965). On Dwight D. Eisenhower, see his own *The White House Years, Mandate for Change* (New York, 1963; paperback, 1965). Very valuable also is *Firsthand Report* by the President's close adviser, Sherman Adams (New York, 1961). Two books relating to the period that are lively as well as informative are: Richard Rovere, *The Eisenhower Years* (New York, 1956), and Emmet Hughes, *The Ordeal of Power* (New York, 1963). Of the extensive literature relating to President John F. Kennedy, two books, written by authors close to him, are especially noteworthy: Arthur M. Schlesinger, Jr, *A Thousand Days* (Boston, 1965); and Theodore C. Sorensen, *Kennedy* (New York, 1965). The Presidency of Lyndon B. Johnson has not been as well covered yet, but a close study might begin with these two recent works: James M. Burns (ed.), *To Heal and to Build: the Programs of President Lyndon B. Johnson* (New York, 1968); and James Deakin, *Lyndon Johnson's Credibility Gap* (Washington, 1968). Finally regarding recent presidential campaigns, see the series on successive elections by Theodore H. White, *The Making of the President, 1960* (etc.) (New York, 1960, 1964, 1968).

The United States Congress

Turning to the American Congress, a good selection from among the many general works on the subject would certainly include: Bertram M. Gross, *The Legislative Struggle: a Study in Social Combat* (New York, 1953); Ernest F. Griffith, *Congress: Its Contemporary Role* (4th ed., New York, 1967); Daniel M. Berman, *In Congress Assembled* (New York, 1964); Louis A. Froman, Jr, *The Congressional Process: Strategies, Rules, Procedures* (Boston, 1967); an anthology, David B. Truman (ed.), *The Congress and America's Future* (Englewood Cliffs, NJ, 1965); and another anthology, Theodore J. Lowi (ed.), *Legislative Politics USA: Congress and the Forces That Shape It* (2nd ed., Boston, 1965). On the members of the two Houses, see: Donald R. Matthews, *U.S. Senators and Their World* (New York, 1962); and Charles L. Clapp, *The Congressman: His Work As He Sees It* (New York, 1964).

Certain more specialised aspects of Congress should also be looked at. On appropriations, see Richard F. Fenno, *The Power of the Purse* (Boston, 1966). On administrative control: Joseph P. Harris, *Congressional Control of Administration* (Washington, 1964). On the parties and leaders: David B. Truman, *The Congressional Party* (New York, 1959). On apportionment: Andrew Hacker, *Congressional Districting*. On constituency relations: Louis A. Froman, Jr, *Congressmen and their Constituents* (Chicago, 1963). And on relations with the President: Louis W. Koenig, *Congress and the President* (Chicago, 1965).

Of many books critical of Congress, among the best are: James M. Burns, *Congress on Trial* (New York, 1959); Joseph S. Clark, *Congress: the Sapless Branch* (New York, 1964); Richard Bolling, *House Out of Order* (New York, 1965); and Roger H. Davidson *et al., Congress in Crisis* (Belmont, Calif., 1966).

If at all possible, use should be made of the publications of the Congressional Quarterly Service (Washington, DC), especially the *Weekly Report,* which is a mine of information in highly accessible form, and the annual *Almanac,* which draws the material together. Among the special publications of this organisation, particularly valuable is, *Congress and the Nation, 1945–1964* (1965).

The Federal Service

The American Federal Service has been much studied against the background of the general study of public administration and in the light of theories of organisation and bureaucracy. In consequence, some of the best works are rather too general and technical to be introduced here. One good short treatment of the subject is Peter Woll's *American Bureaucracy* (New York, 1963). The view from within the Service is well presented in W. Lloyd Warner *et al., The American Federal Executive* (New Haven, Conn., 1963). The view of the Service from the outside, amongst the public, is analysed in some detail in Franklin P. Kilpatrick *et al., The Image of the Federal Service* (Washington, 1964). Some of the basic issues raised by the modern administration are discussed in Norman J. Powell's *Responsible Public Bureaucracy in the United States* (Boston, 1967).

Military and Police

The special problems of military and police administration have been the subject of a number of interesting and controversial works, leaving aside works on the technical aspects of strategy. A detailed analysis of military organisation is Paul Y. Hammond's *Organization for Defense: the American Military Establishment in the Twentieth Century* (Princeton, 1961). Some interesting historical readings on the subject are collected in Russell F. Weigley (ed.), *The American Military* (New York, 1969). A more critical stance is adopted by Jack Raymond in *Power at the Pentagon* (New York, 1964), which should be read in conjunction with C. Wright Mills's *Power Elite*. Praeger have published a descriptive series on individual services: Vernon Pizer, *The United States Army*; James A. Donovan, *The United States Marine Corps*; Monro MacCloskey, *The United States Air Force* (New York, 1967).

Civil-military relations are discussed in an analytically sophisticated way by Samuel P. Huntington in *The Soldier and the State* (Cambridge, Mass., 1957), and personnel aspects of this are analysed in Morris Janowitz, *The Professional Soldier* (New York, 1960). Professor Huntington has also written a critical account of the political aspects of military policy in *The Common Defense* (New York, 1961); and on this topic see also, Robert A. Goldwin (ed.), *America Armed* (Chicago, 1964), an interesting collection of essays by various authors. Finally, on the controversial matter of conscription, see Sol Tax (ed.), *The Draft* (Chicago, 1968).

On police administration, a recent work by a leading scholar in the field of community relations is particularly interesting: *Varieties of Police Behavior: Management of Law and Order in Eight Communities* by James Q. Wilson (Cambridge, Mass., 1968).

Political Parties and Groups

The American political parties are a whole subject of study in themselves, though basic information about them can be garnered from books dealing more generally with the American political system and institutions. A good and thorough standard work on the subject is Hugh A. Bone's *American Politics and the Party System* (3rd ed., New York, 1965). Brief but useful treatments of the two big parties are: Ralph M. Goldman, *The Democratic Party in American*

Politics (New York, 1966); and Charles O. Jones, *The Republican Party in American Politics* (New York, 1965). Two minor classics should not be missed out: E. E. Schattschneider's *Party Government* (New York, 1942), a highly penetrating critical study; and V. O. Key, Jr, *Parties, Politics and Pressure Groups* (5th ed., New York, 1964), a pioneering work of abiding value.

Good general works on pressure and interest groups are: David B. Truman, *The Governmental Process: Political Interests and Public Opinion* (New York, 1951), a highly influential book; L. Harmon Zeigler, *Interest Groups in American Society* (Englewood Cliffs, NJ, 1964); and E. E. Schattschneider, *The Semisovereign People: a Realist's View of Democracy in America* (New York, 1960), which is often scathingly critical.

Most books on voting and elections in America are nowadays highly technical in character. Among the few more readable books are: Angus Campbell *et al., Elections and the Political Order* (New York, 1966); Gerald M. Pomper, *Elections in America* (New York, 1968), and *Nominating the President: the Politics of Convention Choice* (New York, 1966); James W. Davis, *Presidential Primaries: Road to the White House* (New York, 1967); Nelson W. Polsby and Aaron B. Wildavsky, *Presidential Elections: Strategies of American Electoral Politics* (2nd ed., 1968); David A. Leuthold, *Electioneering in a Democracy: Campaigns for Congress* (New York, 1968); and Richard M. Scammon (comp. and ed.), *America Votes: a Handbook of Contemporary American Election Statistics* (Washington, DC: Government Affairs Institute, 1966).

Current Public Affairs: Domestic

In the United States public affairs, domestic and foreign, are conducted very largely through the regular channels and agencies of the legal political system; and for that reason their course can be quite adequately followed by the study of works on the political institutions cited above, especially those on the Presidency and Congress. However, certain aspects of contemporary American public affairs require special attention. In domestic affairs, two areas in particular warrant special study; first, the area of poverty, welfare, and urban decay and renewal; secondly, that of race, rights and riots. Both concern equality.

Welfare, as well as poverty, comes over as a problem in the United States, and is usually treated as such in the literature. For some basic information on the subject, see James N. Morgan *et al., Income and Welfare in the United States* (Survey Research Center publication. New York, 1962). Some interesting recent works that deal with the topic from different standpoints are: Harry C. Bredemeier and Toby Jackson, *Social Problems in America: Costs and Casualties in an Acquisitive Society* (New York, 1960); Richard M. Elman, *The Poorhouse State: the American Way of Life on Public Assistance* (New York, 1966); and David Cushman Coyle, *Breakthrough to the Great Society* (Dobbs Ferry, NY, 1965). On an important special topic related to this, see: Eugene Feingold, *Medicare: Policy and Politics* (San Francisco, 1966).

The literature on poverty generally is very extensive, and one of the best ways of sampling it is through anthologies. See in particular: A. Burton Weisbrod (ed.), *The Economics of Poverty: an American Paradox* (Englewood Cliffs, NJ, 1966); Robert E. Will and Harold G. Vatter (eds), *Poverty in Affluence; the Social, Political, and Economic Dimensions of Poverty in the United States* (New York, 1965); and Louis A. Froman *et al.,* (eds), *Poverty in America: a Book of Readings* (Ann Arbor, Mich., 1965). Among books with a more personal thrust, one that has a particularly strong impact is, Michael Harrington, *The Other America: Poverty in the United States* (Harmondsworth, 1962). On the 'War on Poverty' see especially issue No. xxxi (winter, 1966) of *Law and Contemporary Problems,* which contains many interesting contributions giving a spectrum of views.

On the urban problem, these books offer a fair sample of the available material: Robert Cook and Gordon Mitchell, *Urban America: Dilemma and Opportunity* (New York, 1965); Scott Greer, *Urban Renewal and American Cities: the*

Dilemma of Democratic Intervention (Indianapolis, 1965); and James Q. Wilson (ed.), *Urban Renewal: the Record and the Controversy* (Cambridge, Mass., 1966), and *The Metropolitan Enigma: Inquiries into the Nature and Dimensions of America's 'Urban Crisis'* (Cambridge, Mass., 1968). An interesting but idiosyncratic work written from a completely different point of view, and rather overtaken by events, is Jane Jacobs's *Death and Life of Great American Cities* (New York, 1961), which caused an international stir on publication.

Civil and Social Unrest

The 'urban crisis' is a combination of poverty and civil unrest, both of which are linked to racial inequality. There are some interesting books that draw these themes together in a variety of ways, and among the best of them are: Tom Hayden, *Rebellion in Newark: Official Violence and Ghetto Response* (New York, 1967); Nathan Wright, *Black Power and Urban Unrest; Creative Possibilities* (New York, 1969); and Ben W. Gilbert *et al.*, *Ten Blocks from the White House: Anatomy of the Washington Riots of 1968* (London, 1968), written by staff-members of the *Washington Post*.

On the general issue of equal minority rights, see: Alan P. Grimes, *Equality in America: Religion, Race, and the Urban Majority* (London, 1964), and Witney M. Young, Jr, *To Be Equal* (New York, 1964). A more optimistic view of the matter than is taken in these books is presented in *The Quest for the Dream: the Development of Civil Rights and Human Relations in Modern America* by John P. Roche (New York, 1963). An official document that treats of the genesis of this problem is the *Report of the National Advisory Commission on Civil Disorders* (Washington, DC, GPO, 1968). See especially the Supplemental Study to the *Report* entitled 'Racial Attitudes in Fifteen American Cities', by Angus Campbell and Howard Schuman; and in the same connection, William Brink and Louis Harris, *Black and White* (New York, 1966), which analyses the attitudes of the racial groups towards each other. For some important recent expressions of the Black response, see, for example: Charles E. Lincoln, *The Black*

Muslims in America (Boston, 1964); and E. U. Essien-Udom, *Black Nationalism: a Search for Identity in America* (Chicago, 1963). Especially valuable, however, are more personal expressions, such as: *The Autobiography of Malcolm X* (Harmondsworth, 1968); James Baldwin, *The Fire Next Time* (New York, 1964); Martin Luther King, *Chaos or Community?* (London, 1968); and Stokeley Carmichael and Charles V. Hamilton, *Black Power* (New York, 1967). Finally, it is highly instructive to read a relatively early treatment of the subject, now a classic, in the light of what has happened during the last decade or so: Gunnar Myrdal, *An American Dilemma: the Negro Problem and Modern Democracy* (rev. ed., New York, 1962).

Current Public Affairs: Foreign

Turning to the external aspects of public policy, there are, first, some valuable works dealing with the general topic of America's place in the world, and American ideas on the subject. The view of a friendly outsider is Denis Brogan's *America in the Modern World* (London, 1960), based on lectures delivered by Professor Brogan at Rutgers University in 1959. More restricted in scope, but also more sceptical, is James P. Warburg, *The United States in the Post-War World* (London, 1966). Discussion of the content of United States policies abroad is found in Michael Donelan, *The Ideas of American Foreign Policy* (London, 1963). Up-to-date histories for the period since the second world war are: John W. Spanier, *American Foreign Policy Since World War II* (3rd ed., New York, 1969); Seyom Brown, *The Faces of Power: Constancy and Change in United States Foreign Policy from Truman to Johnson* (New York, 1968); and Dexter Perkins, *The Diplomacy of a New Age: Major Issues in United States Policy Since 1945* (Bloomington, Ind., 1967).

On special aspects of foreign affairs see: Walt W. Rostow and Richard W. Hatch, *American Policy in Asia* (Cambridge, Mass., 1955); Robert Blum, *United States Policy Towards Communist China: the Alternatives* (New York, 1966); Carl Oglesby and Richard Shaull, *Containment and Change* (New

York, 1967); Herbert Feis, *Foreign Aid and Foreign Policy* (New York, 1964); Elliot Zupnick, *Primer of United States Foreign Economic Policy* (New York, 1965); Adam Yarmolinsky, *United States Military Power and Foreign Policy* (Chicago, 1967).

Two highly interesting works deal in a general way with the impact of the American public on foreign affairs: Walter Lippmann's *Public Opinion and Foreign Policy in the United States* (London, 1952); and Gabriel A. Almond, *The American People and Foreign Policy* (New York, 1960), which is less critical and more analytical.

Regarding the most important current problem, see: Wesley R. Fishel and T. A. Bison, *The United States and Viet Nam: Two Views* (New York, 1966); Richard N. Goodwin, *Triumph of Tragedy: Reflections on Vietnam* (New York, 1966); George M. Kahin and John W. Lewis, *The United States in Viet Nam* (New York, 1967); and Howard Zinn, *Vietnam: the Logic of Withdrawal* (Boston, 1967). Two highly critical works that have aroused much controversy concerning America's world role are: Sen. William J. Fulbright, *The Arrogance of Power* (New York, 1967); and Edmund Stillman and William Pfaff, *Power and Impotence: the Failure of America's Foreign Policy* (New York, 1966).

Newspapers

Finally, on all matters of current public interest the major newspapers provide important reading-matter. Consult past as well as current issues of such papers as *The New York Times*; the international edition of *The Herald-Tribune*; *The Wall Street Journal* (especially on business, finance, and other economic matters); *The Washington Post*; and *The Christian Science Monitor*.

3

The Soviet Union

Violet Conolly

Introduction

In presenting this guide to literature on contemporary Russia, we feel the reader should be aware in the first place of its inherent limitations compared to similar lists on more accessible countries. Being a totalitarian regime, controlling all the mass media of publishing, etc. through a rigid censorship, the Soviet Union is able to ensure that writers in every field conform to the party line of the day while certain subjects can be 'taboo' and even disappear from the official records, *pro tem.* The result of this distortion of facts and events is that Soviet source materials on which foreign writers would normally rely are often more misleading than enlightening before 'processing' by experts.

Against this background, further complicated for the western student of Soviet life by the restriction on movement within the Soviet Union and normal communication with Soviet citizens (including free exchange of opinions between Soviet experts and their opposite numbers abroad), it is gratifying to note the impressive *corpus* of works produced since 1917 in the West on the Soviet Union and listed in this guide.

Since the publication of the first Soviet Statistical Yearbook (*Statisticheskiy Ezhegodnik*) in 1956 western economists have had access to much more information on the Soviet economy than formerly and discussion of economic problems has increasingly enlivened the pages of Soviet specialist periodicals and the press. There has been no similar development politically, though the significance of the emergence of clandestine *Samizdat* publications should not be overlooked.

The *Current Digest of the Soviet Press* (Joint Committee on Slavic Studies, NY) provides invaluable English translations of key political materials from the Soviet press, periodicals and other publications for non-Russian reading people. Important information on current Soviet policies is also contained in the daily bulletins of the BBC Monitoring Service Summary of World Broadcasts, Part I: The USSR.

History

Tsarist Background to Bolshevik Revolution (1917)
The Soviet revolution of 1917, like all great historical events, had its roots in the past. Even students of the more contemporary periods of Soviet history since 1945 will therefore need to have some knowledge of Tsarist Russia in order to understand the causes of Bolshevism and the features of the old society it set out to destroy in the new era of Marxist socialism. The two-volume study of *Russia: A History and Interpretation* (London, 1953) by Michael T. Florinsky encompasses the history of Russia from the earliest days to March 1918 and lays bare the main social-political evils of the time. Those seeking a more concentrated reconstruction of the reigns of the last of the Romanov tsars should find *The Twilight of Imperial Russia* (London, 1965) by Richard Charques a very readable, stimulating book. Charques has his own ideas about the controversial role of the Bolsheviks in the 1917 revolution and is concerned 'to chart the tides and currents represented by all the other factions and parties, legal and underground, which swelled the revolutionary cataclysm'. The relevant sections of Professor Hugh Seton-Watson's *The Russian Empire 1801–1917* (London, 1967) also describe the various revolutionary movements of this period.

An admirable introduction to nineteenth-century Russian diplomacy is given in Humphrey Sumner's *A Survey of Russian History* (London, 1944), in which the national geopolitical aims of Russia (Tsarist or Soviet) in the Baltic, the Black Sea, the Caspian and Pacific areas are defined.

The 1917 Revolution

A considerable volume of literature now exists on the 1917 revolution, though a definitive history in either Russian or English must await the unlocking of the Soviet archives still largely inaccessible to scholars. Meanwhile, students can get their bearings on this complex subject by familiarity with the following indispensable works: *The Russian Revolution 1917–1921* (2 vols., London, 1935) by William Henry Chamberlin is a learned and realistic work of scholarship. Chamberlin lived in Moscow from 1922 to 1935 while he was compiling materials for his book and also had the advantage of being able closely to observe many of the revolutionary leaders in action at this time. E. H. Carr's monumental *The Bolshevik Revolution 1917–1923* (London, 1953) is part of his large-scale history of Soviet Russia. It is mainly based on Soviet documents, to which he at times tends to give excessive credence, and he does not have the advantage of Chamberlin's direct knowledge of Soviet Russia in the post-revolution years. It is however an exhaustive source for the available official documentary data.

The essence of the revolution or 'how a group of determined men seized power for themselves in Russia in 1917 and kept others from sharing it' (page v) is the subject of Professor L. Schapiro's most important study: *The Origin of the Communist Autocracy, Political Opposition in the Soviet State, First Phase 1917–1922* (London, 1955). Professor Schapiro incisively destroys the now prevalent myth associated with the Lenin 'mystique' that Stalin, not Lenin, initiated the elimination of political opponents and the terror as a basic element of monolithic Soviet government. The book is soundly based on a massive Russian documentation and is essential to understanding the spirit and substance of the Leninist revolution, then and now.

Apart from these general histories, in which they figure so largely, attention must be directed to the separate biographies of Lenin, Trotsky and Stalin, whose influence dominated the 1917 revolution and the moulding of Soviet Russia. Lenin has had many biographers (the number increased by his centenary in 1970) and opinion is divided as to their merits. *The Life of Lenin* (London, 1965) by Louis Fischer is a most readable, well-documented book and in many ways brilliantly reflects the author's pre-war residence in the Soviet Union and easy familiarity with the Soviet hierarchs of Lenin's generation. Another major and scholarly biography of Lenin is Professor Adam B. Ulam's *Lenin and the Bolsheviks* (London, 1965), which widens the perspective of Lenin's life by tracing the antecedents of the Bolsheviks throughout the nineteenth century in Russia and looking forward to the fate of many of Lenin's chief collaborators and the developing pattern of the Soviet system. In the welter of centenary tributes to Lenin, the perspicacious reappraisal, *Lenin, The Man, The Theorist, The Leader* (London, 1969), edited by Leonard Schapiro and Peter Reddaway, is outstanding. A very detailed sympathetic picture of Lenin during his pre-revolution years in Russia and in exile abroad is given in *Memories of Lenin* by his widow, Nadezhda Krupskaya; it is now available in an English translation by Andrew Rothstein (London, 1970).

Both Trotsky and Stalin have found, somewhat ironically, the same able biographer in Isaac Deutscher. Deutscher's three-volume biography of his tragic hero Leon Trotsky, *The Prophet Armed, The Prophet Unarmed, The Prophet Outcast* (London, 1954–63), recaptures the dramatic quality of Trotsky's life in a vivid fact-filled narrative and acutely analyses the various problems on which he disagreed, to his undoing, with Stalin. His *Stalin: A Political Biography* (London, 1949) is also perforce to a large extent a survey of Stalinist Russia, but it suffers from having been written during Stalin's life and is not on the level of his full-scale biography of Trotsky. Boris Souvarine's *Staline* (Paris, 1935; English translation by C. L. R. James, London, 1939) is a very different type of biography. As a dedicated Marxist and former member of the Executive Committee of the Comintern, Souvarine writes with outraged contempt for Stalin's cruelty and tyrannical domination of all spheres of Soviet life and of the degeneration of Lenin's Russia under his auspices into the 'Etat Knouto-soviétique', before the 1936–8 trials further confirmed his analysis.

Eye-witnesses of the Bolshevik Revolution have left some very vivid and important accounts of these decisive early days of Lenin's triumph. Outstanding among these accounts is John Reed's *Ten Days That Shook the World* (New York, 1935), a book which actually won Lenin's accolade in a personal Foreword. This young American deeply sympathised with the Bolsheviks and knew many of the leaders. His exciting record of events in Petrograd in 1917 and the many official documents are of great historical interest. R. H. Bruce Lockhart's *Memoirs of a British Agent* (London, 1932) tell the story of his life as British Vice-Consul in Moscow from 1911 and subsequently when he remained in charge of British interests till 1918. Lockhart was in close touch with the Bolshevik leaders in his official capacity, and his book contains many details of exceptional interest. Among foreign correspondents who have left useful reminiscences of the revolutionary days may also be mentioned M. Philips Price, *Manchester Guardian* correspondent, who travelled widely in Russia, and author of *My Reminiscences of the Russian Revolution* (London, 1921), and A. R. Williams, author of *Through the Russian Revolution* (London, 1923), who, as an incorrigible early fellow-traveller, relates his experience of the revolution in Petrograd, Moscow and Vladivostok from June 1917 to August 1918. A full list of such works is given in *Books on Soviet Russia 1917–1942* by Philip Grierson (London, 1943).

The Soviet Socialist System

Government and Party

The peculiarities of the Soviet system of government and the disparities between its nominally constitutional structure of an all-Union parliament or Supreme Soviet and Executive or Council of Ministers and these institutions in the western democracies are authoritatively and lucidly described by

Leonard Schapiro in *The Government and Politics of the Soviet Union* (rev. ed., London, 1969). A more detailed exposition of this subject, perhaps for the advanced student, is given in *How Russia Is Ruled* by Merle Fainsod (rev. ed., London, 1963), and John N. Hazard's *Soviet System of Government* (4th rev. ed., London, 1968, also in paperback) can be recommended as the standard textbook on this subject. R. Churchward's *Contemporary Soviet Government* (London, 1968) has the merit of bringing Soviet government down to its grass roots in the local soviets, which he studies in greater detail than any other writer on these problems, apart from his many useful insights on the government and peoples of the Soviet Union.

The important period of reform and innovation in the Soviet regime (1957–64) following Khrushchev's assumption of power and de-Stalinisation and the causes of his fall in 1964 are studied with great acumen in an excellent work by Carl A. Linden, *The Soviet Leadership 1957–1964* (Baltimore, 1966; London, 1967). This is Sovietology at its most useful best, reading between the lines of non-committal Soviet texts and otherwise deciphering the obscurities of the Kremlin oracle and its utterances.

Soviet (i.e., government) and Party affairs are so inseparable in the Soviet Union owing to the Party controls pervading all aspects of life that the Party is inevitably discussed in the above-mentioned works. It is also the subject of separate specialised studies of which some of the most important are: *The Communist Party of the Soviet Union* by Leonard Schapiro (new, rev. and enlarged ed., London, 1970). This is the most fully documented competent history of the Party up to 1968, far surpassing in value any of the official party histories published to-date in the Soviet Union. It also contains an expert analysis of the Party's structure and policies on all major all-Union problems and of the Party's basic ideological framework. Dr T. H. Rigby's impressive work, *Communist Party Membership in the USSR 1917–1967* (Princeton, 1968), concentrates on the hitherto little-known methods of Soviet party cadre selection, though Dr Rigby throws his research net much wider than this dominant subject.

These largely academic studies of the Soviet system may be supplemented with local colour and keen political observation by perusal of Michel Tatu's brilliant book: *Power in the Kremlin* (trans. from the French by Helen Katel, London, 1969). Tatu, who closely studied the Soviet political scene as Moscow correspondent of *Le Monde* for some years, focuses his attention here on the decline of Khrushchev's influence and how collective leadership works in the Soviet Union. Another very stimulating unacademic inside analysis of Soviet political life is given in *The New Class* (first published 1957; paperback, London, 1966) by Milovan Djilas, former Yugoslav Vice-President. From his own experience of the Communist world, Djilas declares that the 'classless society' no longer exists, having been replaced by a 'new class', the political bureaucracy, with special privileges, both economic and administrative.

Ideology

The official statement of Marxism-Leninism and its application to Soviet life is best summarised in *The Programme of the CPSU* (Foreign Languages Publishing House, Moscow, 1961). However, this text with its official jargon needs more than a little informed interpretation to be understood by the 'vulgar'. R. N. Carew Hunt has made a major contribution to understanding in this difficult field of communication in his pioneer works: *Marxism Past and Present* (London, 1954) and *The Theory and Practice of Communism* (London, 1950). The latter study of the ideological development of communism from Marx to Stalin is both succinct and enlightening. Towering over all works in this field is the more philosophically advanced, erudite and objective work: *Soviet Ideology Today: Dialectical and Historical Materialism* by Gustav A. Wetter (London, 1966). A more controversial but very stimulating criticism of Marxism in action in the Soviet Union is given in *The Open Society and Its Enemies* by Karl R. Popper (London, 1957), while those seeking a general introduction to communism in its many guises should find Alfred G. Meyer's *Communism* (New York, 1960) good reading. From the other side of the 'Curtain', a broad beam of light on the devastating realities behind Soviet ideological pretensions was thrown by Academician Andrei D. Sakharov's courageous *Progress, Coexistence and Intellectual Freedom,* first privately circulated in Moscow and then published in London in 1970. This distinguished Soviet nuclear physicist boldly affirms that the party is morally and intellectually bankrupt and its totalitarian system of thought moribund, however powerful it still remains against the relatively powerless educated classes.

The effects of the imposition of official Marxist-Leninist ideology, though all-pervasive, are perhaps most directly felt in the spheres of religion and the creative arts. This materialistic ideology is fundamentally opposed to all transcendental religions upholding belief in God and the supernatural. Promoted by the monopolistic mass media and other agencies of state power, it inspires the Soviet atheist movement directed against the survival of religion in any form in the Soviet Union. The theory and practice of the Soviet anti-religious campaigns are described in detail in Walter Kolarz' comprehensive work: *Religion in the Soviet Union* (London, 1961). Kolarz examines the fate of the various churches in the Soviet Union since 1917: the Russian Orthodox, the Roman Catholic, the western Protestants such as the Baptists, the Russian sects, Soviet Jewry, Islam, Buddhism and even 'scattered' groups like the Yezidis and the Zoroastrians. It is an invaluable exhaustive survey of this important subject, based on a meticulous examination of Soviet and other relevant source materials. More recently, Michael Bourdeaux has turned his dedicated pen to the difficulties of the Orthodox and the Baptists respectively, in two extremely well-informed works: *Patriarch and Prophets* (London, 1970) and *Religious Ferment in Russia* (London, 1970), from which it appears that the fight against religion in the Soviet Union is far from over.

The crippling effect on Soviet literature and the creative arts in general of official censorship and conformity with the theory of 'socialist realism' has become better known outside the Soviet Union with the publication in the West of some major works of contemporary literature, in the first place, Alexander Solzhenitsyn's masterpiece *The First Circle* (London, 1968), still unpublished in the Soviet Union. A chronological survey of Soviet literature, with its writers and problems, is given up to 1963 in Marc Slonim's *Soviet Russian Literature* (New York, 1964). Censorship and ideological controls are discussed in greater detail in a symposium edited by Max Hayward and Leopold Labedz, *Literature and Revolution in Soviet Russia* (London, 1963). The picture can be filled in for the general reader, if not for the specialist, by reference to *Dissonant Voices in Soviet Literature,* a miscellany of Soviet writing from 1917 to 1961, edited with deep knowledge of the subject by Max Hayward and Patricia Blake (*Partisan Review* 3–4, 1961, New York). It is interesting to learn from Max Hayward's Introduction to this miscellany that the Soviet period has been by no means as barren in literary achievement as is often supposed. *The Demonstration in Pushkin Square* (London, 1969) is in many ways symbolic of the present phase of the 'literary revolt' against the Soviet government's interference with writers and their work. It is an English translation of a collection of documents made by Pavel Litvinov (son of the former Foreign Minister) on the trial of young people who demonstrated in Pushkin Square, Moscow, against the arrest of their friends and were in turn themselves imprisoned – as was Litvinov for collecting these documents.

Soviet Law

Soviet citizens live under a legal system which in theory and practice differs fundamentally from that prevailing in western democratic society. It derives its basic concepts of the state, class and property from Marxism, and these ideological concepts have effectively moulded Soviet judicial institutions and practice. This novel system is well explained and analysed in E. L. Johnson's study: *An Introduction to the Soviet Legal System* (London, 1969); John N. Hazard's *Law and Social Change in the USSR* (London, 1953) and H. Berman's *Justice in Russia* (London, 1950) – all reliable well-documented textbooks. *Soviet Penal Policy* by Professor I. Lapenna (London, 1968) is the leading work in this field in English. The differences between the connotation of civil law in western democratic and Soviet regimes is clearly expounded in the authoritative work of Vladimir Gsovski, *Soviet Civil Law: Private Rights and Their Background under the Soviet Régime* (Ann Arbor, Michigan, Vol. I, 1948; Vol. II, 1949). It also contains translations of Soviet legal codes and other basic documents.

Robert Conquest's fully documented *The Great Terror: Stalin's Purges of the Thirties* (London, 1968) reveals in detail the odious perversion of justice for political ends in these pseudo-trials.

Soviet Nationalities Policy

The impact for good or ill of Soviet policies towards the many non-Russian nationalities of the USSR has given rise to a fairly large and controversial literature ranging from works echoing the official claim that there is now no nationality problem in the USSR to those severely criticising Soviet policies. These works may generally be divided into two categories: those dealing with overall Soviet nationality policy and those concerned with a particular nationality or group of nationalities.

The following works belong to the first category: *The Formation of the Soviet Union 1917–1923* by Richard Pipes (rev. ed., Cambridge, Mass., 1964). This is a standard well-documented work and essential to understanding the conflicts and pressures which preceded the establishment of the Soviet Union. Robert Conquest's well-edited *Soviet Nationalities Policy in Practice* (The Contemporary Soviet Union Series, New York, 1967) brings the story up-to-date with pages packed with documentary references and facts. In two other works, Conquest has concentrated on the grim details of the Soviet wartime deportation of certain Caucasian-Volga peoples: *The Nation Killers* (London, 1970), in which he expands the account given in his earlier *The Soviet Deportation of Nationalities* (London, 1960, now out of print) to include the deportation of the Crimean Tartars and the mysterious 200,000 Meskhelians about whom nothing was previously heard in the west. An excellent bird's eye view of the present state of the nationalities is given in *Ethnic Minorities in the Soviet Union* (New York, 1968), to which the editor, Erich Goldhagen, contributes an unusually balanced assessment of the position. Walter Kolarz sees little merit in the Russian attitude to the lesser peoples of the Soviet Union, and their ruthless domination by the Kremlin is the theme of his *Russia and Her Colonies* (London, 1952). He devotes a separate volume to *The Peoples of the Far East* (London, 1954), which contains a mass of local information not easily accessible elsewhere.

The absurdities to which Soviet historians – thus flying in the face of history – have been committed by the party line on the lack of conflict historically between the Russians and the non-Russians of the Empire or Union are the theme of a fascinating, most readable book by Lowell Tillett: *The Great Friendship: Soviet Historians on the Russian Nationalities* (London, 1969).

Apart from these general studies, the individual nationalities have received very unequal treatment from western scholars. This is partly due to the lack of reliable Soviet materials for research coupled with Soviet travel restrictions preventing even the usual superficial acquaintance with areas such as the far North of Siberia, most of the Volga-Tatar-Bashkir region and the vast hinterland shut out behind the now permitted Central Asian oasis towns like Tashkent.

The opening up of the chief cities of the Central Asian Republics to foreign travel in the fifties produced a number of indifferent travelogues, but also stimulated some outstanding works of reference. In the first place, the report published by the League of Nations (Geneva, 1957) incorporating the observations of their delegation, which was granted unusual facilities to visit Uzbekistan and Tadzhikistan in 1957, must be mentioned as of special interest: *Regional Economic Policy in the Soviet Union: The Case of Central Asia.* This delegation examined industrialisation and population trends, immigration, cotton specialisation, terms of trade with other parts of the Soviet Union, etc., and is invaluable. Geoffrey Wheeler, a Central Asian expert of note, attractively presents the history, development and problems of the five Soviet Central Asian republics from the Tsarist annexation in the nineteenth century to the present day in his succinct *The Modern History of Soviet Central Asia* (London, 1964). Islam, the traditional religion of the Turkic peoples throughout the Soviet Union, has been studied with special reference to the Muslim peoples of Central Asia in Alexandre Bennigsen's authoritative *Islam in the Soviet Union* (trans. by G. Wheeler and H. Evans, New York, 1967). Two more popular type of books which vividly convey the colour and flavour of Central Asian life are Sir Fitzroy Maclean's *Eastern Approaches* (London, 1949) and *Back to Bokhara* (London, 1959). The economic resources of this region and their development under Soviet auspices are the subject of detailed examination in *The Soviet Middle East: A Communist Model for Development* by Alec Nove and J. A. Newth (London, 1967) and in *Beyond the Urals* by Violet Conolly (London, 1967).

The Ukraine is of great strategic and economic importance, but it has not so far inspired an up-to-date work in English worthy of its place in the Soviet Union. The history of the Ukraine under the Tsars and the Soviets up to 1939 is ably presented in *The Ukraine* by W. E. D. Allen (London, 1940), who adds an interesting chapter on the economic history of the Ukraine. Clarence Manning's *Ukraine under the Soviets* (New York, 1953) is a less comprehensive study. Since the publication of the clandestine *Internationalism or Russification* (London, 1968) by the Ukrainian nationalist I. Dzyuba and the moving revelations of the outright violation of 'socialist legality' by the Public Prosecutor in his dealings with Ukrainian citizens given by his compatriot V. Chornovil in the *Chornovil Papers* (New York, 1968), Moscow's attitude to Ukrainian nationalism has awakened some interest among western Sovietologists. Unfortunately, under present conditions it is impossible to investigate these problems more closely within the Ukraine itself.

Though not numerically a major nationality, the Jews in Soviet as in Tsarist Russia constitute a considerable problem, mainly because of the persistence in Russia of a seemingly ineradicable and widespread anti-Semitism. Officially, the Soviet government condemns anti-Semitism with all other manifestations of racial discrimination. Nevertheless, since the thirties, when so many important old Bolsheviks of Jewish origin were eliminated, the Jews have felt increasingly insecure and have been the victims of various forms of discrimination, subtle and not so subtle. In his *The Jews in the Soviet Union* (Syracuse, 1951) Solomon M. Schwarz examines in great detail Soviet minority policy with regard to the Jews and the resurgence of anti-Semitism in the Soviet Union from the mid-1920s to the wartime and post-war situation, notable features of which he finds to have been the Soviet silence about the Jewish tragedy under Nazi rule and 'the stealthy advance of discrimination'. Mr Schwarz' study ends in 1951. The investigation is taken up and continued in a later symposium: *The Jews in the Soviet Union Since 1917*, edited by Lionel Kochan and a distinguished group of collaborators (London, the Institute of Jewish Affairs, 1970). There is much common ground between this work and the earlier study by Solomon Schwarz. But the emergence of Israel as a political state and its reaction on the position of the Russian Jews are closely examined in the later work, with the conclusion that its existence and especially the Six Day War has further complicated their difficulties and dilemma.

The secret trial of a group of Crimean Tatars in Tashkent in 1970 focused attention on the fate of this unfortunate people, deported to Central Asia during the War and only partially rehabilitated by the Supreme Soviet in 1967 without the right to return to their traditional homeland. Edige Kirimal, himself a Crimean Tatar who participated in the national movement in the Crimea in the early years of Soviet power, describes these struggles and the situation in the Crimea under the Bolsheviks (1920–41). This is an indifferent study by a naturally partisan author, but the only work specifically devoted to this subject: *Der Nationalkampf der Krimtürken* (Emsdetten, Westfalen, 1952).

Terence Armstrong has made the Far North of Russia his special field of study, and years of research have gone into the making of his *Russian Settlement in the North* (London, 1965). Here he provides both interesting historical background to Russian expansion beyond the Urals and information on current Soviet development policies in this area.

The dramatic vicissitudes of the Georgian peoples under the Tsars and the Soviets have found an enthusiastic historian in Dr D. N. Lang, whose *A Modern History of Georgia* (London, 1962) is an authoritative and very readable book.

While the above references do not cover all the more than a hundred national groups in the Soviet Union, they should adequately illustrate the main common features of the central-ised Soviet nationalities policy, i.e., severe repression of nationalist tendencies accompanied by the promotion of social-economic development of these mostly underdeveloped developing areas.

Economics (Industry and Agriculture)

The nature and results of the revolutionary economic policies of the first Marxist socialist state have been the object of much expert research and comment by western economists. Their task has been greatly complicated, especially in the Stalinist period, by gaps and distortions in the official statistics and other information. Since Stalin's death, more information about the economy has been released; the first Soviet Statistical Yearbook, published in 1956, and the following annual volumes greatly add to the data previously made available.

Russian Economic Development Since 1917 (London, 1928; 3rd ed.: *Soviet Economic Development Since 1917*, London, 1966) by Maurice Dobb, a scholarly Cambridge Marxist, was an early, if not the earliest, attempt in English to explain the first decade of 'the strange new social experiment' in Russia and the operation of a Marxist-Leninist based economy in professional if sympathetic terms. This work of course dealt with the pre-plan period.

Two much later books by Professor Alec Nove very lucidly analyse the complexities of Soviet economic theory and practice during the intervening planned periods: *The Soviet Economy* (rev. ed., London, 1965), in which the structure and problems of the Soviet economy are surveyed, and *An Economic History of the USSR* (London, 1969), in which he critically examines the main developments in the Russian economy from the end of the Tsarist empire to the Khrushchev period, with a note on subsequent prospects and growth rates.

The peculiarities of the Soviet budget are the subject of R. W. Davies' now standard work: *The Development of the Soviet Budgetary System* (London, 1958). Some other individual aspects of the operation of the Soviet system are examined in the following works by experts in their respective fields: David Granick, *Management of the Industrial Firm: A Study in Soviet Economic Planning* (New York, 1954) and *The Red Executive: A Study of the Part Played in the Soviet Industrial System by the Organisation Man* (London, 1960); Joseph Berliner, *Factory and Manager in the USSR* (London, 1957); Abram Bergson and Simon Kuznets (eds), *Economic Trends in the Soviet Union* (Cambridge, Mass., 1963), a systematic survey of Soviet economic growth under the Five-Year plans, by eight experts; Franklyn D. Holzman, *Soviet Taxation: The Fiscal and Monetary Problems of a Planned Economy* (London, 1955).

The place of trade unions in a planned economy like the Soviet one is an important subject that has not yet received the specific attention it deserves in the literature on the Soviet Union. Isaac Deutscher, in his very readable, but now out-of-date, *Soviet Trade Unions* (Oxford University Press for the Royal Institute of International Affairs, 1950) traced their place in Soviet labour policy from 1917 to 1950 and castigated in the strongest words the serf-like conditions imposed on the workers by Stalin. More or less the same line is taken by Victor Feather in *Trade Unions: True or False?* (London, 1951), in which he argues that the worker has no protection in the USSR against government monopolistic controls.

Allowing for factual distortions inevitable in his Stalinist approach, there is much useful information in P. Lyashchenko's Stalinist-prize-winning three volume *History of the National Economy of the USSR to the 1917 Revolution* (English trans., New York, 1949). The still largely obscure subject of forced labour and its economic consequences for the Soviet Union is assessed with cool detachment, in spite of the author's personal experience of Soviet wartime labour camps, in *Forced Labour and Economic Development: An Enquiry into the Experience of Soviet Industrialization* by S. Swianiewcz (London, 1965). The numbers and conditions in these camps are more comprehensively discussed in *Forced Labour in Soviet Russia* by D. J. Dallin and Boris I. Nicolaevsky (London, 1947).

Agriculture

The grim facts accompanying forced collectivisation, on which the present Soviet agricultural system was based, have been studied from different angles by M. Lewin in *Russian Peasants and Soviet Power* (English trans. by A. Nove and J. Biggard, London, 1968), and *Foundations of a Planned Economy 1926-29* by E. H. Carr and R. W. Davies (London, 1969). While Lewin concentrates on the plight of the peasants subjected to the Draconian official measures of collectivisation, Carr and Davies are mainly preoccupied with the more abstract subject of official thinking on the agrarian collectivisation problem, as of 1929. Naum Jasny's *Socialised Agriculture in the USSR* (Stanford, 1949) was 'a remarkable tour de force' when it appeared, providing in Alec Nove's words 'a remarkably accurate picture of the deficiencies of "Stalinist agriculture" up to the early post-war period, in spite of the gaps and distortions in Stalinist official data. Jasny followed this classic work with a highly technical evaluation of the 'aberrations of Khrushchev's agricultural ideas' and their results in *Khrushchev's Crop Policy* (Glasgow, 1965).

Soviet Agriculture in Perspective by Erich Strauss (London, 1969) provides the general reader with a useful review of Soviet successes and failures in agriculture from 1917 to the end of the plan period in 1970. Experts (such as Dr Klatt) believe that Mr Strauss is at his best when dealing with institutional aspects of Soviet agriculture and with Russia's dairy industry as a result of his experience as Chief Economist of the Milk Marketing Board. Other general works on Soviet agriculture which can be recommended are: Jerzy F. Karcz, *Soviet and East European Agriculture* (Berkeley, California, 1967); Roy Laird-Edward, L. Crowley, *Soviet Agriculture:*

The Permanent Crisis (New York, 1965). Incidentally, some of the best work on the constantly shifting Soviet agricultural scene is to be found in periodicals such as *Soviet Survey* (Glasgow); *St Antony's Papers* (London); and *Journal of Agricultural Economics* (London).

The position of Soviet agricultural workers, based on a close examination of official Soviet literature, is the subject of a very informative monograph, *Agricultural Workers in the USSR*, edited by Robert Conquest in the Soviet Studies Series (London, 1968).

Education and the Social Services

The Soviet 'liquidation of illiteracy' campaigns and compulsory education plans following the 1917 revolution are fully but uncritically described in *Changing Man* by Beatrice King (London, 1936). Subsequent changes and developments in Soviet educational policies are more critically discussed in *The Soviet Union: A Concise Handbook, section on Education* by Kenneth R. Whiting (London, 1962); *The Soviet Regime: Communism in Practice*, Part III: *The Worker and Social Stratification, Education* by W. W. Kulski (Syracuse, 1963). John Gunter's personal comments on Soviet education, schools and teachers in his most readable *Inside Russia* (cf. Index for exact references) (New York, 1957) should not be missed. A general survey of the social services provided constitutionally for Soviet citizens is given in *Soviet Society* (Boston, 1961), edited by Alex Inkeles and Geiger Kent. Owing to constant changes in this field, e.g., in the levels of wages, pensions, etc., etc., reference must be made to specialised publications like Soviet Studies for up-to-date accurate information.

Foreign Policy and Military Affairs

The course of Soviet foreign policy in the pre-second world war period (1929–41) and Lenin's formulation (1917–20) of a new 'socialist' foreign policy, combining the conflicting international revolutionary aims, as promulgated by the Comintern, with the establishment of normal diplomatic relations with the non-socialist capitalist part of the world, are critically examined in Max Beloff's *The Foreign Policy of Soviet Russia* (2 vols., London, 1947–9). In regard to the official activities of the Comintern, it is most effectively supplemented by the *Documents,* very ably selected and edited by Jane Degras (issued under the auspices of the Royal Institute of International Affairs, London, 1955–66). Its activities are further 'unmasked' in F. Borkenau's *The Communist International* (London, 1938). Pre-war Soviet foreign policy is also studied to advantage in *The Soviets in World Affairs 1917–1929* (New York, 1969) by Louis Fischer, whose personal knowledge of men and events of this period adds unusual insights to his book. George Kennan's succinct little study, *Soviet Foreign Policy 1917–1941* (New York, 1960), should also be consulted, as the work of a scholar diplomat with first-hand experience of the Soviet Union.

The post-war period with the death of Stalin, the Sino-Soviet conflict and various shifts in Soviet foreign policy is relatively well covered by special studies. In a massive work, *Expansion and Coexistence* (London, 1968), Professor Adam Ulam surveys half a century of Soviet foreign policy with painstaking scholarship and includes an excellent account of Soviet-American relations since the end of the second world war. In *Russia and the West under Lenin and Stalin* (London, 1961), George Kennan reviews Soviet-Western relations with his characteristic skill and detachment, pinpointing, however, the consistent innocence of the western leaders in their wartime dealings with Stalin. Sir William Hayter's *Russia and the World* (London, 1970) is a little classic of precise knowledge and informed views. No better introduction to the aims and methods of Soviet foreign policy 'with its lunatic passion for secrecy' can be recommended than this latest work by the former British Ambassador to Moscow.

Apart from these general studies of Soviet foreign policy, Soviet aims and operations in individual countries are the subject of a voluminous literature from which the following works dealing with major areas of Soviet interest have been selected.

The history of Soviet-German relations during the inter-war years is recorded in an interesting work, *The Incompatible Allies* (New York, 1953), by Gustav Hilger, whose recollections as a high-ranking official of the German Embassy in Moscow are invaluable and are supported by Alfred G. Meyer, a distinguished American authority on Marxist communism. The immediate post-war period is studied in John P. Nettl's scholarly book, *The Eastern Zone and Soviet Policy in Germany, 1945–1950* (London, 1951). Soviet diplomatic methods from the Berlin crisis and Khrushchev's ultimatum of 1958 to the building of the Wall in August 1961 are analysed in *Divided Berlin: The Anatomy of Soviet Political Blackmail* by Hans Speier (London, 1961).

The uneasy course of Soviet-Finnish relations from the War of Liberation of 1918 to his resignation as President of Finland in 1946 is given by Marshal Mannerheim, an active Finnish participator in these events, in his *Memoirs* (trans. from the Finnish, London, 1953). The Soviet campaign aimed against Finnish independence in 1939–40 is also vividly recorded from the Finnish standpoint by Väino A. Tanner in *The Winter War: Finland against Russia, 1939–1940* (trans. from the Finnish, Stanford, 1957). Soviet-Finnish relations are further examined in *Finland between East and West* by Anatole G. Mazour (London, 1956).

The first comprehensive account of the Soviet invasion of Czechoslovakia and Czech resistance and of the pre-invasion reforms is given in an impressive work: *Czechoslovakia 1968: Reform, Repression and Resistance* (The Institute of Strategic Studies, London, 1969).

An excellent historical background to the present controversial subject of Soviet objectives in the various regions of the Middle East, including the Arab world and Israel, is to be found in the pages of A. R. C. Bolton's *Annotated Bibliography: Soviet Middle-East Studies* (Central Asian Research Centre for the Royal Institute of International Affairs, London, 1959). This examination of the 'hitherto uncharted sea of Soviet material on the Middle East', while not claiming to be exhaustive, pinpoints the permanent and more ephemeral elements in the often confused picture of Russian approaches to the history, economics and current problems of this region. Bolton, moreover, stresses that Soviet Oriental studies are 'poles apart from Oriental studies in the West' because, like all the social sciences studied in the Soviet Union, they are dominated by Marxist-Leninist concepts. Nevertheless, the Soviet Union inherited a valuable legacy of Oriental scholarship from Tsarist Russia and, however adulterated, this still inspires the wide range and achievements of much Soviet research in this field.

The contemporary situation resulting from the recent Soviet penetration of the Middle East is analysed in detail in Walter Laqueur's *The Struggle for the Middle East* (London, 1969). Here, the interesting, but surely controversial, thesis is expounded that Soviet penetration of this region is the predictable result of the vacuum created by the British withdrawal and gives it a significance it would not otherwise have.

Soviet Russia and Asia 1917–1927 by Harish Kapur (for the Geneva Institute of International Studies, London, 1966) contains a few introductory chapters on 'Marxism and Asia', the Soviet attitude to 'the national and colonial question', 'Soviet diplomacy in the Far East' and 'Colonial Asia', but then passes to a more detailed analysis of Soviet policy in Turkey, Iran and Afghanistan during the first decade of Soviet power, when Moscow was feeling its way to establishing a new socialist relationship with these Near Eastern neighbours, to replace the former domination of Tsarist Russia. This is a fairly well-documented book about a very interesting period in Soviet diplomatic history. Though some of Kapur's views on Soviet aims and policies may not find general agreement among his critics, his conclusion that the ultimate aim of Soviet policy in this area was the neutralising and finally the elimination of British influence is well supported by the evidence.

As far as Iran is concerned, Kapur's study is usefully extended to 1948 in *Russia and the West in Iran 1918–1948* by George Lenczowski (Ithaca; London, 1949). His main theme is the rivalry between the big powers for influence and especially Soviet efforts to undermine western influence and interests in Iran.

Before the Sino-Soviet conflict produced an open division

of loyalties in the Indian Communist Party, an excellent, fully documented study of the post-war evolution of international communist strategy with special reference to India was contained in John H. Kautsky's *Moscow and the Communist Party of India* (published jointly by The Technology Press of the Massachusetts Institute of Technology and John Wiley & Sons, New York, 1956). Moscow's lack of interest in and ignorance of Indian affairs in the immediate post-war years emerge inescapably from Mr Kautsky's acute analysis. This in turn was reflected in its incompatible and confusing directives to the CPI during this period.

Peter Sager in *Moscow's Hand in India* (Berne, 1966) studies Soviet policy in India from the point of view of Moscow's propaganda agencies. The detail collected by Sager shows that India is covered with an immense network of propaganda services, including angled films, periodicals and floods of all kinds of miscellaneous papers tending to extol the virtues and successes of Soviet Socialist Russia, with booklets specially edited for all levels of Indian society. A main feature of this propaganda is to obscure the real extent of Soviet economic aid compared to American aid, which is in fact much larger than Moscow's.

It may be because of the difficulties of separating the ambiguous Soviet state and Indian Communist activities in India that the publications in English on these matters concentrate primarily on the Indian Communist Party and only incidentally on Soviet-Indian state relations. A most detailed survey of Indian communism and its links with Moscow is given in *Communism in India* by Gene D. Overstreet and Marshall Windmiller (Berkeley, 1959). This is an authoritative study and traces the history of the movement from its earliest stages to the victory of the Communists in the Kerala State election of 1957 and subsequent developments.

Marxism and Asia by two experts on this subject, Hélène Carrère d'Encausse and Stuart R. Schram (original French ed. 1965, trans. Harmondsworth, 1969) is an 'essay accompanied by illustrative materials' which examines the 'metamorphoses of a system of ideas' or the widening gulf between the disciples of Marx in Europe and Asia in the period 1853–

D

1964. The culmination of these political-ideological differences is of course the now overt Sino-Soviet conflict, to which the selected documents in this volume provide an enlightening background.

A documentary survey of the early Soviet post-revolutionary activities in Asia, with an historical introduction on Russian expansion in Asia and 'the nationality and colonial policies of the Russian Communists', is given in *Soviet Russia and the East 1920–1927* by Xenia Joukoff Eudin and Robert C. North (Stanford, 1957). Soviet policies in the Far East during and before the second world war are more generally examined in David J. Dallin's work: *Soviet Russia and the Far East* (New Haven, 1948).

Relations between Soviet Russia and Communist China, especially since the overt breach between them, have inspired a voluminous literature, including a mass of expert articles in periodicals like *The China Quarterly*. John Gittings' excellent *Survey of the Sino-Soviet Dispute 1963–1967* (issued under the auspices of the Royal Institute of International Affairs, London, 1968) discusses the origins of the conflict, but concentrates on developments from 1963 to 1967 in a well-written narrative reinforced by the texts of the major relevant historical documents, to which he also supplies a useful check list. Wisely cutting repetition to the minimum, Gittings pays tribute to the following works which preceded his own: Donald Zagoria's pioneering study, *The Sino-Soviet Conflict 1956–61* (Princeton, 1962); William E. Griffith's *The Sino-Soviet Rift* (Cambridge, Mass., 1964); Klaus Mehnert's first-hand reportage, *Peking and Moscow* (trans. L. Vernewitz, London, 1963).

Frontier problems between the Soviet Union and China are carefully examined in *Territorial Claims in the Sino-Soviet Conflict* by Dennis J. Doolin (Stanford, 1965).

The many complexities underlying the study of *Communism in South East Asia* were admirably handled on the basis of much research and first-hand knowledge of the far-flung area in a book of this name by the late J. H. Brimmell (for the Institute of International Affairs, London, 1959). A later work by Professor Charles McLane concentrated on *Soviet*

Strategy in South East Asia and Eastern Policy under Lenin and Stalin (Princeton, 1966), in which the author shows his mastery of Soviet documentation in this field.

Outer Mongolia or the Mongolian People's Republic officially ranks as an independent country with its own government, foreign missions and other regalia of sovereignty. Soviet influence has however been dominant there since the twenties, and as a result Mongolia has been precipitated from its traditional nomadic society into a socialist form of government with collectivisation of its livestock wealth and some rudimentary industrialisation. These developments are examined with scholarly acumen and knowledge of the country by Dr C. R. Bawden in his *The Modern History of Mongolia* (London, 1968).

Before the Cuban crisis of 1962, Latin America was generally regarded as only of marginal interest to the Soviet Union. The attempt to set up Soviet missile bases in an area traditionally regarded as America's 'backyard' brusquely undermined these assumptions. In fact, the Soviet Union today maintains a wide and increasing range of political, economic and cultural contacts with Latin American countries. In a pioneer work, edited with admirable command of the subject by Stephen Clissold, *Soviet Relations with Latin America 1918–1968* (issued under the auspices of the Royal Institute of International Affairs, London, 1970), the fluctuating course of Soviet relations with Latin America, from the extraordinary mission of Mikhail Borodin to Mexico in 1919, where he converted the young Indian M. N. Roy to Communism, to Castro's speech supporting the Soviet action in Czechoslovakia in 1968, is graphically unfolded in these pages of documents and very informative notes by Clissold. He also provides an invaluable Introduction, in which he summarises most lucidly the main phases in the development of Soviet-Latin American relations and then gives a country-by-country survey of the situation between them and Moscow. A wealth of little known, most interesting Soviet material on this subject is brought to light in this volume.

An admirably comprehensive guide to *Soviet African Studies 1918–59* is given in Mary Holdsworth's annotated bibliography of that name (for the Royal Institute of International Affairs, London, 1961). Mrs Holdsworth discusses the origins and intensive development of Soviet African studies, the objectives of Soviet Africanists and the organisation of Soviet African studies in her General Introduction. Apart from the main bibliography, she includes selected biographies of some of the chief Soviet scholars in this field, an Index of Authors and an Index of Subjects. It is only regrettable that this invaluable guide has not been brought up to date to cover the mass of new work on Africa which has been published in the Soviet Union since 1959. *Mizan,* the journal of the Central Asian Research Centre, will however be found to contain interim comments on the more important Soviet works in this field.

Soviet Policy in West Africa by Robert Legvold (Cambridge, Mass., 1970) contains much of interest about the largely frustrated Soviet ambitions in Africa and the Chinese challenge to the Russians in this area, with its furious denunciations of Soviet foreign-policy priorities. According to Legvold, Soviet hopes of 'reliable socialism' in Africa have at least for the moment evaporated, while the lack of a genuine working class has prevented the formation of communist parties in West Africa.

Pan-Africanism or Communism (London, 1956) is interesting in spite of its highly controversial views because the author, George Padmore, is a West Indian negro and writes as a supporter of pan-Africanism. According to Padmore, if the African peoples are not granted independence, they will veer towards Communism through despair. His attitude to the Soviet Union is very naive and shows no understanding of Soviet aims or policies in Africa. A more balanced, informed survey of *Africa and the Communist World* is given in Zbigniew Brzezinski's book under this title (2nd ed., London, 1967).

A comprehensive symposium, *Soviet Policy in the Developing Countries* (Waltham, Mass., 1970), edited by W. Raymond Duncan, studies many aspects of this subject and stresses its emergence in Soviet strategy since Stalin's death. One general conclusion of the survey is that Soviet national objectives have now superseded the more purely ideological former goals of expanding communist movements throughout the Third World, i.e. the evolving nations of Africa, Asia, the Middle East and Latin America. It is interesting to learn, incidentally, that modern Asian and African history are now compulsory courses for all Soviet graduates in history. The importance of the Soviet military assistance programme as a means of influencing regional balances of power and its steeply mounting costs are emphasised. David Morison contributes an extremely well-argued, cogent analysis of Soviet Arab policies before and after the June War of 1967. He takes the somewhat original view that it is more appropriate to speak of Moscow's present Arab policy in terms of liability than of opportunity, but the contrary would be true if Soviet policy were in an adventurous phase. He suggests that the 'Soviet man's burden in the Afro-Asian world is beginning to be appreciated in its various dimensions'.

As a permanent member of the Security Council, the Soviet Union's tactics and policies in the United Nations are obviously of paramount international importance. Alexander Dallin has written a well-documented analysis of this difficult subject, which throws much-needed light on the often bewildering Soviet tactics: *The Soviet Union at the United Nations: An Inquiry into Soviet Motives and Objectives* (New York, 1962). The book requires an up-to-date sequel.

It is not surprising that far less has been written about Soviet military affairs and strategy than on Soviet foreign policies in view of the even tighter security restrictions obscuring this important subject from prying foreign eyes. Nevertheless, Professor John Erickson produced a most impressive reconstruction of the organisation and tensions in the Soviet armed forces in *The Soviet High Command: A Military-Political History 1918–1941* (London, 1962). This was followed up by *Juggernaut: A History of the Soviet Armed Forces* by Malcolm Mackintosh (London, 1967), also a remarkable contribution to knowledge, not only of the organisation of the Soviet armed forces, but of the many campaigns in which they were engaged from the Civil War to the short action against the Japanese in the Far East in 1945.

91

All this is illustrated by excellent maps, including a map of the military districts of the USSR in 1966. His informed discussion of party-military relationships is of great and continuing importance to all interested in this crucial aspect of the balance of power in the Kremlin.

The flood of Soviet military memoir material, much of it of indifferent quality, yet yielding important information about Stalin's role and capacity as Generalissimo of the Soviet armed forces, which has been published in the Soviet Union in the 1960s, has found a very competent, scholarly commentator in Professor Seweryn Bialer. His *Stalin and His Generals: Soviet Memoirs of World War II* (London, 1970) will be invaluable to many lacking his ability to plough through this mass of evidence yet interested to know what it contains.

Foreign trade and economic aid are also important adjuncts of Soviet foreign policy, and are all interrelated in the Soviet world view. The structural organisation of Soviet foreign trade on the eve of the second world war and a breakdown of Soviet trade with the more important countries are clearly described in Professor A. Baykov's *Soviet Foreign Trade* (London, 1946). This is essentially a theoretical study. The subject is more realistically analysed by Alec Nove and Desmond Donnelly in their joint study *Trade with Communist Countries* (the Institute of Economic Affairs, London, 1960). While Professor Nove examines the prospects for East-West trade, bilateralism and strategic controls, Desmond Donnelly looks at the practical operation of trade with communist countries in the light of his extensive experience in the Soviet Union and Eastern Europe.

The development of economic aid from Stalin's death to the early 1960s, in particular in Asia and the Middle East, is fully documented in Joseph S. Berliner's informative study: *Soviet Economic Aid: The New Aid and Trade Policy in Underdeveloped Countries* (for the Council of Foreign Relations, New York, 1958; abridgment with new material, London, 1960).

Subsequent *Soviet Foreign Aid* is examined in some detail in a book of this name by Marshall I. Goldman (New York,

1967). It gives, for example, an almost incredible description of the chaotic conditions underlying Soviet aid to Indonesia before the 'crash'. According to Goldman, the Soviets soon found that anything involving activity on Indonesian territory or participation of Indonesian workmen seemed to falter or collapse. Many expensive and even grotesque mistakes were made owing to Soviet ignorance of local conditions. There are useful insights in these pages showing why the Soviets have been successful and why they failed in this field of activity.

For more recent information, consult the interim reports of the countries concerned, special Russian publications and *The United Nations Statistical Yearbook* (Statistical Office of the UN, New York).

Geography (Human and Physical)

Russian Land, Soviet People by James S. Gregory (London, 1968) is an encyclopedic reference work on the physical divisions (republics, krays, oblasts, etc.) of the Soviet Union and its multi-national population. There is also some information on Soviet economic resources and development, but it would need supplementing from more specialised sources, for research purposes. An older, but still very useful book is the admirably accurate and concise *Geography of the Soviet Union* by T. Shabad (New York, 1951). This early work has been succeeded by a comprehensive survey of the Soviet resource base (i.e., fuel and energy, metals and other minerals for the chemical industry – all most important for the understanding of Soviet economic power today) by T. Shabad: *Basic Industrial Resources of the USSR* (New York, 1969). This book is arranged in two parts. In the first part, general production trends and locational patterns of each resource sector (coal, oil and gas fields and pipelines, metals, etc.) are discussed, while part two is a survey of the mining and related resource complexes of the major regions, e.g., the Ukraine, the Urals, etc. There are admirable regional maps and a good index.

Though somewhat dated on the score of economic resources

and development, Erich Thiel's *The Soviet Far East* (English translation from the German by A. and R. M. Rookwood, London, 1957) still provides the best guide in English to the physical features of the Soviet Far Eastern region.

In his standard work: *The Population of the Soviet Union* (Geneva, 1946), Frank Lorimer examines in considerable depth and great expertise the multi-national Soviet population statistics and problems on the basis of the 1939 census. He prefaces this study with a very useful analysis of the position from the 1897 Imperial Russian census to 1939. Unfortunately, no similar work on the Soviet 1959 census has been published, though the main census statistics, as published in the Russian texts, are generally available in English reference works, e.g., *Russian Land, Soviet People,* listed above.

The great increase in Soviet urban centres and populations, especially since the war, has in turn produced a spate of new urban buildings, most of them uninspired and dully monotonous, if not also extremely unsightly. This was not always so, according to a survey of the role of Soviet architects in the development of modern architecture in the period 1917–1935, by Anatole Kopp. His book, *Town and Revolution: Soviet Architecture and City Planning, 1917–1935* (trans. Thomas E. Burton, London, 1970), describes the hey-day of avant-garde Russian architecture and the blossoming of constructivist buildings in Moscow before the Party intervened to destroy architectural initiative as well as so many fine old buildings of architectural interest. In the thirties, the new Moscow and its Soviet institutions were still very much in the making. In order to investigate the new type of municipal government of this large city or *Mossoviet* administering housing, building schemes, education, public order, communications and innumerable other branches of public business, four English experts (including Sir E. D. Simon and Lady Simon), spent some time in Moscow in 1936 and published their survey in an interesting professional book: *Moscow in the Making* (London, 1937). It is probably the most detailed breakdown of the activities of Mossoviet in English, and of considerable interest to students of local government.

Finally, a few outstanding works may be mentioned which reflect the intellectual frustration and politcal dissent of a highly educated sector of the Soviet people. This atmosphere is vividly described with inside knowledge by Svetlana Alliluyeva in her second book, *Only One Year* (London, 1969). A more active, very brave opponent of the present régime, Andrei Amalrik, has written an absorbing account of the realities and strains in Soviet Russian life today, published in English under the title: *Can the Soviet Union Survive until 1984?* (New York, 1970). His forecast of the collapse of the present Soviet system with the 'inevitable' outbreak of war between Russia and China in 1984 is probably inspired by mere wishful thinking rather than political intelligence, but he is on more interesting ground when he writes of the demands for physical and intellectual freedom and respect for law coming from 'the specialists' and the political weakness created by the lack of moral criteria in the Russian 'middle class' since the replacement of Christian morality by the so-called official 'class morality'. Among many rather indifferent travelogues, the lively acute observations of Soviet life and people from Central Russia to Central Asia and Siberia contained in Laurens van der Post's *Journey into Russia* (London, 1964) are in quite another class, both good reading and very enlightening.

Other Recommended Reference Works

Russia and the Soviet Union. A bibliographical guide to Western-language publications, Paul L. Horecky (ed.), (London, 1965).

Soviet Foreign Relations and World Communism. A selected, annotated bibliography of 7000 books in 30 languages. Compiled and edited by Thomas T. Hammond (Princeton, 1965). This work contains references to Soviet diplomatic and economic relations with all major countries since 1917 and communist movements throughout the world since 1917; major internal developments in all communist countries except the USSR.

Books on Soviet Russia, 1917–1942. A bibliography and a guide to reading by Philip Grierson (London, 1943).

The Essentials of Lenin. Two-volume edition (London, 1947). Contains a selection of the more important works of Lenin, arranged so as to provide his comments on the course of the Revolution and its problems, and an understanding of the principles on which he aimed at building the new Soviet society.

The History of the Russian Revolution by Leon Trotsky. Translated by Max Eastman (London, 1934). A brilliantly written history of the Bolshevik Revolution and its causes, seen through the eyes of one of its most dynamic leaders.

Concise Encyclopaedia of Russia. S. V. Utechin (London, 1961). An invaluable easily accessible source of information on Russian history and general affairs.

Books on Communism. A bibliography. Walter Kolarz (ed.). New revised edition (London, 1963). Contains reliable details of publications in English on the development of Communism in the USSR, China and all the principal countries of the world.

Soviet Treaties Series. L. Shapiro (ed.), Vol. I: 1917–28 (published Washington, 1950); Vol. II: 1929–39 (1955). A most valuable work of reference for all students of Soviet foreign policy.

The Theory, Law and Policy of Soviet Treaties. Jan. F. Triska and Robert Slusser. An analysis of more than 2000 Soviet treaties between 1917 and 1957 with notes, bibliography and classified indices (Stanford, 1962).

Russian Works on China 1918–1960, in American Libraries. Tung-Li Yuan (ed.). Yale University Far Eastern Publications, 1961. With an index, a very useful reference work, also listing English translations of Russian works mentioned.

Soviet Russia and the East 1920–1927: a documentary survey with an excellent general introduction and comments on the various regional sections into which the book is divided. Xenia Joukoff Eudin and Robert C. North (Stanford, 1957).

Soviet Russia and the West, 1920–1927. A companion volume to the above work. Same authors and publisher, 1957.

Economic Geography of the USSR. S. S. Balzak, V. F. Vasyutin and Y. G. Feigin (eds). American edition ed. Chaucy D. Harris (New York, 1949).

The Economy of the USSR during World War II (trans. from the Russian), by Nikolay Voznesenskii (Washington, 1948). The author, who was Chief of the State Planning Commission and a Deputy Premier of the USSR (purged in 1949), draws on his official experience and knowledge to show how the Soviet economy overcame many crucial problems during the war.

The Political Economy of Communism by P. J. D. Wiles (Oxford, 1963). An original critical study of Communist theory and practice. Probably too sophisticated for under-graduates, but stimulating for more mature students.

Karl Marx by Isaiah Berlin (London, 1949). A classic of concise brilliant biography.

Archaeology in the USSR by A. L. Mongait. Trans. from the Russian by M. W. Thompson (Harmondsworth, 1961).

Russia, 1917: the February Revolution by G. Katkov (London, 1967). An exhaustive examination of the source materials dealing with the prelude to the October Revolution, on which the author holds strong and often controversial views.

4

Eastern Europe

Heinz Schurer

Introduction

The study of post-war Eastern Europe presents similar problems to the reader as did the study of Russia after the October Revolution. Then serious students had to admit that in order to understand bolshevist Russia they had to grapple with the writings of Karl Marx and learn about the history of the international socialist movement. A distinguished writer on Eastern Europe in the inter-war period has stated that his book could not be written without a profound knowledge of Marxism-Leninism, the history of European Communism, and without a comprehension of the main events of Russian history since 1917. Study of the recent history of Eastern Europe demands some grasp of these subjects, and particularly a grasp of events in Soviet Russia since the end of the War. The rule of Stalin, Stalin's death, the twentieth congress of the Soviet Communist Party of 1956, the Sino-Soviet rift, have had profound repercussions on Eastern Europe.

That the establishment of one party states and the political patterning of the new East European states presents difficulties to the writing of detached and well-informed current history, involving the authors frequently in guess work, hardly needs emphasising. Equally characteristic of this field of study is that a high proportion of the authors dealing with the area are émigrés. It is remarkable that many volumes are nevertheless written in a spirit of scholarly detachment inspired by the search for a balanced presentation. What is natural and must be expected as inevitable is that the writing in some monographs, however valuable for their factual information and for their able interpretation, is often undistinguished, if not dull. However, we would be much less informed about the complex area under review if it was not for the great number of brilliant expatriates who have contributed so much to the understanding of this particularly difficult corner of the world.

General Surveys

The one attempt so far at presenting the history of the people's democracies from 1944 to the Soviet intervention in Czechoslovakia in August 1968 is a book written by a Hungarian author in French. As it is the only work covering such a wide field it should be given pride of place. F. Fejtö, *Histoire des démocraties populaires* (2 vols, Paris, 1952–68) is remarkable not only for its rich factual information, but also as an ambitious attempt at a synthesis of the main currents and strains and stresses in this part of the communist world. A translation has recently appeared.[1] For the early period of the communist take-over after the end of the war, the standard work is H. Seton-Watson, *The East European Revolution* (London, 1950; 3rd ed. 1956). This remains the authoritative survey. In addition to its analysis of the communist triumph, there is also a chapter devoted to the exception, Greece. As a companion piece, the collection of essays edited by R. R. Betts, *Central and South East Europe 1945–48* (London, 1950) should be consulted. These concise chapters by experts give accurate factual information with a conclusive summing up by the editor.

A different approach, emphasising the transformation of the countryside by the communist victory is presented by a distinguished student of the East European peasantry, D. Warriner, in her *Revolution in Eastern Europe* (London, 1950). She stresses the economic changes and – in 1950 – considered that 'the new regimes offer real progress, an incredible advance on the past'. Y. Gluckstein, *Stalin's Satellites in Europe* (London, 1952) on the other hand, lays strong emphasis on Russia's dominating role in the post-war developments in the political as well as the economic sphere. The last third of the book is devoted to the rise of Titoism and its repercussions. For the Balkan region there is an outstanding survey, R. L. Wolff, *The Balkans in Our Time* (Cambridge, Mass., 1956; reprinted 1967). The second half of this very solid scholarly work deals with the post-war period up to 1955. Economic as well as political developments are treated in considerable depth. Particular attention is given to Yugoslavia, but there are also separate sections for Rumania, Bulgaria and Albania. Z. K. Brzezinski, *The Soviet Bloc: Unity and Conflict* (Cambridge, Mass., 1960; revised ed. 1967) is a very ambitious attempt at a synthesis of the impact of the theory and practice of the Soviet Union on the people's democracies. Separate chapters deal with Yugoslavia, Hungary and Poland. R. V. Burks, *The Dynamics of Communism in Eastern Europe* (Princeton, 1961) is an original attempt at a typology of East European Communism within a very restricted space. Of particular interest is the first part discussing Greek communism. H. Ripka, *Eastern Europe in the Post-War World* (London, 1961) is a stimulating essay of the period which had experienced the impact of the events of 1956. While the author emphasised the need for a democratic development in Eastern Europe, he did not consider that the forms of democracy suitable for the region should be an exact copy of West European models. S. D. Kertesz (ed.), *The Fate of East Central Europe* (Notre Dame, Indiana, 1956) has short informative chapters on the individual countries, but the main interest lies in the discussion of US policy towards East Central Europe since 1945. S. D. Kertesz (ed.), *East Central Europe and the World* (Notre Dame, Indiana, 1962) follows the same patterns of essays written by experts on the individual states and their political developments since 1945. There are sections on economic policy as well and on West European and American policy towards East Central Europe. S. Fischer-Galati (ed.), *Eastern Europe in the Sixties* (New York, 1963) follows the same arrangement of chapters on the new social order, the economy, and the politics of the area. There are chapters on relations with international communism and on relations with the non-communist world. W. E. Griffith (ed.), *Communism in Europe* (Cambridge, Mass., 1964–6. 2 vols.) emphasises – as a collection of substantial essays – how the Sino-Soviet dispute has affected Yugoslavia, Poland, Hungary, East Germany and Czechoslovakia. The stress in the essays is on the developments in these countries since 1956. H. G. Skilling, *Communism, National and International: Eastern Europe after Stalin* (Toronto, 1964) is a stimulating collection of articles by the same author reprinted from journals. The collection has as its unifying theme the various responses of the East European countries to the Khrushchev era. V. L. Benes and others, *Eastern European Government and Politics* (New York, 1966) presents in the form of separate essays concise up-to-date information on Poland, Czechoslovakia, East Germany, Hungary, Yugoslavia and Rumania. There are no chapters on Albania and Bulgaria. J. F. Brown, *The New Eastern Europe: the Khrushchev Era and After* (London, 1966) summarises the main events since the death of Stalin. Special attention is given to nationalist trends emerging in Albania and Rumania in connection with the Sino-Soviet dispute. H. G. Shaffer (ed.), *The Communist World* (New York, 1967) has had the worthwhile idea of confronting communist and non-communist views of the Soviet Union, China and the people's democracies, the chapters being arranged in country-by-country order. G. Ionescu, *The Politics of the East European Communist States* (London, 1967) is a serious attempt at a synthesis of the experience of the last twenty years as far as the political structure of the people's democracies is concerned. The author proposes the interesting thesis that the mass organisations created in a totalitarian spirit are likely to develop autonomous trends of their own and to form the basis of a pluralist political structure of the future. As a piece of highly original political theorising the work deserves a very special place. N. Spulber, *The Economics of Communist Eastern Europe* (Cambridge, Mass., 1957) is the most comprehensive survey of the great economic changes sweeping over East Europe since 1945. Substantial chapters deal with agricultural policy, nationalisation, and planning, treating the area as a whole. A. Zauberman, *Industrial Progress in Poland, Czechoslovakia, and East Germany, 1937–62* (London, 1964) focuses on the impact of central planning on industrial growth. Energy, metals and chemicals are given separate chapters. The emphasis throughout is on developments in Poland. The final chapter discusses economic relations within the Soviet bloc. M. Gamarnikov, *Economic Reforms in Eastern Europe* (Detroit, 1968) discusses the recent changes in economic policy by main themes such as the problem of combining planning and the market economy, and the issues raised by economic decentralisation. The bibliography is advantageously arranged by countries. L. Sirc, *Economic Devolution in Eastern Europe* (London, 1969) emphasises the dangers and risks inherent in the new trend of the economic reforms. M. Kaser, *Comecon: Integration Problems of the Planned Economies* (London, 1965; 2nd ed. 1967) presents a lucid and well organised account of the Council for Mutual Economic Assistance. The second edition takes account of the considerable changes that had taken place since 1965 in the economic relations between the USSR and the people's democracies. The trend has been away from rigid central management with its implications for international coordination.

J. F. Triska (ed.), *The Constitutions of the Communist Party-States* (Stanford, 1968) presents a useful collection of the texts of the constitutions of all communist countries of the world, including those of all East European countries.

N. Grant, *Society, Schools, and Progress in Eastern Europe* (Oxford, 1969) discusses one of the genuine achievements of the East European revolution, the broadening out of education. After dealing with the general pattern of schooling in Eastern Europe, there is a country-by-country survey, each chapter discussing the old system and the post-war developments, thus making the book a useful factual description of the post-war educational scene in the area.

Poland

So far there is no large-scale up-to-date authoritative work on post-war Poland. The most recent concise summary of the main developments is J. F. Morrison, *The Polish People's Republic* (Baltimore, 1969) published as a volume of a series of small monographs dealing with the individual East European countries. R. Hiscocks, in his *Poland: bridge for the abyss?* (London, 1963) devotes about two thirds of his volume to the post-war period. He considers that Poland, owing to her history and geographical position might find her role as a mediator between East and West. H. Stehle, *The Independent Satellite: society and politics in Poland since 1945* (London, 1965) surveys the Polish scene mostly in the period since 1956. The author is a West German journalist. Of considerable interest are the chapters on state–church relations and on relations between Poland and West Germany since 1956. H. Roos, *A History of Modern Poland* (London, 1966) covers the period from 1914 onwards, but devotes the last third to a useful sketch of the developments from 1945 to 1965. The book was first published in West Germany. P. E. Zinner (ed.), *National Communism and Popular Revolt in Eastern Europe: a selection of documents on events in Poland and Hungary, February–November 1956* (New York, 1957) presents a useful documentation of the crucial year 1956. A. Bromke, *Poland's Politics: idealism vs. realism* (Cambridge, Mass., 1967) surveys Polish politics since 1945, with interesting chapters on Catholic movements such as the *Pax* and the *Znak* groups. The author stresses the extreme importance of Polish–West German relations for the future of Poland. N. Bethell, *Gomulka: his Poland and his communism* (London, 1969) sketches the history of the Polish Communist Party and then surveys the developments up to the 'October Revolution' of 1956. The subsequent developments are discussed rather briefly. The author sums up, 'Gomulka had power thrust upon him. His greatness was that he helped make viable a form of communism which both his people and the Soviet leaders were able to find generally tolerable. His weakness was in his stubbornness and lack of flexibility.' M. K. Dziewanowski's *The Communist Party of Poland* (Cambridge, Mass., 1959) is an outstanding scholarly study and remains the standard work on the subject. The second half of the book deals with the post-1945 period.

J. J. Wiatr (ed.), *Studies in Polish Political System* (Warsaw, 1967) is a collection of essays published under the auspices of the Polish Academy's Institute of Philosophy and

Sociology. It discusses topics such as the changes in the class structure of post-war Poland, the role of the party system, and problems of interest groups and their representation. As a sample of recent Polish sociological science the volume is of considerable interest. T. P. Alton, *The Polish Post-War Economy* (New York, 1955) lays its main emphasis on the problems of economic planning. The impact of the Soviet model on Polish economic policy is discussed in detail. For the later period and for the changes in economic policy since 1956, there is J. M. Montias, *Central Planning in Poland* (New Haven, 1962). A. Kotarbinski, *The Politics of Socialist Agriculture in Poland, 1945–1960* (New York, 1965) gives a well-documented account of the attempts at large-scale collectivisation in the Stalin era and the gradual drastic modification of this policy, which has now made Poland the communist country *par excellence,* where private property predominates in the countryside. In addition to the chapters on church–state relations in the general works listed above, for the famous *Pax* group and its founder there is a good journalistic account in L. Blit, *The Eastern Pretender: Boleslaw Piasecki* (London, 1965).

East Germany

East Germany has not attracted the attention of many scholars writing in English. For many years, the one serious comprehensive survey – of the first phase only – of what has been since 1949 the German Democratic Republic, was J. P. Nettl, *The Eastern Zone and Soviet Policy in Germany, 1945–50* (London, 1951). This remains the standard work for the first years of the Republic. The book was a considerable achievement for a very young man who had also written a biography of Rosa Luxemburg. (Nettl died in 1970.) Carola Stern (pseud.), *Ulbricht: a political biography* (London, 1965) has gathered all the facts which could be ascertained about Ulbricht. The book is a work of a former East German writer who has made her home in West Germany. It was originally published in West Germany. A. M. Hanhardt, Jr, *The German Democratic Republic* (Baltimore, 1968) is a concise survey useful for its outline of the developments since 1961. Considerably more ambitious is an English volume of the 'Nations of the Modern World' series: D. Childs, *East Germany* (London, 1969) is a scholarly study by a young British academic. The emphasis is on the political and economic structure, and there are also chapters on the army and on the international situation of the DDR. While not uncritical in his approach, the author gives fair recognition to the achievements of the last decade. Very positive and sympathetic towards the present East German regime is Jean Edward Smith, *Germany Beyond the Wall: people, politics and prosperity* (Boston, 1969). This profile of the DDR presents a large amount of factual information on daily life, economic development, the political structure, and the new system of education. The author considers that an increasing acceptance of the present regime has taken place.

Czechoslovakia

Czechoslovakia, although having a large communist party in the inter-war period, was the last European country to join the Soviet bloc. We are fortunate in having a very detailed study of the first twelve years of communist rule. E. Taborsky, *Communism in Czechoslovakia 1948–1960* (Princeton, 1961) is the most comprehensive account of the period surveyed. The author was a personal aide of Beneš in the years of wartime emigration. The communist seizure of power of February 1948, one of the crucial events of the post-war period, yielded a crop of books which in most cases build up the background of the sensational events of that year. P. E. Zinner, *Communist Strategy and Tactics in Czechoslovakia 1918–1948* (London, 1963) devotes its second half to a succinct sketch of the post-war developments. This can be supplemented by J. Korbel, *The Communist Subversion in Czechoslovakia, 1938–1948* (Princeton, 1959) which studies the activities of the Communist Party in considerable detail. For a book written soon after the event by a distinguished Czech politician who was a member of the Beneš government in exile, there is H. Ripka, *Czechoslovakia Enslaved* (London, 1950) which discusses the background to the 1948 events very thoroughly. There is no comprehensive survey comparable to Taborsky's valuable study for the sixties, but naturally the introductions to the works on the 1968 crisis present some material. A short account discusses the 1968 events primarily from the point of view of the military situation and from the aspect of Soviet developments which resulted in the fateful decision to intervene. P. Windsor and A. Roberts, *Czechoslovakia 1968* (London, 1969) is written by two British academics. Z. A. B. Zeman, *Prague Spring* (Harmondsworth, 1969) surveys the reform movement. The author spent some time in Prague in 1968 and his survey has the value of an eyewitness report. W. Shawcross, *Dubcek* (London, 1970) is a journalist's biography. While critical of Dubček's tactics in 1968 and presenting an account of the events of this year which will remain controversial, the author has gathered considerable new material on Dubček's pre-1968 activities. R. Rhodes James, *The Czechoslovak crisis 1968* (London, 1969) is based on the proceedings of a conference held under the auspices of the Institute for the Study of International Organisation of the University of Sussex in October 1968. The Czech events are discussed from the international relations aspect. There is a useful chronology of events from January to December 1968. There are two particularly useful collections of documents on the 1968 events, R. A. Remington (ed.), *Winter in Prague* (Cambridge, Mass., 1969) where most of the documents are translated from Czech and Slovak, and R. Littell (ed.), *The Czech Black Book* (London, 1969) which is an abridged translation of a collection of documents in Czech, produced by the Historical Institute of the Czechoslovak Academy of Sciences. G. R. Feiwel, *New Economic Patterns in Czechoslovakia* (London, 1969) describes the search for a new type of market socialism characteristic of the developments of the sixties. A long final chapter deals with the trend towards political liberalisation culminating in the 1968 events.

Yugoslavia

By its break with Stalin in 1948, Yugoslavia anticipated the trends which in later years were to become known as 'national communism' and 'polycentrism'. As a result, the attitude of many authors towards the Tito regime is considerably more sympathetic than in the case of other East European countries. Such a positive approach is characteristic of the most comprehensive account so far, A. W. Hoffman and F. W. Neal, *Yugoslavia and the New Communism* (New York, 1962), which gives considerable attention to the economic development of the country and the importance of decentralisation. The authors conclude that 'Titoism has achieved remarkable successes in its short life.' In 1965, a conference on modern Yugoslavia was held at Stanford University; the papers read there form the basis of W. S. Vucinich (ed.), *Contemporary Yugoslavia: twenty years of socialist experiment* (Berkeley, 1969). The volume is of a sound scholarly standard and deals with Yugoslav politics and economic developments. F. W. Neal, *Titoism in Action: the reforms in Yugoslavia after 1948* (Berkeley, 1958) is a well written account of 'Tito's separate way'. Political and economic developments are given equal attention in this scholarly work. A book written under the fresh impact of the events of 1948 which retains its value today, as its author is one of the best writers on Russia and Eastern Europe, is A. B. Ulam, *Titoism and the Cominform* (Cambridge, Mass., 1952). It is an excellent study of the Soviet–Yugoslav conflict of 1948. The most recent biography of Tito is by a distinguished British academic who is clearly sympathetic to her subject, Phyllis Auty, *Tito: a biography* (London, 1970). Considerable research into Yugoslav source material has gone into the making of this work. On the other hand, a highly critical analysis of Yugoslav society is presented by a former high official in the Yugoslav Foreign Office who fled to the West in 1961. N. D. Popovic, *Yugoslavia: the new class in crisis* (Syracuse, 1968) emphasises that underneath the surface powerful processes of political ferment are at work. F. W. Hondius, *The Yugoslav Community of Nations* (The Hague, 1968) studies the present federal system. The 1963 constitution is seen as a watershed. Its provisions, the author considers, worked out the principles of polycentrism, recognising the nations as essential components of the federal community. P. Shoup, *Communism and the*

Yugoslav National Question (New York, 1968) on the other hand, emphasises the powerful centrifugal forces arising from rapid industrialisation and economic devolution. The author stresses the fact that Yugoslav communism remains in a state of transition. F. E. I. Hamilton, *Yugoslavia: patterns of economic activity* (London, 1968) presents a scholarly survey of developments since 1945, discussing agriculture as well as industry. The importance of regional planning receives special emphasis.

Hungary

F. A. Váli, *Rift and Revolt in Hungary* (Cambridge, Mass., 1961) is the most comprehensive scholarly study of post-war Hungary. In the central section, it outlines the events leading up to and discusses the October Revolution of 1956, of which the author was an eyewitness. There is a substantial chapter on the five years following 1956, the author applying the basic concept of a clash between indigenous nationalism and communism imposed from outside. P. E. Zinner, *Revolution in Hungary* (New York, 1962, p. 380) pays particular attention to developments within the Communist Party. P. Kecskemeti, *The Unexpected Revolution: social forces in the Hungarian uprising* (Stanford, 1961), in the author's words, 'deals with the genesis of a revolutionary situation in Hungary, rather than with the revolutionary events themselves'. The author considers that both the imposition of the Stalinist regime and the violent upheaval causing its break-up make Hungary an extreme example of a regime enforced from above and with disruptive tendencies leading to an explosion at a favourable moment. The small book is a useful attempt at a sociological analysis of a highly important episode of the post-war period. T. Aczél and T. Méray, *The Revolt of the Mind: a case history of intellectual resistance behind the Iron Curtain* (London, 1960) is a journalistic account of opposition trends in the Hungarian intelligentsia in the years before 1956. There are two useful collections of documents which give the flavour of contemporary experience to the events illustrated: M. J. Lasky (ed.), *The Hungarian Revolution* (London, 1957) and P. E. Zinner (ed.), *National Communism and Popular Revolt in Eastern Europe: a selection of documents on events in Poland and Hungary, February–November 1956* (New York, 1957) which has already been mentioned in the section on Poland. T. Aczél (ed.), *Ten years After: a commemoration of the tenth anniversary of the Hungarian revolution* (London, 1966) is a useful collection, mostly by distinguished Hungarian émigrés surveying the main trends since 1956. There is also a bibliography on the Hungarian revolution. B. A. Balassa, *The Hungarian Experience in Economic Planning* (New Haven, 1959) bases his study on the Hungarian practice of the period before 1956. The author's purpose is to discuss the theory of centralised planning and to demonstrate by the Hungarian example how such a system really works.

Rumania

Two of the most distinguished authors writing on East European problems today have contributed monographs on Rumania's post-war development: Stephen Fischer-Galaţi and Ghiţa Ionescu. S. Fischer-Galaţi, *Twentieth Century Rumania* (New York, 1970) devotes about a third of its space to the period under review. Very ably written chapters discuss the 'loss of national identity' in the Stalin era and the reclamation of the 'national legacy' in the period after 1953, culminating in the sensational assertion of Rumanian independence in 1964. The author concludes that Rumania today is vastly different from the country of the forties and fifties. G. Ionescu, *Communism in Rumania 1944–1962* (London, 1964) is the most comprehensive account of post-war developments published so far. The book is a work of real distinction. After an introduction outlining the history of the Communist Party, the establishment of Soviet domination and the impact of Russian events on Rumania's recent history is discussed. For additional factual material covering the first post-war decade, S. Fischer-Galaţi (ed.), *Romania* (New York, 1957) should be consulted. Numerous experts contribute chapters under headings such as government and party, culture, and economy, but the work is principally for reference. D. Floyd, *Rumania: Russia's dissident ally* (London, 1965) discusses the 'new type relations' emerging between Soviet Russia and Rumania in the sixties. J. M. Montias, *Economic Development in Communist Rumania* (Cambridge, Mass., 1967) presents a detailed treatment of the industrialisation of a peasant country under communist rule. The author stresses the parallels between the Soviet Russian and Rumanian experience under central planning.

Bulgaria

Post-war Bulgaria has not attracted the attention of many writers. There have not been the dramatic episodes which have focused interest on other countries in Eastern Europe, such as the Hungarian events of 1956 or the sensational break of Tito with Stalin. The most useful compilation of essays by numerous experts discussing government, society, and the economy was published in the series East-Central Europe under the Communists, L. A. D. Dellin (ed.), *Bulgaria* (New York, 1957). Only recently has a comprehensive survey of Bulgaria been published, a work which is likely to remain a standard text for some time to come, by an author who has made other useful contributions to the recent history of Eastern Europe, J. F. Brown, *Bulgaria under Communist Rule* (London, 1970).

Albania

Albania, undoubtedly the most backward region of East Europe, has drawn more attention to her post-war history than she would normally receive, owing to her break with Soviet Russia and her alliance with China following the Sino-Soviet rift. N. C. Pano, *The People's Republic of Albania* (Baltimore, 1968) presents a concise survey of post-war developments. S. Skendl (ed.), *Albania* (New York, 1956) is a collection of essays by several experts. A good deal of the information supplied refers to the period before 1945. The work is one of the series East-Central Europe under the Communists. H. Hamm, *Albania – China's beachhead in Europe* (London, 1963) is the translation of a book first published in West Germany. It is a good journalistic account of the period 1960–3 when Albania first swung round to her present pro-Chinese position. A. Dallin (ed.), *Diversity in International Communism: a documentary record, 1961–63* (New York, 1963) is of particular relevance owing to its 100-page collection of documents concerning Albania and the impact of the Sino-Soviet conflict on Soviet-Albanian relations. W. E. Griffith, *Albania and the Sino-Soviet rift* (Cambridge, Mass., 1963) consists of a factual account as well as a collection of documents relevant to the subject of the book.

Greece

Greece is the great exception in the area under discussion. After a bitter civil war in the immediate post-war years, communism failed in its bid for power. Since 1967 the country has been living under a military dictatorship. An able essay in political sociology describes and analyses the present political system: K. R. Legg, *Politics in Modern Greece* (Stanford, 1969) with interesting chapters on the political parties in the post-war era and a chapter discussing the coup of 1967. For a brief, unambitious chronicle of the main events of the last quarter of a century, stopping at the 1967 coup, there is a useful concise account, J. P. C. and A. G. Carey, *The Web of Modern Greek Politics* (New York, 1968). For the crucial period of the immediate post-war years, D. G. Kousoulas, *Revolution and Defeat: the story of the Greek Communist Party* (London, 1965) is a well documented history of the party from 1918 onwards. The very last section deals with the civil war. W. H. McNeill, *The Greek Dilemma* (London, 1947) is a concise scholarly account of war and post-war developments, with the emphasis on the civil war and the great difficulties facing Greek society at the time. S. G. Xydis, *Greece and the Great Powers, 1944–47: prelude to the Truman doctrine* (Salonika, 1963) puts the Greek crisis in its international setting, with the British army opposing communism while active support was given it by Albania, Bulgaria, and Yugoslavia. The impact on American-Soviet relations is discussed. For a highly personal survey of Greek post-war history, the autobiographical account by the son of a former liberal prime minister is worth consulting. A. Papandreou, *Democracy at the Gun Point: the Greek front* (Garden City, NY, 1970) tells the general story up to the 1967 coup. W. O. Candilis, *The Economy of Greece, 1944-66* (New York, 1968) is a highly professional account of the efforts for achieving economic stability in post-war Greece.

1 There is an English translation of the second volume, *A History of the People's Democracies: Eastern Europe since Stalin* (London 1971).

5

India, Pakistan and Ceylon

K. N. Chaudhuri

General Problems and Background

In surveying the bibliographical material on the contemporary history of South Asia one can discern a number of distinct themes, on which major studies have been made in depth and detail. Of these the problems of independence and the transfer of power naturally dominated the years from the end of the second world war in 1945 to the granting of independence to all three South Asian countries in 1947. This was the starting-point of a whole series of related developments in government and politics: the task of setting up effective government, the drafting of a constitution, the formation of political parties, problems of foreign policy and defence, and finally the handling and resolution of conflicting forces latent in South Asian societies, which began to manifest themselves in the late 1950s and 1960s in the form of a breaking down of the democratic process of government, tension between centre and regional politics, and a clash of ideas between the forces of tradition and modernity. These urgent tasks were overshadowed all along by the intensity of Asian poverty. Consequently, popular demand for rapid economic development and growth has been a major characteristic of South Asian affairs in recent years, and has led to an incessant search for economic policies that would raise the standards of living and bring about large-scale industrialisation.

One of the main difficulties in compiling a bibliographical guide on such a varied range of topics as that outlined above is of course that of selection, particularly as the volume of material available is very large. Another one is that we live so close to the events that authoritative studies become rapidly obsolete either due to sudden political or economic changes or to the discovery of new facts. Bearing in mind these limitations, the current material on South Asian history can perhaps be classified under three categories: those works which come under the heading of sources, such as printed official documents, writings and speeches of leading political figures, and biographical material. The second category comprises books which provide a general account and outline of the main events, while the third includes detailed monographs and standard works of scholarship. In a different class are the various bibliographical guides themselves. The three most useful ones which cover all aspects of South Asian material for recent years as well as historical periods are *South Asia: A Bibliography for Undergraduate Libraries* edited by Louis A. Jacob and others (Williamsport, Pennsylvania, 1970), Patrick Wilson, *Government and Politics of India and Pakistan, 1885–1955, a Bibliography of Works in Western Languages* (Berkeley, 1956), and Margaret H. Case, *South Asian History, 1750–1950: A Guide to Periodicals, Newspapers, and Dissertations* (Princeton, 1968). On the historical background to the period before 1945, introductory accounts will be found in C. H. Philips (ed.), *Politics and Society in India* (London, 1963), P. J. Griffiths, *The British Impact on India* (London, 2nd ed. 1965), and K. M. Panikkar, *Asia and Western Dominance* (London, 1953). A critique of historical writings on South Asian history and some of the more important documents are provided in C. H. Philips (ed.), *Historians of India, Pakistan, and Ceylon* (London, 1961), and Philips (ed.), *The Evolution of India and Pakistan, 1858–1947, Select Documents* (Oxford, 1962).

Independence and Transfer of Power

The most important documentary source at the British government's end is the projected *India: The Transfer of Power 1942–47*, under the editorship of N. Mansergh, which will cover the whole period in several volumes; volume I (London, HMSO, 1970) covers the period from January to

April, 1942. A detailed survey of the main problems and events leading up to the partition of India is given in C. H. Philips and M. D. Wainwright (ed.), *The Partition of India, Policies and Perspectives 1935–1947* (London, 1970). Two general accounts of the partition period are H. Tinker, *Experiment With Freedom: India and Pakistan 1947* (London, 1967), and B. N. Pandey, *The Break-up of British India* (London, 1969). A day-to-day eye-witness account of the political events during Lord Mountbatten's viceroyalty is given by A. Campbell-Johnson, *Mission With Mountbatten* (London, 1951), while similar detailed accounts are also provided by two former leading officials connected with the Government, V. P. Menon, *The Transfer of Power in India* (London, 1957) and *The Story of the Integration of the Indian States* (New York, 1956); H. V. Hodson, *The Great Divide* (London, 1969). The events that took place in the Indian state of Bhopal in 1947 are described in P. Moon, *Divide and Quit* (London, 1961). Most of these books perhaps come under the category of political biographies and source material, and a thorough scholarly treatment of the partition and the transfer of power in British India by an independent historian is still lacking.

Government and Politics

The volume of literature under this heading is extremely large, although no comprehensive collection of printed documents is available either on India, Pakistan, or Ceylon. The two exceptions are perhaps, S. L. Poplai (ed.), *India 1947–50, Select Documents on Indian Affairs* (New York, 1959), vols. I and II, and Girija Kumar and V. K. Arora (ed.), *Documents on Indian Affairs 1960* (Bombay, 1965), both of which cover internal and external affairs and provide valuable primary material on Indian history and politics since 1947. A number of works are available which contain the writings and speeches of leading political personalities. The speeches of Jawaharlal Nehru are published under the title *Independence and After: A Collection of the more Important Speeches of Jawaharlal Nehru* (Delhi, 1949–68), vols. I–V, 1946–64.

Mohammad Ali Jinnah's speeches have been edited by M. R. Afzal, *Selected Speeches and Statements of the Qaid-i-Azam Mohammad Ali Jinnah* (1911–34 and 1947–8) (Lahore, 1966), and more recently we also have M. Ayub Khan, *Speeches and Statements* (Lahore, 1961–4), vols. I–III.

There are a large number of good secondary works which provide a general analysis and description of government and politics in South Asia since 1947. On India two particularly lucid introductory works are W. H. Morris-Jones, *The Government and Politics of India* (London, 1965) and H. Tinker, *India and Pakistan: A Political Analysis* (London, 1963). Another work which analyses the recent structure and function of Indian political machinery in outline is by N. D. Palmer, *The Indian Political System* (Boston, 1961). Selig S. Harrison in his *India: The Most Dangerous Decades* (Princeton, 1960) provides a journalist's assessment of the probable direction of Indian political events, predicting the collapse of India's present form of democratic structure. On Pakistan one of the best general works dealing with the period from 1947 to the capture of power by President Ayub Khan is Khalid Bin Sayeed, *Pakistan: the Formative Phase* (Karachi, 1960). The two other general works dealing with the same theme are K. B. Callard, *Political Forces in Pakistan* (New York, 1959) and M. Ahmad, *Government and Politics in Pakistan* (Karachi, 1959). The latter systematically surveys the various component parts of political life in Pakistan, such as the head of state, the role of the prime minister and cabinet, the political parties and the civil service. While both India and Pakistan have attracted a high level of historical scholarship, Ceylon is rather thinly represented, and there are only two introductory works: E. F. C. Ludowyk, *The Modern History of Ceylon* (New York, 1966), which covers a long period of history, and B. H. Farmer, *Ceylon A Divided Nation* (Oxford, 1963).

At the level of detailed monographs and studies that deal with specific aspects of political behaviour are R. L. Park and I. Tinker (ed.), *Leadership and Political Institutions in India* (Princeton, 1959) and Myron Weiner, *The Politics of Scarcity: Public Pressure and Political Response in India*

(Chicago, 1962). The former examines in detail the influence of pressure groups, the role of political parties, the decision-making process in government and the relationship between the government of India and local political leadership, while Weiner concentrates mainly on pressure groups such as religious communities, linguistic groups, trade unions, and organised business, and seeks to isolate the effects of their activities. The relationship between traditional ideas and forces and the concept of a secular state has been investigated by D. E. Smith in great depth in his *India As A Secular State* (Princeton, 1963) and *South Asian Politics and Religion* (Princeton, 1966). M. Brecher's *Nehru's Mantle: The Politics of Succession in India* (New York, 1966) provides a most perceptive insight and analysis of the Indian political system since the death of Nehru and examines all the major public issues. On Pakistan Khalid Bin Sayeed's *The Political System of Pakistan* (Boston, 1967) examines the conflict between the politicians and bureaucracy, while Karl von Vorys in *Political Development in Pakistan* (Princeton, 1965) attempts to apply some new techniques of analysis such as quantitative methods and content analysis to Pakistan's political system. An analysis of the problem of becoming an Islamic state is provided by L. Binder, *Religion and Politics in Pakistan* (Berkeley, 1961). The major themes and problems of Ceylonese politics since independence are examined by W. H. Wriggins, *Ceylon: Dilemmas of a New Nation* (Princeton, 1960) and M. R. Singer, *The Emerging Elite: A Study of Political Leadership in Ceylon* (Cambridge, Mass., 1964).

Apart from studies dealing with politics at the centre and at the all-India level, there are a number of good monographs on regional politics and on the relationship between the central government and states. A. Chanda, a former high-ranking government official, examines some of the practical problems in his *Federalism in India: A Study of Union-State Relations* (London, 1965). The best general account of regional Indian politics is perhaps that by M. Weiner (ed.), *State Politics in India* (Princeton, 1968). The regional politics of Bengal and the problem of its federal relationship is studied by M. F. Franda, *West Bengal and the Federalizing Process*

117

in India (Princeton, 1968). P. R. Brass, *Factional Politics in an Indian State: the Congress Party in Uttar Pradesh* (Berkeley, 1965) gives a penetrating account of local politics in one of India's most important states as well as a major study of a political party. The first full-scale examination of Punjab politics following independence, particularly the emergence of Sikh political consciousness expressed in the demand for a separate state, is undertaken by B. R. Nayar in his *Minority Politics in the Punjab* (Princeton, 1966).

One of the principal difficulties encountered by the recently independent countries of Asia in general, and those of South Asia in particular, has been associated with the problem of forming stable political parties capable of offering alternative government in a democratic system. The importance of the subject is reflected in the number of serious and well-documented studies that have been made for India at least. M. Weiner, *Party Politics in India: the Development of a Multi-Party System* (Princeton, 1957) traces the history of the major political parties through a series of case-studies, and the book serves as a useful introduction to the subject. The study of the Congress Party in Uttar Pradesh made by P. R. Brass, *Factional Politics in an Indian State*, has already been mentioned. A detailed and full-length analysis of the central structure of the Congress can be found in S. A. Kochanek, *The Congress Party of India; the Dynamics of One-party Democracy* (Princeton, 1968). On right-wing politics and the attempt to form a distinctly conservative party in India there are two important works: H. L. Erdman, *The Swatantra Party and Indian Conservatism* (Cambridge, 1967), and C. Baxter, *The Jana Sangh: A Biography of an Indian Political Party* (Philadelphia, 1969). The Communist Party of India has attracted a considerable amount of attention. M. R. Masani, *The Communist Party of India, a Short History* (New York, 1954) is now somewhat out of date. The standard work on the Communist Party is G. D. Overstreet and M. Windmiller, *Communism in India* (Berkeley, 1959). From the point of view of international communism, particularly the line followed by Moscow, there is J. H. Kautsky, *Moscow and the Communist Party of India, a Study in the Postwar Evolution of International Communist Strategy* (Cambridge, Mass., 1956). A collection of documents on the Indian Communist Party has been published by Democratic Research Service, *Indian Communist Party Documents 1930–1956* (Bombay, 1957). Though some of the documents have been acknowledged by the party as officially genuine, others have been denounced as forgeries.

On constitution and elections, the standard work on India is by G. Austin, *The Indian Constitution: Cornerstone of a Nation* (Oxford, 1966). W. H. Morris-Jones, *Parliament in India* (Philadelphia, 1957) describes in detail the position of Parliament in India's constitution and its practical functioning. A general account of Pakistan's constitutional problems around 1947 is provided in Sir Ivor Jennings, *Constitutional Problems in Pakistan* (Cambridge, 1957), and G. W. Choudhury, *Constitutional Development in Pakistan* (Lahore, 1959) gives a resumé of the main events from 1947 to 1958. The Indian General Election of 1962 has been studied by two scholars: V. M. Siriskar, *Political Behavior in India: A Case-Study of the 1962 General Elections* (Bombay, 1965) and M. Weiron, *Indian Voting Behavior, Studies of the 1962 General Elections* (Calcutta, 1965).

Administration and Bureaucracy

It has now been clearly recognised both by practising politicians in South Asia and academic scholars that the success of centrally planned economic development depends to a large extent on the efficacy of the administrative machinery. This is the theme of R. Braibanti and J. J. Spengler (ed.), *Administration and Economic Development in India* (Durham, North Carolina, 1963), which examines the various aspects of Indian administration in relation to the problem of economic development. A. Chanda, *Indian Administration* (London, 1958) is a major contribution for the specialists, which describes the problems of setting up a closely integrated central administration and preparing the government for public responsibility. A valuable critique for Indian administration is provided by P. H. Appleby, *Re-examination of*

India's Administration System (New Delhi, 1956), while N. C. Roy, *The Civil Service of India* (Calcutta, 1958) discusses the history of recruitment and training of public servants since 1947. A comprehensive bibliographical essay is given in R. Braibanti, *Research on the Bureaucracy of Pakistan: A Critique of Sources, Conditions, and Issues with Appended Documents* (Durham, North Carolina, 1966). On Pakistan's civil service there is M. A. Chaudhuri, *The Civil Service in Pakistan: the Centrally Recruited Civil Service* (Dacca, 1969).

Education

Despite its importance, education is one of the subjects that has attracted comparatively little attention. Most of the emphasis has been placed on the problem of policy, and there has been as yet no serious effort to evaluate the role of modern education either in relation to economic development or the larger national life in general. On policy aspects of Indian education there are two works: G. Ramanathan, *Educational Planning and National Integration* (Bombay, 1965), and J. P. Naik, *Educational Planning in India* (New Delhi, 1965). Some of the general problems are touched upon by a former Indian minister of education, Humayuun Kabir, *Education in New India* (London, 2nd ed. 1959). A short and able survey of educational planning in Pakistan, based on personal experience as a foreign adviser, is given by A. Curle, *Planning for Education in Pakistan: A Personal Case-Study* (Cambridge, Mass., 1966).

External Relations and Defence

Studies that deal with the general problem of Indian foreign policy and defence are the following: K. P. Karunakaran, *India in World Affairs: A Review of India's Foreign Relations* (Oxford, 1952–8), A. B. Shah, *India's Defence and Foreign Policy* (Bombay, 1966), and L. Karvic, *India's Quest for Security: Defence Policies, 1947–65* (Berkeley, 1967). Conversations with one of the leading figures in Indian foreign policy are reported by M. Brecher, *India and World Politics:*

Krishna Menon's View of the World (London, 1968). Documents on Pakistan's foreign policy in the early 1960s can be found in Z. A. Bhutto, *Foreign Policy of Pakistan: A Compendium of Speeches made in the National Assembly of Pakistan 1962–64* (Karachi, 1964). One of the most important topics under the heading of this section is naturally the continued existence of tension and conflict between India and Pakistan, which has been studied from various aspects. A general account from the Indian side has been presented by J. B. DasGupta, *Indo-Pakistan Relations (1947–55)* (Amsterdam, 1958) which examines briefly the history of the Kashmir dispute, the dispute concerning canal water, the problem of evacuee property, and the position of the minorities. Covering the same ground from Pakistan's point of view is G. W. Choudhury, *Pakistan's Relations with India, 1947–1966* (London, 1968). The conflict over Kashmir has been examined by a number of scholars. A. Lamb, *The Kashmir Problem* (New York, 1967) gives a general outline, while more detailed treatment is offered by J. B. DasGupta, *Jammu and Kashmir* (The Hague, 1968) and S. Gupta, *Kashmir: A Study in India-Pakistan Relations* (Bombay, 1967). The more recent history of Indo-Pakistan relationships, particularly the short armed-conflict of 1965, is treated in R. Brines, *The Indo-Pakistani Conflict* (London, 1968). There are many works that deal with the history of India's uneasy relations with China. The most useful are the following ones: G. Jain, *Panchsheela and After: A Re-appraisal of Sino-Indian Relations in the Context of the Tibetan Insurrection* (Bombay, 1960), A. Lamb, *The China-India Border: The Origins of the Disputed Boundaries* (Oxford, 1964), S. P. Varma, *Struggle for the Himalayas* (Delhi, 1965), and R. Rowland, *A History of Sino-Indian Relations; Hostile Co-Existence* (Princeton, 1967).

Biographies and Political Memoirs

Considering the extent of the geographical area covered, the amount of biographical material on South Asia is not large, and attention has mainly focused on a few leading political figures. The life of Mahatma Gandhi has been the object of an eight-volume study; D. G. Tendulkar's *Mahatma: Life of Mohandas Karamchand Gandhi* (Bombay, 1951–4), vols. I–VIII. The last two volumes survey Gandhi's political and other activities during 1945–8. B. R. Nanda, *Mahatma Gandhi* (London, 1958) provides a most readable and scholarly biography. The best biographical work on Jawaharlal Nehru is that by M. Brecher, *Nehru: A Political Biography* (Oxford, 1959), which is also one of the most balanced and careful surveys of political events in India since 1945. Nehru's political thinking has been studied by D. E. Smith, *Nehru and Democracy* (New York, 1959). On Jinnah there is only one work, H. Bolitho, *Jinnah, Creator of Pakistan* (London, 1954). Other important political memoirs by Pakistani politicians are Chaudhuri Muhammad Ali, *The Emergence of Pakistan* (New York, 1967), Chaudhry Khaliquzzaman, *Pathway to Pakistan* (Lahore, 1961), M. Ayub Khan, *Friends not Masters: A Political Autobiography* (London, 1967), and Z. A. Bhutto, *The Myth of Independence* (London, 1969). On Ceylon there is Sir John Kotelawala, *An Asian Prime Minister's Story* (London, 1956).

Economics

Appraisal of the economies of South Asian countries and a critical evaluation of the various plans for economic development have occupied as much attention as the developments in politics and government. An excellent background to the pre-Independence period can be found in Vera Anstey, *The Economic Development of India* (London, 4th ed., 1952). It provides a systematic survey of all sectors of the economy. The most ambitious and comprehensive attempt to describe and analyse the economy of India, Pakistan, and Ceylon since 1947 is Gunnar Myrdal, *Asian Drama: An Inquiry into the Poverty of Nations* (London, 1968), vols. I–III. The work examines the problem of economic development in the context of South Asian countries from different aspects, political machinery, social factors, and strictly economic criteria, and also contains invaluable primary data on South Asian economic history. However, its value as an objective study is somewhat marred by Myrdal's idiosyncratic approach to the science of economics and the attempt to write an encyclopedia of facts. At a different level, but still concerned with the general performance of the Indian economy during the period from 1951 to 1961, is Wifred Malenbaum, *Prospects for Indian Development* (New York, 1962). H. Venkatasubiah, *Indian Economy since Independence* (Bombay, 1959) is another survey of some of the more important events in India, though it lacks in critical analysis. The theoretical problems in economic growth are examined by N. A. Khan, *Problems of Growth of an Underdeveloped Economy* (Bombay, 1961), and mention must also be made of Daniel and Alice Thorner, *Land and Labour in India* (Bombay, 1962) which contains a number of powerful essays on various aspects of Indian economic planning, source material, and Indian economic history in general. On the economy of Pakistan since 1947 there are two excellent studies, J. R. Andrus, *The Economy of Pakistan* (London, 1958) and J. R. Andrus and A. F. Mohammed, *Trade, Finance, and Economic Development in Pakistan* (Stanford, 1966). Some of the basic statistical data will be found in W. Nelson Peach, Mohammad Uzair and George W. Rucker, *Basic Data of the Economy of Pakistan* (Karachi, 1959). There are no recent studies on Ceylon, and the only survey of its economy is that by Sir Ivor Jennings, *The Economy of Ceylon* (London, 1951).

The Indian effort to promote economic development through central state planning has provoked some particularly penetrating and powerful economic analysis. Details of the four *Five Year Plans* (Delhi, 1953–66) have been published by the Planning Commission. One of the first attempts to evaluate the targets and the rationale of Indian planning is C. N. Vakil and P. R. Brahmananda, *Planning for a Shortage Economy: The Indian Experiment* (Bombay, 1952), while another critique is provided by one of India's leading economists and now the chairman of the Planning Commission, D. R. Gadgil, *Economic Policy and Development* (Poona, 1955). W. B. Reddaway, *The Development of the Indian Economy* (London, 1962) is a rigorous economic and statistical analysis of Indian planning during the period of the Third Plan.

The economic difficulties experienced by India in the critical years of the mid 1960s are discussed in Paul Streeten and Michael Lipton (ed.), *The Crisis of Indian Planning: Economic Policy in the 1960's* (Oxford, 1968). A major study of the political aspects of Indian planning is that of A. H. Hanson, *The Process of Planning: A Study of India's Five-Year Plans 1950-64* (London, 1966). On social attitudes to economic development there are two studies; Kusum Nair, *Blossoms in the Dust* (London, 1961) is a first-hand account of social conditions in India, and K. W. Kapp, *Hindu Culture, Economic Development and Economic Planning in India* (Bombay, 1963) which is a more theoretical analysis. The problems of economic policy and development in Pakistan are discussed by M. L. Qureshi, *Strategy of Industrial Planning and Developments in Pakistan* (Karachi, 1965) and S. R. Lewis, *Pakistan: Industrialization and Trade Policies* (London and Paris, 1970).

On foreign trade, investment, and industrialisation the ground is covered in a somewhat uneven manner and there is no authoritative overall work. S. Sen, *India's Bilateral Payments and Trade Agreements 1947-48 to 1963-64* (Calcutta, 1965) is a detailed factual survey; a little more analytical is the work by M. Singh, *India's Export Trends and the Prospects for Self-Sustained Growth* (Oxford, 1964). An excellent analysis of investment made by foreign enterprise in India is given by M. Kidron, *Foreign Investments in India* (London, 1965), while D. L. Spencer, *India: Mixed Enterprise and Western Business* (The Hague, 1959) discusses the relationship between the private and public sectors and gives brief accounts of the various industries under private and public management. The general problems of industrialisation in India are discussed by R. Rosen in two books, *Industrial Change in India* (Illinois, 1958) and *Democracy and Economic Change in India* (Berkeley, 1966). Investment in public works and other essential industrial services is analysed by J. M. Healey, *The Development of Social Overhead Capital in India 1950-60* (Oxford, 1965). On specific industries there are a number of detailed case-studies: W. A. Johnson, *The Steel Industry of India* (Cambridge, Mass., 1966), G. B. Baldwin,

Industrial Growth in South India (Illinois, 1959), and J. J. Berna, *Industrial Entrepreneurship in Madras State* (New York, 1960).

Despite its importance, agriculture is not very well represented in the economic literature on South Asia, though there are many minor works. A good general survey is given in J. W. Mellor (ed.), *Developing Rural India; Plan and Practice*; M. R. Haswell, *Economics of Development in Village India* (London, 1967) is a collection of case-studies. On policy aspect there is D. R. Gadgil, *Planning for Agricultural Development of India* (Poona, 1960), and a detailed study of agriculture in Ceylon has been made by an economic geographer, B. H. Farmer, *Pioneer Peasant Colonization in Ceylon: A Study in Asian Problems* (London, 1957).

Problems of industrial labour, urbanisation, and demography have attracted considerable attention in South Asia. On the first two topics there is V. B. Singh and A. K. Saran (ed.), *Industrial Labour in India* (London, 1960), which contains contributions from the leading experts on industrial labour, and N. V. Sovani, *Urbanization and Urban India* (Bombay, 1966). On Pakistan there is a study undertaken by UNESCO, *Dacca: Human and Social Impact of Technological Change in East Pakistan* (1956). The relationship between economic development and population growth is examined in S. N. Agarwala (ed.), *India's Population: Some Problems in Perspective Planning* (Bombay, 1960). Other aspects of demographic factors operating in Indian society are discussed by S. Chandrasekhar, *Population and Planned Parenthood in India* (New York, 1961) and B. C. Mamoria, *Population and Family Planning in India* (Allahabad, 1963). A classic study of the pre-Independence period is Kingsley Davis, *The Population of India and Pakistan* (Princeton, 1951). Population in Ceylon has been investigated by N. K. Sarkar, *The Demography of Ceylon* (Colombo, 1957).

Sociology and Anthropology

Two classic works on the history of social change in modern India are M. N. Srinivas, *Caste in Modern India and Other*

Essays (New Delhi, 1962), and *Social Change in Modern India* (Berkeley, 1966). The sociological aspects of political change are discussed by Lloyd I. Rudolph and Susanne H. Rudolph, *The Modernity of Tradition: Political Development in India* (Chicago, 1967). Detailed case-studies of Indian society at the village level are given by F. G. Bailey, *Caste and the Economic Frontier*; *A Village in Highland Orissa* (Manchester, 1958), *Politics and Social Change: Orissa in 1959* (Berkeley, 1963), and A. C. Mayer, *Caste and Kinship in Central India*; *A Village and Its Region* (Berkeley, 1960). G. Obeyesekere, *Land Tenure in Village Ceylon* (Cambridge, 1967) provides an exhaustive analysis of the historical evolution of land rights in Ceylon. On the Muslim communities of India and Pakistan and Islamic religious institutions there are two good studies, A. Ahmad, *Islamic Modernism in India and Pakistan 1857–1964* (London, 1967) and M. Mujeeb, *The Indian Muslims* (London, 1967).

6

The Middle East

M. E. Yapp

Introduction

Three particular problems confront the would-be student of recent Middle Eastern history. The first is that of language. It is impossible to penetrate deeply into the subject without a knowledge of one or more of the major languages of the area – Arabic, Persian and Turkish. Secondly, the type of basic source material which is taken for granted by students of western Europe is lacking, partly owing to the secrecy observed by many governments and partly because of the problems of obtaining important publications. Thirdly, it is essential for a student to acquire some general understanding of the cultural and historical background of the area, especially of the rôle of Islam and of the structure of traditional communities. Although both participants in and commentators on events habitually employ the terminology of western politics they frequently disguise thereby a more ancient and fundamental idiom. Accordingly, students are wise to scrutinise with more than ordinary care the credentials of writers on the Middle East.

General

Two descriptive geographies provide a general conspectus of the area. These are W. B. Fisher, *The Middle East* (London, 1956) and W. C. Brice, *South West Asia* (London, 1966). A briefer introduction is S. H. Longrigg, *The Middle East: A Social Geography* (London, 1963). Of the general histories S. N. Fisher, *The Middle East. A History* (2nd ed., New York,

1969) although not always reliable for earlier periods does provide a detailed narrative for the nineteenth and twentieth centuries. The two volumes of the *Survey of International Affairs* witten by George Kirk, *The Middle East in the War* (Oxford, 1952) and *The Middle East 1945-50* (Oxford, 1954) are still worth reading. For students beginning work on the area Maurice Harari, *Government and Politics in the Middle East* (New Jersey, 1962), is a short text book which gives considerable space to the pre-1945 period. For the Arab area Hisham Sharabi, *Nationalism and Revolution in the Arab World* (New York, 1966), is especially valuable for its comments on the vocabulary of Arab politics. Malcolm Kerr, *The Arab Cold War 1958-67* (2nd ed., Oxford, 1967), is primarily useful for its account of the abortive negotiations for Arab union in 1963. Some collections of translations of documents may also be mentioned here. Helen Miller Davis, *Constitutions, Electoral Laws and Treaties of States in the Near and Middle East* (2nd ed., Durham, N. Carolina, 1956) and Abid al-Marayati, *Middle Eastern Constitutions and Electoral Laws* (New York, 1968) can save much time. Muhammad Khalil, *The Arab States and The Arab League* (2 vols., Beirut, 1962), is much more wide ranging than the title suggests and is probably the most comprehensive general collection of documents on Arab internal and external politics. For subsequent years the translations of Arabic documents published by the American University of Beirut, entitled *Arab Political Documents* and covering the years 1963 to 1965 in annual volumes may be consulted.

Several important books have been concerned with changing ideas. Leonard Binder, *The Ideological Revolution in the Middle East* (London, 1964), is an interesting example of the approach of a political scientist to the problems of the Middle East. In Manfred Halpern's book *The Politics of Social Change in the Middle East and North Africa* (Princeton, 1963), the nature of change, the political alternatives and the instruments of innovation are dissected and analysed over a large area extending to Pakistan. A recent book by Majid Khadduri, *Political Trends in the Arab World* (Baltimore, 1970), considers the rise of ideas of nationalism, socialism, etc. in the Arab world from the late nineteenth century to the present. An excellent collection of extracts from nationalist writers with a most lucid introduction by the editor is Sylvia Haim (ed.), *Arab Nationalism* (Berkeley, 1962). A similar collection exists for socialism, Sami A. Hanna and George H. Gardner, *Arab Socialism* (Leiden, 1969). A wider-ranging anthology including extracts from Persian and Turkish writers is Kemal H. Karpat (ed.), *Political and Social Thought in the Contemporary Middle East* (New York, 1968).

International Relations

The rise of communism, Soviet policy and the Middle Eastern reaction are the subject of three books by Walter Z. Laqueur. *Communism and Nationalism in the Middle East* (London, 1956) is still useful for the account of the growth of communist parties in the area although more recent information has modified certain details. *The Soviet Union and the Middle East* (London, 1959) contains two essays, one on the Soviet image and the other on the major shift in Soviet policy towards the Middle East which took place in the mid-1950s. *The Struggle for the Middle East* (London, 1969) analyses Russian policy from 1958 to 1968, and includes several documents. William R. Polk, *The United States and the Arab World* (2nd ed., Cambridge, Mass., 1969) is useful for US popular, but well balanced *Turkey* (London, 1968) by Andrew Mango and Geoffrey Lewis, *Turkey* (3rd ed., London, 1965). evolution of American policy towards the Baghdad pact, taking the story down to the 1956 crisis. An interesting collection of papers is contained in J. C. Hurewitz (ed.), *Soviet-American Rivalry in the Middle East* (New York, 1969) in which military, economic and cultural competition are all considered. The same editor's collection of documents, *Diplomacy in the Near and Middle East* (2 vols., New York, 1956) is indispensable. A second revised edition in four volumes is now in preparation.

Of all aspects of international rivalry it is the Arab-Israeli conflict which has attracted most attention. Christopher

Sykes, *Crossroads to Israel* (London, 1965), is probably the best general account of the period of the Palestine Mandate, although J. C. Hurewitz, *The Struggle for Palestine* (New York, 1950), despite its age is still worth reading. For the 1948-9 war see Jon and David Kimche, *Both Sides of the Hill* (London, 1960), which gives particular emphasis to British policy. There is no good general account of the refugee problem although Don Peretz, *Israel and the Palestine Arabs* (Washington, 1958), is a useful discussion of some of the main issues. For the period 1948-56 Earl Berger, *The Covenant and the Sword* (London, 1965) and Ernest Stock, *Israel on the Road to Sinai, 1949-56* (Ithaca, NY, 1967), are both soundly based on available published material. A detailed study of one of the enduring problems of this period is N. Bar-Yaacov, *The Israel-Syrian Armistice* (Jerusalem, 1967). A large literature exists on the 1956 Suez war. Of the more recent works Hugh Thomas, *The Suez Affair* (London, 1967), is a reliable outline although concentrating primarily on the Anglo-French role and irritatingly, if understandably, failing to identify many sources. More comprehensive is Kennett Love, *Suez, the Twice Fought War* (New York, 1969), the product of much research by an American journalist. Memoirs of participants continue to appear. Andre Beaufré, *The Suez Expedition, 1956* (London, 1969), is good for the military planning and execution while Anthony Nutting, *No End of a Lesson* (London, 1967), is much the frankest on British political involvement. Moshe Dayan, *Diary of the Sinai Campaign* (London, 1966), is good for the Israeli military side. The memoirs of Eden (understandably) and Macmillan (tiresomely) are so selective as to be quite misleading. Two documentary collections on this episode will also be found helpful. These are US Department of State, *The Suez Canal Problem*, 1956, which covers the negotiations of July to September 1956 and James Eayrs, *The Commonwealth and Suez* (London, 1964) which presents the reactions of Commonwealth leaders to the various stages of the developing crisis. Treatment of the period 1958 to 1967 is inevitably more speculative. Bourguiba's peace initiative of 1965 is the subject of Samuel Merlin, *The Search for Peace in the Middle East*

(New Jersey, 1968). Nadav Safran, *From War to War* (New York, 1969) surveys the whole period since 1948 in terms of Zionist, Pan-Arab and Great Power aspirations and contains good material on the arms build-up. Fred J. Khouri, *The Arab-Israeli Dilemma* (Syracuse, 1968), is a moderate, well informed study sympathetic to the Arab case and contains a long account of the 1967 war. Well based on Hebrew sources and informative on Israeli attitudes towards the Arabs is Aharon Cohen, *Israel and the Arab World* (London, 1970). Walter Laqueur, *The Road to War* (Harmondsworth, 1969), is a useful survey of the political aspects of the war and Peter Young, *The Israeli Campaign 1967* (London, 1967), of the military. Maxime Rodinson, *Israel and the Arabs* (Harmondsworth, 1968), is also worth reading for the novelty of its viewpoint. A good scholarly study of the role of the United Nations in the crisis with important documents is Arthur Lall, *The U.N. and the Middle East Crisis 1967* (New York, 1968).

Several collections of documents exist. The Institute for Palestine Studies in Beirut has produced three volumes of documents on Palestine edited by Sami Hadawi. The first contains UN resolutions on Palestine 1947–68, the second and third the UN discussions on the subject in 1965 and 1966. The collection is entitled *Palestine Before the United Nations*. The scope of the series has now been widened. The latest volume entitled *International Documents on Palestine in 1967* contains speeches and documents drawn from the UN, Arab countries and the Great Powers (including a very restricted collection from Israel). A further collection of UN materials with an analysis is in Rosemary Higgins, *United Nations Peacekeeping Documents and Commentary, I, The Middle East* (London, 1969). A useful short collection is Walter Laqueur (ed.), *The Israel-Arab Reader* (London, 1969).

Economics (Including Oil)

There is no general economic history of the Middle East. The nearest approach is Alfred Bonne, *State and Economics in the*

Middle East, 2nd ed. (London, 1964), which is primarily historical but contains sections on recent developments. On industry generally see Kurt Grunwald and Joachim O. Ronall, *Industrialization in the Middle East* (New York, 1960) and on agriculture, Doreen Warriner, *Land Reform and Development in the Middle East* (London, 1957). The economic development of individual countries is considered under the appropriate headings.

The standard history of oil exploration and production is S. H. Longrigg, *Oil in the Middle East* (3rd ed., London, 1968). On the associated political problems see Benjamin Shwadran, *The Middle East, Oil and the Great Powers* (2nd ed., New York, 1959) and George Lenczowski, *Oil and State in the Middle East* (Ithaca, 1969) which looks at effects on Europe and the Middle East and contains a case study of the repercussions of the 1956 Suez crisis on the oil industry, and the more general J. L. Hartshorn, *Oil Companies and Governments* (London, 1962), which is not limited to the Middle East. Two good studies of the financial and economic aspects of oil production are Charles Issawi and Muhammad Yeganeh, *The Economics of Middle Eastern Oil* (London, 1962) which examines the period 1948–60 in detail and E. Penrose, *The Large International Firm in Developing Countries* (London, 1968), which is primarily concerned with the organisation of the petroleum industry in the Middle East.

Military

The prevalence of military regimes in the Middle East has led to some interesting comparative studies of the phenomenon and its implications. The most comprehensive attempt to date is that of J. C. Hurewitz, *Middle Eastern Politics, The Military Dimension* (London, 1969), which is particularly interesting for its demonstration of the apparent lack of connection between military regimes and arms expenditure. An important, comparative sociological analysis written in an historical framework is Eliezer Be'eri, *Army Officers in Arab Politics and Society* (New York, 1970). Also worthy of attention are S. N. Fisher (ed.), *The Military in the Middle East* (Columbus,

1963); John J. Johnson (ed.), *The Role of the Ministry in Underdeveloped Countries* (Princeton, 1962); and D. A. Rustow, *The Military in Middle Eastern Society and Politics* (Washington DC, 1963).

The History of Individual Countries and Areas

The Arabian Peninsula

There has been very little serious historical writing on the Arabian peninsula which relates to the recent past and it is often necessary to use the work of journalists and the memoirs of participants. Manfred W. Wenner, *Modern Yemen, 1918–66* (Baltimore, 1967), is a genuine attempt at serious history and contains a good bibliography. It has however been heavily criticised on certain points. Dana Adams Schmidt, *Yemen. The Unknown War* (New York, 1968), is a journalist's account. Another journalist, Tom Little, *South Arabia* (London, 1968), has written the only general account of the formation of the South Arabian Federation and the events leading up to the British withdrawal from Aden. The work has no references and new information is already modifying certain conclusions. There is virtually nothing on Saudi Arabia since H. St John Philby, *Saudi Arabia* (London, 1955) although this devotes most space to the pre-1945 period. David Holden, *Farewell to Arabia* (London, 1966), which covers the entire peninsula, is a very neat piece of journalism. The situation is somewhat better with regard to the Gulf area. J. B. Kelly, *Eastern Arabian Frontiers* (London, 1964), is a detailed study of the background to the Buraimi dispute by a professional historian opposed to the Saudi claims. Robert G. Landen, *Oman since 1856* (Princeton, 1967), is also a careful and competent piece of historical writing. Husain M. Albaharna, *The Legal Status of the Arabian Gulf States* (Manchester, 1968), is a study of the position of the Gulf states and of their territorial claims and boundary disputes from the viewpoint of an international lawyer, but contains much incidental historical information.

Egypt

There are several sound general histories of Egypt in the

nineteenth and twentieth centuries which can provide a background. P. J. Vatikiotis, *The Modern History of Egypt* (London, 1969), is particularly strong on internal developments, notably on social and ideological change. Two thirds of Tom Little, *Modern Egypt* (London, 1967), which is an enlarged version of his 1968 *Egypt,* is devoted to the post-1945 period.

Contemporary Egypt is also well-served by some important general descriptive and analytical studies. The writings of Charles Issawi are always full of interest and his *Egypt at Mid-Century* (Oxford, 1954) and *Egypt in Revolution* (Oxford, 1963), are characterised by his customary incisive economic and political analyses. Jean and Simone Lacouture, *Egypt in Transition* (London, 1958), the work of two French journalists, has become almost a source book for its account of the origins of the 1952 revolution but is also valuable for its discussion of the early years of the revolutionary government. Anouar Abdel-Malek, *Egypt, Military Society* (New York, 1968), is a socio-political analysis by a well-known Egyptian Marxist who now lives in France. His untranslated studies of intellectual currents in Egypt, written in French, also repay study. At a more elementary level, Peter Mansfield, *Nasser's Egypt* (Harmondsworth, 1965), is worth reading. Finally P. J. Vatikiotis (ed.), *Egypt since the Revolution* (London, 1968) is a good collection of essays which includes a useful bibliographical study by Derek Hopwood entitled 'Works in English on Egypt since 1952'.

Among exclusively political studies are two works on the most significant, purely indigenous, political party which has so far emerged within the Arab world – the Muslim Brotherhood. Christine P. Harris, *Nationalism and Revolution in Egypt* (The Hague 1964), is one and the other, more recent account of the movement, down to its 1954 suppression is Richard P. Mitchell, *The Society of the Muslim Brothers* (London, 1969) which makes good use of Arabic sources and of interviews with participants. No other political party has achieved a comparable following but the *Charter of the Arab Socialist Union* (UAR Information Department, Cairo, 1962), is a fundamental document for understanding the ideology of the revolution. The memoirs of three Egyptian leaders are available and repay study. These are Mohammed Neguib, *Egypt's Destiny* (London, 1955), by the figurehead of the 1952 revolution; Gamal Abdel Nasser, *The Philosophy of the Revolution* (Cairo, 1955) and Anwar Sadat, *Revolt on the Nile* (London, 1957). The biography of *Nasser* by Peter Mansfield (London, 1969), is also worth reading, despite the absence of references, because of the author's familiarity with and sympathy for his subject.

The major achievements of the post-1952 regime have been in economic and social development. A good account is Patrick O'Brien, *The Revolution in Egypt's Economic System 1952–65* (Oxford, 1966), which singles out the sharp movement towards state direction in 1959–61 as a decisive event. Gabriel S. Saab, *The Egyptian Agrarian Reform 1952–62* (London, 1967), is a very careful study of the operation of the land reform, which was at the heart of the early changes wrought after 1952. The successes of reform since 1952 have owed much to the high quality of upper civil servants in Egypt and Morroe Berger, *Bureaucracy and Society in Modern Egypt* (Princeton, 1957), is an absorbing study of these based upon extensive interviews. Of the many books on the Suez Canal it is worth considering D. A. Farnie, *East and West of Suez* (Oxford, 1969), which is a mine of obscure information about the operation and impact of the Canal from its opening until 1956.

Iran

Considering its size and importance Iran has attracted less scholarly attention than almost any area of the Middle East. Peter Avery, *Modern Iran* (London, 1965), is a fair outline of the nineteenth and twentieth centuries, by a writer with a good knowledge of Persian, but less than one-third is given to the post-1945 period. A quite fascinating book is Leonard Binder, *Iran, Political Development in a Changing Society* (Berkeley, Los Angeles, 1962) which attempts to analyse the Persian political system in categories comprehensible to political scientists. It is however a difficult book and in no sense a narrative political history. No more is George B. Baldwin,

Planning and Development in Iran (Baltimore, 1967), a description of Iranian economic development, but only an analysis of the planning process in Iran, based upon the author's experiences in 1958–65, although it contains some useful information. Two studies of the Abadan crisis of 1951–4 are worth noting although neither of them very satisfying. They are Alan W. Ford, *The Anglo-Persian Oil Dispute of 1951–2* (Berkeley, 1954) which contains a description of events to July 1952 and an analysis in terms of international law and L. P. Elwell-Sutton, *Persian Oil. A Study in Power Politics* (London, 1955), by a writer with good Persian, poor economics and pronounced political sympathies. Land Reform has come off much better: A. K. S. Lambton, *Landlord and Peasant in Persia* (Oxford, 1953), is a long historical study of tenurial problems while *The Persian Land Reform 1962–66* (Oxford, 1969), describes the effect of land reform, both from a study of official sources and from an extensive series of visits to villages to observe the progress on the spot. Unfortunately, it says very little about either the political motivation or the political effects, although land reform appears to be destined to change forever the face of Iranian politics. There is little of real value on Iranian foreign relations. George Lenczowski, *Russia and the West in Iran 1918–48* (Ithaca, 1949), is really out of date although it does contain an account of the 1946 Azerbaijan crisis. M. K. Sheehan, *Iran: the impact of United States Interests and Policies 1941–54* (New York, 1968), is useful. Finally Sipehr Zabih, *The Communist Movement in Iran* (Berkeley, 1966) is a good study of left-wing politics in Iran, including the role of the Tudeh party.

Iraq

Stephen H. Longrigg, *Iraq 1900–1950* (Oxford, 1953), is now rather out of date, but still contains much valuable detail. The more recent period is best covered by two scholarly studies by Majid Khadduri. These are *Independent Iraq 1932–1958* (Oxford, 1960) and *Republican Iraq 1958–66* (Oxford, 1969). The author concentrates largely on political development, using Arabic sources. His second book may be compared with another careful study by an Israeli scholar, Uriel Dann, *Iraq under Qassem 1958-63* (New York, 1969) which also concentrates upon political developments. Information about economic developments is less easily available. Fahim I. Qubain, *The Reconstruction of Iraq 1950-57* (New York, 1958), is a study of the economic projects of the Hashemite government and was written before the 1958 revolution. Abbas Alnasrawi, *Financing Economic Development in Iraq* (New York, 1967), presents a less optimistic picture showing that the efforts to diversify the economy since 1950 have failed to change either the basic structure or to lessen the dependence upon oil. See also K. Haseeb, *The National Income of Iraq 1953-61* (London, 1961), especially for the author's healthy approach to the statistics and Kathleen M. Langley, *The Industrialization of Iraq* (Cambridge, Mass., 1961).

Israel

Material in English relating to the contemporary history of Israel is more abundant than for any other country of the Middle East. Two general surveys are Norman Bentwich, *Israel Resurgent* (London, 1960), a revised and enlarged version of his 1952 work and L. F. Rushbrook Williams, *The State of Israel* (London, 1957). A useful political survey is Leonard J. Fein, *Israel, Politics and People* (Boston, 1968). So is Nadav Safran, *The United States and Israel* (Cambridge, Mass., 1963) which, despite its title, is primarily concerned with internal political developments within Israel. Marver H. Bernstein, *The Politics of Israel* (Princeton, 1957), provides a helpful analysis, divided according to subject, of the first decade of the state. Although Israel does not have a formal constitution, Emanuel Backman, *Israel's Emerging Constitution 1948-51* (New York, 1953), is a good account of how the political system evolved in the period of the Provisional government and the first Knesset. Asher Zidon, *The Knesset,* (New York, 1967), although basically descriptive of the powers and procedures of the Parliament does contain valuable historical information, including detailed information about members of Parliament. Another study of members of the

Knesset, based on work done in 1960–1, is Lester G. Seligman, *Leadership in a New Nation* (New York, 1964). The slow rate of change in the outlook of the Israeli political elite in the first half of the 1960s is the subject of Alan Arian, *Ideological Change in Israel* (Cleveland, 1968). On the Israeli Communist Party and its role in the 1961 elections see Moshe M. Czudnowski and Jacob M. Landau, *The Israeli Communist Party* (Stanford, 1965). Jacob Landau is also the author of a detailed study of the Arab community in Israel, *The Arabs in Israel. A Political Study* (Oxford, 1968). In fairness, an Arab view of the same community should also be mentioned, Sabri Jirgis, *The Arabs in Israel* (Beirut, 1969). Civil-military relations and the development of the Israeli army are the themes of a heavily conceptualised book by Amos Perlmutter, *Military and Politics in Israel* (London, 1969).

The economic development of Israel has been the subject of many studies, a number of them deriving from the extensive programme organised in 1962–5 by the List Institute at Basel and later published by Praeger. Among these one general study can be mentioned by Nadav Halevi and Ruth Klinov-Malut, *The Economic Development of Israel* (New York, 1968). A shorter survey is David Horowitz, *The Economics of Israel* (Oxford, 1967). Alex Rubner, *The Economy of Israel* (London, 1960) is a detailed account of the years 1948–58. The draft Plan *Israel, Economic Development* (Jerusalem, 1968), published by the Prime Minister's Office and the Economic Planning Authority, contains a general historical survey and massive statistical information. Particular attention has always been given to Agricultural development and especially the various forms of organisation of rural communities. The most detailed study of the communal (*kibbutz*) and co-operative (*moshav*) systems is the massive work by Harry Vitales, *A History of the Co-operative Movement in Israel* (6 vols.) [7 projected], London, 1966–70). The relative neglect of the important, individually owned system (*moshava*) has been partly remedied by an interesting study by D. Weintraub, M. Lisak and Y. Azmon, *Moshava, Kibbutz and Moshav* (Ithaca, 1969), in which the three systems are compared. The purely economic aspects of the *kibbutz* are explored in a balanced, but moderately critical study by Eliyahu Kanovsky, *The Economy of the Israeli Kibbutz* (Cambridge, Mass., 1966). Also interesting in this general connection is the detailed anthropological analysis of rural land settlement in the period 1948–58 by Dorothy Willner, *Nation Building and Community in Israel* (Princeton, 1969). For general social developments see S. N. Eisenstadt, *Israeli Society* (London, 1967).

Jordan

Few studies of Jordan are of much value. Ann Dearden, *Jordan* (London, 1958), is a history which rests too heavily upon interviews with Jordanian and British officers of the Arab Legion but, despite this and its popular style, is still fairly reliable. Less than half of Benjamin Shwadran, *Jordan, A State of Tension* (New York, 1957), is given to the post-1945 period but it is informative on internal developments and has a good bibliography. P. J. Vatikiotis, *Politics and the Military in Jordan 1921–57* (New York, 1967), is a study of the Arab Legion in politics and contains much useful information about political history. Students may also like to look at the memoirs of Jordan's rulers. The English version of Abdullah's memoirs, edited by Philip Graves (London, 1950), is incomplete. The second volume (the *Takmilah*) has been translated by H. W. Glidden with the title *My Memoirs Completed* (Washington, 1954). *Uneasy Lies the Head* (London, 1962), is the autobiography of King Hussein.

Lebanon

A good general history of Lebanon is Kamal S. Salibi, *The Modern History of Lebanon* (London, 1965), although only a very small part is given to the post-1945 period. The 1958 crisis is the subject of M. S. Agwani, *The Lebanese Crisis 1958* (London, 1965), which is a collection of documents reflecting the development of the dispute and the attitudes of interested parties with some explanatory matter. Michael Suleiman, *Political Parties in Lebanon* (Ithaca, 1967), is a survey and history of the political groups in Lebanese politics, including those based in Lebanon which aspire to figure on a wider Arab stage.

Syria

A. L. Tibawi, *A Modern History of Syria* (London, 1969), will provide a general background of nineteenth and twentieth century developments. Two excellent studies of Syrian politics between 1945 and 1958 are Gordon H. Torrey, *Syrian Politics and the Military, 1945–58* (Columbus, 1964) and Patrick Seale, *The Struggle for Syria 1945–58* (London, 1965), both of which, because of the central position of Syria within the Arab world, shed much incidental light on the foreign policies of Iraq and Egypt. What was formerly one of the major political parties (also active in Lebanon) is the subject of Labib Zuwiyya Yamak, *The Syrian Social Nationalist Party* (Cambridge, Mass., 1966), while the recently more successful Ba'th party is considered in Kamal S. Abu Jaber, *The Arab Ba'th Socialist Party* (Syracuse, 1966), although the publication of new evidence has cast some doubt upon the author's account of the origins of the party.

Turkey

Two useful general guides to recent Turkish affairs are the popular, but well balanced *Turkey* (London, 1968) by Andrew Mango and Geoffrey Lewis, *Turkey* (3rd ed., London, 1965). The best general account of Ottoman and Turkish history in the nineteenth and twentieth centuries is Bernard Lewis, *The Emergence of Modern Turkey* (London, 1961), which takes the story down to 1950. The recent period may be studied in Ronald Robinson, *The First Turkish Republic* (Cambridge, Mass., 1963), a discursive work without any narrative form in which, effectively, about half is devoted to the post 1945 period, and in Kemal H. Karpat, *Turkey's Politics* (Princeton, 1959), a sound narrative with a good account of the rise and organisation of the Democratic Party. The 1960 revolution is the subject of a short study by Walter H. Weiker, *The Turkish Revolution, 1960–1* (Washington, 1963), and its aftermath and the return to a parliamentary system may be traced in C. H. Dodd, *Politics and Government in Turkey*

(Manchester, 1969). This last work is analytical rather than descriptive of political developments during the years 1960–5 and may be difficult to follow for those without an outline knowledge. Another analytical study of first rate importance is Frederick W. Frey, *The Turkish Political Elite* (Cambridge, Mass., 1965), which contains the results of an investigation into the social backgrounds of members of the Grand National Assembly from 1920–57 and an analysis of their party membership and voting behaviour. The comparative work by R. E. Ward and D. Rustow, *Political Modernization in Japan and Turkey* (Princeton, 1964), is also valuable.

Of several useful works on the Turkish economy Z. Y. Hershlag, *Turkey, An Economy in Transition* (2nd ed., The Hague, 1966) may be mentioned as the most recent general survey with a useful bibliography. On social change the far-ranging book by Andreas Kazamias, *Education and the Quest for Modernity in Turkey* (London, 1966), can be read with profit.

There is little of real value on Turkish foreign relations. *Turkey and the United Nations* (New York, 1961), is in the well known series and was prepared at the University of Ankara, using Turkish materials and a public opinion poll conducted in 1954. Mehmet Glönlübol, *Turkish Participation in the United Nations, 1945–54* (Ankara, 1963), is a detailed account of Turkish attitudes on a range of problems and is based on UN documents. A most useful work for the student of Turkish foreign relations is A. Gündüz Ökçün, *A Guide to Turkish Treaties 1920–64* (Ankara, 1966), which lists all Turkish treaties and international agreements and the dates when they came into force.

Current Affairs

Of the journals concerned with the Middle East, published in English, *The Middle East Journal* (Washington) and *Middle Eastern Affairs* (NY) both contain articles on recent events and chronological information. Neither, however, are as useful as *Orient* (Paris) or *Oriente Moderno* (Rome) for the serious student. The *New Middle East* (London) is a more popular

141

publication, primarily concerned with the Arab-Israeli dispute, but material of much interest does appear in it. *The Middle East and North Africa* (Europa Publications) is a gazeteer-type work revised at yearly, or two yearly, intervals and contains articles on economic and historical developments as well as statistical and other information. The student who wishes to make a comprehensive search of periodical literature is advised to consult J. D. Pearson (ed.), *Index Islamicus* (Cambridge, 1958), and later supplements. One of the basic works of reference although primarily concerned with earlier history is the *Encyclopaedia of Islam* (2nd ed., Leiden, 1954-   ).

7

Latin America

Alistair Hennessy

Introduction

The truism that contemporary history is conditioned by contemporary problems is nowhere more evident than in developing and ex-colonial nations. Many of the historiographical problems facing Latin Americans are those common to historians in other ex-colonial nations – a complex of issues raised by cultural dependence and by the problem of 'decolonising the mind'.

The historian in the newly independent nation may be inhibited by his metropolitan training either in the historical tradition in which he has been formed or in the colonising power's interpretation of his own country's history. But liberation from what may have been a restricting strait jacket can lead to a bewildering variety of alternative historiographical models once the close cultural links with the metropolitan power have been severed. A yearning for modernity can make the new urbanised intellectual elite anxious to acquire the latest historical expertise irrespective of whether this is applicable to its own country's situation or not.

Techniques acquired abroad may be too sophisticated to be sustained by inadequate archives and library facilities and the ideological presuppositions on which these techniques are based may be irrelevant to the needs of that society. Under such conditions the able young historian might choose to study the colonial period in the well-organised archives and intellectually exciting atmosphere of the metropolitan power, eschewing the political overtones of working on the contemporary history of his own country.

143

The concept of objective history presupposes that the historian operates in a social and cultural milieu where the norms of the professional historian are openly acknowledged. In new nations socially conscious historians, anxious to play an active part in the process of development, may well reject this concept in favour of one of commitment – to become the soothsayer, the party ideologist or the mythmaker of nationalism, or to write history in the words of Dr Eric Williams, as a 'manifesto of a subjugated people'.[1] These may be seen as legitimate roles for the historian to play in societies seeking justificatory sanction for their actions in an exclusive interpretation of their own past.

Latin American historians are less fortunate than their European or North American colleagues in that they do not enjoy similar professional immunity. Few have occupational or financial security; the number of full-time teaching and research posts is small; the number of History Departments limited; the concept of the professional historian almost nonexistent; the audience for serious historical work minimal; the publishing and distribution facilities inadequate. It must be remembered too that the Latin American university is not an academic so much as a political institution. Throughout the continent universities have traditionally been critics of governments. A few private institutes exist but these are largely dependent on foreign foundations for support and this can have serious repercussions at a time of rising nationalism such as we are now witnessing.

The historian in Latin America is not only circumscribed by his social situation but also by the nature of his subject matter. One hundred and fifty years of nominal independence have created historiographical traditions from which it is hard to escape. The most pervasive of these has been the tendency to study people rather than processes. The attention lavished on the leaders of the Emancipation movement and on political leaders since has been at the expense of broader studies of social groups and their interaction. History writing has tended to be legalistic, political and constitutionally oriented, written

[1] E. Williams, *History of the people of Trinidad and Tobago* (London, 1964, p. x).

144

by amateur historians, trained as lawyers who were often active politicians and for whom the study of history was a means of learning the secrets of manipulation. Elitist and European-centred attitudes meant the depreciation of the non-European elements in the national culture: study of these had to wait until the *indigenista* revival of the 1920s which followed on from the Mexican Revolution. Inevitably, the bulk of the historiography of the independent period has been national history: historians have been the creators of national myths for nations which were largely artificial entities. When wars over frontier disputes broke out in the latter half of the nineteenth century historians became as adept as their European counterparts in ransacking archives to substantiate national claims and counter-claims. It is economists and not historians who have been in the forefront of the contemporary movement to look at Latin America in continental terms, emphasising that the experience of economic dependence common to all Latin American states is more important than the national experiences which divide them.

Under this influence historians have belatedly found a new role. The inability of development economists to provide satisfactory explanations applicable to Latin America has encouraged historians to provide historical analyses for structural blockages, cultural factors inhibiting or enhancing growth, the role of foreign capital or of immigrants. Similarly, the inadequacy of the political scientists' models to explain political behaviour has prompted historians to test their hypotheses against the historical evidence. Only within recent years has this necessary and fruitful interdisciplinary dialogue begun to occur although even now it may be threatened by the arrogance of statistical positivists.

The foreign historian operates within the same restrictive framework as regards available evidence. The main differences between him and his Latin American counterpart lie in the imperatives of the discipline which often define the type of problem studied, and the scale of available finance. The acceleration of knowledge and the development of new disciplines such as the econometric techniques of the 'new' economic history, historians' increasing recognition of the relevance of sociology and social anthropology, of social communications theory and basic personality theory can mean that research projects are chosen mainly with methodological considerations in mind. Some aspects of this work, especially that by United States researchers, has been criticised in Latin America as a new form of cultural imperialism, introducing research techniques into an area where not only their relevance is questioned but also the assumption that they are value-free. Academic considerations doubtless explain much of the explosion of interest in Latin America but these rarely work in isolation. Without the Cuban Revolution the academic study of Latin America might still be in the doldrums. Now there is a concern with prediction – to anticipate the next revolutionary outburst. Some North American research is explicitly couched in Cold War categories and is policy-oriented as in the instance of Operation Camelot, which raised doubts about the motives behind United States sociological research in Latin America.[2] Policy considerations have unleashed such a flood of funds from governmental agencies as well as from private foundations that the major part of serious research on the contemporary history of Latin America is either being done by North Americans or is financed by US funds. No one would deny the high quality of a great deal of this work; what is in question is whether such a preponderance is desirable.

As far as Latin America is concerned there is a danger in adhering too closely to a limited concept of 'contemporary' history. Nineteen hundred and fifty-nine clearly inaugurated a new era with the Cuban Revolution and the involvement of Latin America in the Cold War but this could only be used as a starting point at the level of exposition not explanation. Nor is 1945, where this reading list begins, a meaningful date in Latin American history. It did not constitute a sharp break

[2] For this see I. L. Horowitz (ed.), *The Rise and Fall of Project Camelot: studies in the relationship between social science and practical politics* (Boston, 1967), and for an example of how it affected one sociologist working in the sensitive field of student attitudes see M. Glazer, 'Field Work in a Hostile Environment: a chapter in the sociology of social research in Chile', in *Comparative Education Review* (10, no. 2, June, 1964).

between colonial status and independence as in Africa and Asia; it did not inaugurate a period of reconstruction after the ravages of war nor was Latin America markedly affected by the opening of the Cold War.

It is difficult, in fact, to make much sense of contemporary events without some understanding of the formative years of the 1920s and the 1930s. This was the period of adaptation to economic crises and the Great Depression and which saw the emergence of multi-class populist movements which cannot easily be characterised in terms of the left-right dichotomy of European politics – fascism is not a useful concept (even assuming its utility in Europe) in elucidating the nature of the Vargas regime in Brazil or Peronism in Argentina – but without some understanding of the origins of these two movements later politics are difficult to understand. Nor can the complexities of present industrialisation processes, the role of the military and of violence or the imbalance between ultra-modern metropoli and backward 'internal colonies' be explained without reference to earlier developments.

A further difficulty in studying contemporary Latin American states arises from the fact that they are 'old' new nations – nations which have been independent for 150 years but which are still extensions of Europe, rooted in a European, or more specifically a southern European culture, in a way which makes them quite distinct from other parts of the Third World.[3] For the European, the very familiarity of many aspects of Latin American culture is a pitfall and has led to the uncritical application of linear models of historical development and of stage theories of economic growth. The complexity of Latin American society derives from the inter-penetration of deeply traditional forms of behaviour with modern attitudes co-existing within a framework of rapid

---

[3] For example, an Arab or a Hindu can define himself and the history of his people by reference to philosophical and religious systems which owe nothing to Europe: for the Latin American this is not possible, as his culture is rooted in European presuppositions. The Aztec past might provide an inspiration for a nationalist revival; it cannot provide a philosophy of life or of history. It is the tension between the promise of a 'New World' culture and the brake of 'Old World' behaviour patterns which has prompted so many ontological quests by Latin American intellectuals.

change. Furthermore, in a nationalist situation where problems of national identity are paramount there is an obsession with the unassimilated past: a variety of historical relationships demand explanation – that between the independent and colonial periods, between colonial and pre-colonial periods, between pre-colonial and independent periods as well as the nature of the neo-colonial relationship between nominally independent nations and the economically dominant industrialised powers. Revolutionary movements seek the respectability and sanction of historical pedigrees. One of the contemporary historian's most difficult tasks is to weed out spurious continuities and to explain those instances where discontinuities do occur.

There is a formidable undertaking as the contemporary historian has to base his judgements on an inadequately studied past both in terms of factual and conceptual content, and for the reason that the historiography of modern Latin America is still in its infancy many of the books which follow will be found to pose questions rather than give answers.

General Surveys

C. Veliz (ed.), *Latin America and the Caribbean: a Handbook* (London, 1968), contains a mass of information in country-by-country and thematic chapters. L. Hanke, *Contemporary Latin America: a History* (New York, 1968), has a long introduction to a wide range of readings by country and theme. J. J. Johnson, *Political Change in Latin America: the emergence of the middle sectors* (Stanford, 1958), is a useful starting point for the 'middle class controversy'. P. Calvert, *Latin America: internal conflict and international peace* (London, 1969), is a short thematic introduction. Among a host of general overall surveys see K. Schmitt and D. Burks, *Evolution or Chaos* (London, 1963); Tad Szulc, *The Winds of Revolution: Latin America today and tomorrow* (London, 1964); J. Gerassi, *The Great Fear in Latin America* (New York, 1965); J. TePaske and S. N. Fisher, *Explosive Forces in Latin America* (Ohio, 1964).

Three excellent geographic surveys are J. P. Cole, *Latin America: an economic and social geography* (London, 1965), J. E. Preston, *Latin America* (3rd ed., New York, 1959), and R. C. West and J. P. Augelli, *Middle America: its lands and peoples* (New York, 1966).

General Political Surveys

An incisive introduction is M. Needler, *Latin American Politics in Perspective* (New York, 1963). More detailed but lucid is J. Lambert, *Latin America: social structure and political institutions* (trans. H. Katel, Berkeley, 1967). M. Needler (ed.), *Political Systems of Latin America* (2nd ed., New York, 1970), is a country-by-country treatment. H. E. Davis (ed.), *Government and Politics in Latin America* (New York, 1958), is thematic in treatment. W. S. Stokes, *Latin American Politics* (New York, 1959), emphasises cultural conditioning factors. B. G. Burnett and K. F. Johnson, *Political Forces in Latin America: dimensions of the quest for stability* (Belmont, Calif., 1968), is a country-by-country survey with a useful chapter on ideas. G. Blanksten's chapter in G. A. Almond and J. S. Coleman, *The Politics of Developing Nations* (Princeton, 5th ed., 1966), is a useful introductory analysis.

From a wide selection of readings the following may be noted: J. D. Martz (ed.), *The Dynamics of Change in Latin America* (New York, 1965); P. Snow (ed.), *Government and Politics in Latin America* (New York, 1967); R. D. Tomasek (ed.), *Latin American Politics* (New York, 1966); D. B. Heath and R. N. Adams (eds.), *Contemporary Cultures and Societies of Latin America* (New York, 1965).

There are few biographies of Latin American politicians. For short studies see R. J. Alexander, *Prophets of the Revolution* (New York, 1962) and R. Bourne, *Political Leaders of Latin America* (Harmondsworth, 1969).

Occupational Groups

For studies of occupational groups see J. J. Johnson (ed.),

Continuity and Change in Latin America (Stanford, 1964) and
S. M. Lipset and A. Solari (eds), *Elites in Latin America*
(Oxford, 1967). The military are now attracting scholarly
attention although most works tend to be general as in
E. Liewen's *Arms and Politics in Latin America* (New York,
1960) and his *Generals versus Presidents* (London, 1964).
J. J. Johnson's *The Military and Society in Latin America*
(Stanford, 1964) is a standard work. There are also three
essays on Latin America in his edited *The Role of the Military
in Underdeveloped Countries* (Princeton, 1962). K. Silvert
and G. Germani propound an interesting typology of the
military in 'Politics, Social Structure and Military Intervention in Latin America' in *Archives européenes de sociologie*
(II, i, 1961). See also J. Nun's 'The Middle Class Military
Coup' in Veliz, *Politics of Conformity* for an influential hypo-
thesis. The problem of internal security is dealt with in W. F.
Barker and C. N. Ronning, *Internal Security and Military
Power: counterinsurgency and civic action in Latin America*
(Ohio, 1966). The crucial problem of the police awaits its
researcher.

Students are attracting serious attention as in S. M. Lipset
(ed.), *Student Politics* (New York, 1967) with four essays on
Latin America and in D. K. Emmerson, *Students in Developing Countries* (London, 1968) with essays on Venezuela,
Brazil and Cuba. A detailed analysis of students, professors
and universities is to be found in J. Maier and L. Weatherhead, *The Latin American University* (New York, 1971).

Little has been written on the important new trends in the
Catholic Church. For its political expression see E. J.
Williams, *Christian Democrat Parties in Latin America* (Nash-
ville, 1967). F. B. Pike (ed.), *The Conflict between Church and
State in Latin America* (New York, 1964) is a short collection
of readings. F. Houtart and E. Pin, *The Church in the Latin
American Revolution* (New York, 1965) and F. B. Pike and
W. Y. d'Antonio, *Religion, Revolution and Reform: new forces
for change in Latin America* (New York, 1964) are general
discussions.

Interpretative Works

Two important collections of essays which break away from established categories, edited by C. Veliz, are *Obstacles to Change in Latin America* (Oxford, 1965) and *The Politics of Conformity in Latin America* (Oxford, 1967). Other stimulating interpretations may be found in A. O. Hirschman (ed.), *Latin American Issues – essays and comments* (New York, 1961); J. Maier and L. Weatherhead (eds), *Politics and Change in Latin America* (New York, 1964); K. Silvert, *The Conflict Society; reaction and revolution in Latin America* (New Orleans, 1961); L. Bryson (ed.), *Social Change in Latin America Today: its implications for U.S. policy* (New York, 1960), mainly written by social anthropologists, and S. Andreski, *Parasitism and Subversion in Latin America* (London, 1966). S. and B. Stein, *The Colonial Heritage of Latin America* (New York, 1970), challengingly puts economic dependence into historical perspective.

The complex problem of nationalism has been inadequately treated but see A. P. Whitaker and D. Jordan, *Nationalism in Contemporary Latin America* (Glencoe, 1966). G. Masur, *Nationalism in Latin America* (New York, 1966) lacks conceptual depth. K. Silvert (ed.), *Expectant Peoples* (New York, 1965) attempts to provide a conceptual framework. V. Alba, *Nationalists without Nations: the oligarchy versus the people in Latin America* (London, 1968) is polemical but has some interesting insights. A useful collection of essays is *Latin America's Nationalist Revolutions*, a special number in March 1961 of the *Annals of the American Academy of Political and Social Sciences*, Philadelphia. For the analysis of ideas and the intellectual background see L. Zea, *The Latin American mind* (tr. J. H. Abbott and L. Dunham, Norman, 1963). A short introduction is S. Clissold, *Latin America: a cultural outline* (London, 1965) and more detailed J. Franco, *The Modern Culture of Latin America* (London, 1967).

Agrarian Reform and the Peasantry

The most detailed analyses are those produced by CIDA,

the Inter-American Committee for Agricultural Development, an agency of the Alliance for Progress on Argentina, Brazil, Chile, Colombia, Ecuador, Guatemala and Peru published by the Pan American Union, Washington, between 1965 and 1967. The Land Tenure Centre of the University of Wisconsin has produced a number of mimeographed studies on various countries.

T. Lynn Smith (ed.), *Agrarian Reform in Latin America* (New York, 1965) is a collection of readings. D. Warriner, *Land Reform in Principle and Practice* (Oxford, 1969) has chapters on Brazil, Chile and Venezuela. Colonisation is studied in C. L. Dozier, *Land Development and Colonization in Peru, Bolivia and Mexico* (New York, 1969).

H. Landsberger (ed.), *Latin American Peasant Movements* (Cornell, 1969), is the only detailed examination of peasants in various countries.

Economics

An introductory survey is F. Benham and H. Holley, *A Short Introduction to the Economy of Latin America* (Oxford, 1960). General descriptive works are W. P. Glade, *The Latin American Economies: a study of their institutional evolution* (New York, 1966); C. W. Anderson's *Politics and Economic Change in Latin America* (Princeton, 1967), shows the dominant role of economic development in politics; Celso Furtado, *Economic Development of Latin America* (Cambridge, 1970). For inflation see W. Baer and I. Kerstenetzky (eds), *Inflation and Growth in Latin America* (Homewood, Ill., 1964).

The most pungent critique of development theories as applied to Latin America is K. Griffin, *Underdevelopment in Spanish America* (London, 1969). An influential critique is A. G. Frank, *Capitalism and Underdevelopment in Latin America: historical studies of Chile and Brazil* (New York, 1967). A. O. Hirschman, *Journeys to Progress* (New York, 1963) puts development problems in Chile, Colombia and North-East Brazil into historical perspective. H. S. Ellis and H. G. Wallich (eds), *Economic Development for Latin America*

(New York, 1961), is a collection of conference papers. V. Urquidi, *The Challenge of Development in Latin America* (London, 1964), and R. de Oliviera Campos, *Reflections on Latin American Development* (Austin, 1967) are the views of two prominent Latin American experts.

Social factors of development are treated in E. de Vries, *Social Aspects of Economic Development in Latin America* (vol. I. 1963, and vol. II, ed. J. M. Echevarría and B. Higgins, UNESCO, 1963). See also P. Hauser (ed.), *Urbanization in Latin America* (Paris, 1961). For population problems see J. M. Stycos and J. Arias (ed.), *Population Dilemmas in Latin America* (Washington, 1966).

Latin American integration is covered in M. S. Wionczek, *Latin American Economic Integration* (New York, 1966); S. Dell, *A Latin American Common Market* (Oxford, 1966); V. Urquidi, *Free Trade and Economic Integration in Latin America: the evolution of a common market policy* (California, 1964). For a general collection on integration see R. H. Hilton (ed.), *The Movement towards Latin American unity* (New York, 1969). For the Alliance for Progress see S. G. Hanson, *Five Years of the Alliance for Progress* (Washington, 1967); J. W. Nystrom and N. A. Haverstock, *The Alliance for Progress* (New York, 1966); H. K. May, *Problems and Prospects for the Alliance for Progress* (New York, 1968); R. M. Sommerfeld, *Tax Reform and the Alliance for Progress* (Austin, 1970); and the polemical V. Alba, *Alliance without Allies: the mythology of progress in Latin America* (New York, 1965); D. Joslin examines the most important foreign bank in *A Century of Banking in Latin America: the Bank of London and South America, 1862-1962* (Oxford, 1963); H. S. Perloff, *Alliance for Progress: a social invention in the making* (Baltimore, 1969).

Inter-American Affairs

G. Connell-Smith, *The Inter-American System* (London, 1966) is a standard account of the Organisation of American states. Other studies are O. C. Stoetzer, *The Organization of American States* (New York, 1965); J. C. Dreier, *The*

Organization of American States and Hemisphere Problems and Perspectives (Oxford, 1962); A. van Wynen Thomas and A. J. Thomas, Jr, *The Organization of American States* (Dallas, 1963); J. Slater, *The Organization of American States and United States Foreign Policy* (Ohio, 1967); M. M. Ball, *The O.A.S. in Transition* (Durham, NC, 1969); C. N. Ronning, *Law and Politics in Inter-American Diplomacy* (New York, 1963); A. P. Whitaker, *The Western Hemisphere Idea: its rise and decline* (Ithaca, 1954); D. Perkins, *A History of the Monroe Doctrine* (London, 1960); J. L. Mecham, *The United States and Inter-American Security, 1889–1960* (Austin, 1963); R. N. Burr, *Our Troubled Hemisphere: perspectives on U.S.–Latin American relations* (Washington, 1967); E. Liewen, *U.S. Policy in Latin America* (London, 1966) is a useful introduction; R. W. Gregg, *International Organization in the Western Hemisphere* (Syracuse, 1968). The foreign policies of Argentina, Brazil and Mexico are discussed in C. Astiz (ed.), *Latin American International Politics* (Notre Dame, 1969). Bryce Wood, *The United States and Latin American Wars 1932–42* (New York, 1966) is crucial.

The Left

Two important collections of articles are I. L. Horowitz, J. de Castro and J. Gerassi, *Latin American Radicalism: a documentary report on left and nationalist movements* (New York, 1969) and M. Zeitlin and J. Petras (eds), *Latin America: reform or revolution?* (New York, 1968). Guerrilla movements are exhaustively covered in R. Gott, *Defeat of the Revolution? Guerrilla movements in Latin America* (London, 1970), and more theoretically in L. Mercier-Vega, *Technique of the Counter-State: the guerrillas in Latin America* (London, 1968). The theory of guerrilla warfare is contained in Guevara's *Guerrilla Warfare* (London, 1968) and R. Debray's *Revolution in the Revolution* (London, 1968) and in R. Blackburn's edition of Debray's writings *Strategy for Revolution* (London, 1970). A critique of Debray is the collection of essays in the special issue of the *Monthly Review* (vol. 20, no. 3, July, 1968) 'Regis Debray and the Latin American Revolution'.

Communism

R. J. Alexander, *Communism in Latin America* (New Brunswick, 1957) is a detailed country-by-country survey. R. Poppino, *International Communism in Latin America* (New York, 1964), is short and D. Dillon, *International Communism in Latin America: perspectives and prospects* (Gainesville, 1962) even shorter. S. Clissold (ed.), *Soviet Relations with Latin America 1918–1968: a documentary survey* (Oxford, 1970), is a useful collection of documents with a perceptive introduction. L. E. Aguilar (ed.), *Marxism in Latin America* (New York, 1968), is a short collection of readings. For communism in Latin America generally, see the special issue of *Problems of Communism* (Washington) July/August, 1970, and D. B. Jackson, *Castro, the Kremlin and Communism in Latin America* (Baltimore, 1969). *The World Marxist Review* (Prague) is useful for the orthodox line. A comprehensive analysis of Chinese attitudes is C. Johnson, *Communist China and Latin America, 1959–67* (New York, 1970).

Labour

An introductory account is R. Troncoso and R. Burnett, *The Rise of the Latin American Labour movement* (New York, 1960). The fullest account is V. Alba, *Politics and the Labour Movement in Latin America* (Stanford, 1968). Shorter is R. J. Alexander, *Organized Labour in Latin America* (New York, 1965); his *Labour relations in Argentina, Brazil and Chile* (Cambridge, Mass., 1962) is a standard work.

W. Form and A. A. Blum (eds), *Industrial Relations and Social Change in Latin America* (Gainesville, 1965), is short. See also J. R. Ramos, *Labour and Development in Latin America* (New York, 1970).

The Bureau of Labor Statistics of the US Department of Labor publishes useful reports on labour in separate countries as does the International Labour Office. See also the *Bulletin* of the International Institute for Labour Studies.

Argentina

A brief introduction is T. F. McGann, *Argentina: the divided land* (New York, 1966). A standard, excellent thematic treatment is J. Scobie, *Argentina: a city and a nation* (New York, 1966). Two reliable general works are G. Pendle, *Argentina* (3rd ed., Oxford, 1963) and H. S. Ferns, *Argentina* (London, 1969). An important analysis of the Argentinian elite is J. L. de Imaz, *Los que mandan,* tr. C. A. Astiz (Berkeley, 1970). Relations with the United States are covered in H. F. Peterson, *Argentina and the United States, 1810–1960* (Albany NY, 1964). A. P. Whitaker, *The United States and Argentina* (Cambridge, Mass., 1954) is an introductory study. For foreign policy see A. C. Paz and G. Ferrari, *Argentina's Foreign Policy, 1930–62* (Indiana, 1966).

Until Peronism has been studied in depth the following general treatments must serve: the most detailed is G. Blanksten, *Perón's Argentina* (New York, 1953); shorter is R. J. Alexander, *The Perón Era* (New York, 1965). The end of the Peronist regime is briefly treated in A. P. Whitaker, *Argentine Upheaval; Perón's fall and the new regime* (New York, 1956). P. Lux Wurm, *Le péronisme* (Paris, 1965) is a useful analysis. Two books which throw much light on the background of Peronism are P. Smith, *Politics and Beef in Argentina* (New York, 1969) and R. Potash, *The Army and Politics in Argentina, 1928–45* (Stanford, 1969). J. Barager (ed.), *Why Perón Came to Power?* (New York, 1968) is a short collection of readings. A study which brings out the weakness and contradictions of middle class politics is P. G. Snow, *Argentine Radicalism: the history and doctrine of the Radical Civic Union* (Iowa, 1965). Various aspects of the complex problem of Argentinian nationalism are covered in S. Baily, *Labor, Nationalism and Politics in Argentina* (New Brunswick, 1967); C. Solberg, *Immigration and Nationalism: Argentina and Chile 1890–1914* (Austin, 1970); J. J. Kennedy, *Catholicism, Nationalism and Democracy in Argentina*

(Notre Dame, 1958) and in K. Silvert's chapter in K. Silvert, *Expectant Peoples* (New York, 1965). The important student movement has only received attention in English from R. J. Walter, *Student Politics in Argentina* (New York, 1968).

Surprisingly little exists in English on the Argentine economy. The best coverage is A. Ferrer, *The Argentine Economy* (Berkeley, 1967). Social determinants are discussed in T. R. Fillol, *Social Factors in Economic Development: the Argentine case* (Boston, 1961). The OECD study *Education, Human Resources and Development in Argentina* (2 vols, Paris 1967 and 1968) is invaluable. C. F. Diaz Alejandro, *Essays on the Economic History of the Argentine Republic* (New Haven, 1970) has useful selective analyses. J. L. Romero's *A History of Argentine Political Thought*, tr. T. F. McGann (Stanford, 1963) is useful on ideas.

Bolivia

The standard account of the 1952 Revolution, now largely outdated, is R. J. Alexander, *The Bolivian National Revolution* (New Brunswick, 1958). The origins of the Revolution have been expertly studied in H. Klein's key *Parties and Political Change in Bolivia, 1880–1952* (Cambridge, 1969). H. Osborne, *Bolivia: a land divided* (3rd ed., London, 1964) is strong on geography and the economy but weak on politics. H. J. Pühle, *Tradition und Reformpolitik in Bolivien* (Hannover, 1970) is a short analysis with detailed and excellent bibliographical references. An analysis by a political scientist J. M. Malloy, *Bolivia; the uncompleted revolution* (Pittsburgh, 1970). The key role of the army has been little studied apart from the short, W. H. Brill, *Military Intervention in Bolivia: the overthrow of Paz Estenssoro* (Washington, 1967).

The economy is examined in C. H. Zondag, *The Bolivian Economy, 1952–65* (London, 1966). The crucial question of relations with the United States has been incisively analysed in L. Whitehead, *The United States and Bolivia – a case of neo-colonialism* (Beckenham, 1969). For a quantitative analysis see J. W. Wilkie, *The Bolivia Revolution and U.S. Aid since*

1952 (Los Angeles, 1969). The agrarian situation and the peasantry is briefly examined in R. W. Patch's chapters in L. Bryson, *Social Change in Latin America* (New York, 1960) and in K. Silvert, *Expectant Peoples* (New York, 1963). D. W. Heath *et al, Land reform and Social Revolution in Bolivia* (New York, 1969) is the most detailed treatment. The Indian problem is best studied in J. Vellard, *Civilisations des Andes* (Paris, 1963) and more generally in H. Osborne, *Indians of the Andes* (London, 1952). For Aymaras see W. E. Carter, *Aymara communities and the Bolivian Agrarian Reform* (Gainesville, 1964).

Brazil

R. Poppino, *Brazil: the land and the people* (New York, 1968) is a general history treated thematically. J. M. Bello, *A History of Modern Brazil, 1889–1964* (Stanford, 1966) is a narrative account. The most detailed political history is T. Skidmore, *Politics in Brazil, 1930–1964: an experiment in democracy* (New York, 1967). A useful introductory account by an anthropologist is C. Wagley, *An Introduction to Brazil* (5th ed., New York, 1966). An authoritative analysis of Brazilian society is T. Lynn Smith, *Brazil: people and institutions* (Baton Rouge, 1963). A useful hotch-potch of readings is I. L. Horowitz, *Revolution in Brazil* (New York, 1964). A short political analysis is V. Reisky de Vudnic, *Political Trends in Brazil* (Washington, 1968). The Vargas regime has not received much attention but see K. Loewenstein, *Brazil under Vargas* (New York, 1942) and J. M. Young, *The Brazilian Revolution of 1930 and the Aftermath* (New Brunswick, 1966). A full length study of Vargas is J. W. F. Dulles, *Vargas of Brazil: a political biography* (Austin, 1967).

Various aspects of modern Brazil are discussed in two books by E. Baklanoff (ed.), *The Shaping of Modern Brazil* (Baton Rouge, 1969) and *New Perspectives of Brazil* (Nashville, 1966). A pungent analysis of the contemporary crisis is O. Ianni, *Crisis in Brazil* (New York, 1970). A general economic history is C. Furtado, *The Economic Growth of Brazil* (Berkeley, 1963). His *Diagnosis of the Brazilian Crisis*

(Berkeley, 1965) analyses the development of the economy since 1930. See also his *Development and underdevelopment* (Berkeley, 1964). General development problems are discussed in S. Kuznets *et al.*, *Economic Development, Brazil, India, Japan* (Durham, NC, 1955). The Brazilian economy has attracted considerable attention as in W. Baer, *Industrialization and Economic Development in Brazil* (Homewood, Ill., 1965); N. H. Leff, *The Brazilian Capital Goods Industry, 1929–64* (Cambridge, Mass., 1968); H. Jaguaribe, *Economic and Political Development: a theoretical approach and Brazilian case-study* (Cambridge, Mass., 1968). The problem of the North-East is discussed historically in A. Hirschman, *Journeys toward Progress* (New York, 1963, chap. 1) and specifically in S. H. Robock, *Brazil's Developing North-East: a study of regional planning and foreign aid* (Washington, 1963).

Political aspects of development are discussed in J. D. Wirth, *The Politics of Brazilian development, 1930–54* (Stanford, 1970). Two important historical studies of the industrialisation and modernisation processes are R. Graham, *Britain and the Modernization of Brazil, 1850–1914* (Cambridge, 1969) and W. Dean, *The Industrialization of São Paulo, 1880–1945* (Austin, 1969). For agrarian problems see A. K. Ludwig and H. W. Taylor, *Brazil's New Agrarian Reform: an evaluation of its property classification and tax system* (New York, 1969).

Administrative problems are discussed in L. S. Graham, *Civil service Reform in Brazil: principles versus practice* (Austin, 1968) and R. T. Daland, *Brazilian Planning: development politics and administration* (Chapel Hill, 1967). For problems of national identity and nationalism see G. Freyre, *New World in the Tropics: the culture of modern Brazil* (New York, 1959); J. H. Rodrigues, *The Brazilians, their character and aspirations* (Austin, 1967); E. B. Burns, *Nationalism in Brazil: a historical survey* (New York, 1968), and F. Bonilla's chapter in K. Silvert, *Expectant Peoples* (New York, 1965). Brazil's African legacy is discussed in the context of foreign policy in J. H. Rodrigues, *Brazil and Africa* (Berkeley, 1966). For racial problems see D. Pierson, *Negroes in Brazil* (Carbondale, 1967) and F. Fernandes, *The Negro in Brazilian Society* (New York, 1969). There is a dearth of analyses of either the Brazilian Left or the Right in English except for the detailed study of the Catholic radical movement of the 1960s in E. de Kadt, *Catholic Radicals in Brazil* (London, 1970). The urban guerrilla handbook by C. Marighela has been translated as *For the Liberation of Brazil* (Harmondsworth, 1971). Educational problems are examined in F. de Azevedo, *Brazilian Culture* (New York, 1950) and R. J. Havighurst and J. M. Moreira, *Society and Education in Brazil* (Pittsburgh, 1965), and more concisely in F. Bonilla's chapter in J. S. Coleman, *Education and Political Development* (Princeton, 1965). Brazil's attitude to nuclear power politics is analysed in H. J. Rosenbaum and G. M. Cooper, 'Brazil and the Nuclear Non-Proliferation Treaty' in *International Affairs* (vol. 46, no. 1, Jan. 1970). An interesting comparative analysis of social values is J. Kahl, *The Measurement of Modernism: a study of values in Brazil and Mexico* (Austin, 1968).

Chile

There is no study of recent Chilean history in English. Short introductions are K. Silvert, *Chile* (New York, 1965) and G. Butland, *Chile* (3rd ed., London, 1956). F. B. Pike, *Chile and the United States* (Notre Dame, 1963) is wider than its title indicates and contains a mass of bibliographical detail. F. C. Gil, *The Political System in Chile* (Boston, 1966) is a general analysis. An attempt to analyse political culture in relation to colonial legacies is F. J. Moreno, *Legitimacy and Stability in Latin America: a study of Chilean political culture* (New York, 1969). The Left is authoritatively discussed in E. Halperin, *Nationalism and Communism in Chile* (Cambridge, Mass., 1965). For a leftist analysis see J. Petras, *Politics and Social Forces in Chilean Development* (Berkeley, 1969).

The economy is discussed in M. Mamalakis and C. W. Reynolds, *Essays on the Chilean Economy* (Homewood, Ill., 1965) and from a Christian Democrat standpoint in M. Zañartu and J. J. Kennedy (eds), *The Overall Development of*

Chile (Notre Dame, 1969). For the agrarian situation see W. C. Thiesenhusen, *Chile's Experiments in Agrarian Reform* (Madison, 1967). Labour is covered in J. O. Morris, *Elites, Intellectuals and Concensus: a study of the social question and the industrial relations system in Chile* (Ithaca, 1966) and in A. Angell, 'Labour and Politics in Chile' in *St Antony's Papers: Latin American affairs,* ed. R. Carr (Oxford, 1970).

Colombia

There is no general history of Colombia in English except the old-fashioned J. M. Henao and G. Arrubla, *History of Colombia* (Chapel Hill, 1938). W. Galbraith, *Colombia* (2nd ed., London, 1968) is a general survey. J. D. Martz, *Colombia: a contemporary political survey* (Chapel Hill, 1962) is factually useful. More interesting for their analyses are R. A. Dix, *Colombia: the political dimensions of change* (New Haven, 1967) and J. L. Payne, *Patterns of Change in Colombia* (New Haven, 1967) and O. Fals Borda, *Subversion and Social Change in Colombia* (New York, 1969). See also V. Fluharty, *Dance of the Millions: military rule and social revolution in Colombia, 1930–1956* (Pittsburgh, 1957).

A comprehensive study of Colombian society is T. Lynn Smith, *Colombia: studies of social structure and the process of development* (Gainesville, 1966). A useful short introduction to Colombian politics is A. Angell, 'Co-operation and Conflict in Colombian Party Politics', *Political Studies* (vol. xiv, no. 1, Feb. 1966). The complex problem of the 'violencia' has been studied in detail in O. Fals Borda, G. Guzman and E. Umaña Luna in *La violencia en Colombia* (2 vols, Bogotá, 1962–4); in English there are two short articles – R. S. Weinert, 'Violence in Pre-Modern Societies: rural Colombia', in *American Political Science Quarterly* (vol. LX, no. 2, June, 1966) and E. Hobsbawm, 'The Anatomy of Violence', in *New Society,* April 1963. The labour movement has been lucidly treated in M. Urrutia, *The Development of the Colombian Labour Movement* (New Haven, 1969). The Left has not been studied in detail in English although there is a biography of the guerrilla priest Camilo Torres by G. Guzman, tr. R. D.

Ring (New York, 1969) and a collection of his writings, *Camilo Torres: revolutionary writings*, ed. M. Zeitlin (New York, 1971). For agrarian reform see E. A. Duff, *Agrarian Reform in Colombia* (New York, 1968) and for peasants O. Fals Borda, *Peasant Society in the Colombian Andes* (Gainesville, 1962) and the classic anthropological study, Reichel – Dolmatoff, *The People of Aritama: the cultural personality of a Colombian mestizo village* (London, 1961).

Central America

The best general treatment is F. D. Parker, *The Central American Republics* (Oxford, 1964). J. D. Martz, *Central America: the crisis and the challenge* (Chapel Hill, 1964) is a useful factual survey. A short introduction is T. V. Kalijarvi, *Central America: land of lords and lizards* (New York, 1962).

There are no adequate national histories in English. Guatemala has been covered in most detail. The Guatemalan Revolution has been studied from one point of view by R. M. Schneider, *Communism in Guatemala, 1944–54* (New York, 1958). For government see K. Silvert, *A Study in Government: Guatemala* (New Orleans, 1954). For a leftist analysis of Guatemala see E. Galeano, *Guatemala: occupied country* (New York, 1969). The military has been studied by R. N. Adams, 'The Development of the Guatemalan Military' in vol. IV, no. 5 of the publications of the Social Science Institute of Washington University, St Louis. N. L. Whetten's *Guatemala, the land and the people* (New Haven, 1961) is an excellent account of society. See also R. N. Adams, *Crucifixion by Power: essays on Guatemalan social structure, 1944–66* (Austin, 1970).

For Honduras see W. S. Stokes, *Honduras: an area study in Government* (Madison, 1950). For Panama see L. Pippin, *The Remón Era: an analysis of a decade of events in Panama, 1947–57* (Stanford, 1964) and S. B. Liss, *The Canal, Communism and Chaos: aspects of U.S.–Panama relations* (Notre Dame, 1967). For Costa Rica, see J. L. Busey, *Notes on Costa Rican Democracy* (Boulder, 1962), and D. Goldrich, *Sons of the Establishment: Elite Youth in Panama and Costa*

Rica (Chicago, 1966). D. R. Reynolds studies one economy in his *Rapid Development in Small Economies: the example of El Salvador* (London, 1967). Industrialisation in a wider context is discussed in D. E. Ramsett, *Regional Industrial Development in Central America* (New York, 1969). For Nicaragua see IBRD report *The Economic Development of Nicaragua* (Baltimore, 1952). For the 'Football War' of 1968 between Honduras and El Salvador see V. Cable, ' "The Football War" and the Central American Common Market', in *International Affairs* (October, 1969). For an important Nicaraguan forerunner of guerrillas see N. Macauley, *The Sandino Affair* (Chicago, 1967). A standard work on British Honduras is D. Waddell, *British Honduras* (Oxford, 1962). The diplomatic background to the Belice-Guatemala dispute is covered by R. A. Humphreys, *A Diplomatic History of British Honduras, 1638–1901* (Oxford, 1961).

For the Central American Common Market see C. M. Castillo, *Growth and Integration in Central America* (New York, 1966) and J. S. Nye, *Central American Regional Integration* (New York, 1967).

Cuba

The only comprehensive study of Cuban history in English apart from the five-volume, idiosyncratically translated *History of the Cuban Nation* by R. Guerra Sanchez *et al.* (Havana, 1952) is H. Thomas's crucial *Cuba: or the pursuit of freedom* (London, 1971). Half of its 1600 pages are devoted to the post-1952 period. R. E. Ruiz, *Cuba: the making of a revolution* (Coral Gables, 1968) is an excellent thematic treatment of historical factors conditioning the Revolution. W. MacGaffey, C. Barnett, *Cuba: its people, its society, its culture* (New Haven, 1962) is a comprehensive analysis of Cuban society put in a historical perspective. R. F. Smith (ed.), *What Happened in Cuba?* (New York, 1963) and his *Cuba: background to Revolution* (New York, 1966) are good collections of readings and articles. A good study of the struggle against Batista is R. Taber, *M-26, the Biography of a Revolution* (New York, 1963).

Early sympathetic Marxist analyses of the Revolution are L. Huberman and P. Sweezy, *Cuba: anatomy of a revolution* (New York, 1961) and J. P. Morray, *The Second Revolution in Cuba* (New York, 1962). The two books by T. Draper – *Castro's Revolution: myths and realities* (London, 1962) and *Castroism: theory and practice* (New York, 1965) were early and influential attempts to interpret the Revolution as variants of communism but his analysis is vitiated by a lack of awareness of Cuban history. The relationship between Castroism and Communism is analysed in A. Suarez, *Cuba: Castroism and Communism, 1959–1966* (Boston, 1967). B. Goldenberg, *The Cuban Revolution and Latin America* (London, 1965) gives the wider setting whilst his *Zehn Jahre Kubanische Revolution* (Hannover, 1970) is the most concise analysis of Castroism.

Few attempts at detailed political or sociological analysis of Castro's Cuba exist apart from M. Zeitlin's revealing *Revolutionary Politics and the Cuban Working Class* (Princeton, 1967) and R. Fagen, *The Transformation of Cuban Political Culture* (Stanford, 1969). The same author has written, together with R. A. Brody and T. O'Leary, *Cubans in Exile: disaffection and revolution* (Stanford, 1968). J. Suchlicki describes the important role played by students in his *University Students and Revolution in Cuba, 1920–1968* (Coral Gables, 1969). The best analysis of pre-Castro rural society is Lowry Nelson, *Rural Cuba* (Minneapolis, 1950).

From a spate of early encomia the most influential were H. Matthews, *The Cuban Story* (New York, 1961); J. P. Sartre, *Sartre on Cuba* (New York, 1961) and C. Wright Mills, *Listen Yankee* (New York, 1960). Among later eye-witness accounts see Lee Lockwood, *Castro's Cuba: Cuba's Fidel* (New York, 1967), E. Sutherland, *The Youngest Revolution* (New York, 1969) and J. Iglesias, *In the Fist of the Revolution* (London, 1970). J. Clytus, *Black Man in Red Cuba* (Miami, 1970) is the critical account of a Black Nationalist. From the considerable French literature the following may be noted: C. Julien, *La révolution cubaine* (Paris, 1961) and K. S. Karol, *Les guerrilleros au pouvoir: l'itinéraire politique de la révolution cubaine* (Paris, 1970).

Until an adequate biography of Castro appears, H. Matthews' adulatory, *Castro: a political biography* (London, 1968), and E. Meneses, *Fidel Castro* (London, 1968) will have to serve. Among a number of reminiscences by ex-colleagues the following may be noted – T. Casuso, *Cuba and Castro* (New York, 1961); R. Lopez Fresquet, *My Fourteen Months with Castro* (New York, 1966) and M. Urrutia, *Fidel Castro and Company Inc.* (New York, 1964). For Batista's apologia see his *The Growth and Decline of the Cuban Republic* (New York, 1964).

Economic aspects of the Revolution are discussed in D. Seers (ed.), *Cuba: the economic and social revolution* (Chapel Hill, 1964); J. Alvarez Diaz (ed.), *A study on Cuba* (Coral Gables, 1965); C. Mesa-Lago, *The Labor Sector and Socialist Distribution in Cuba* (New York, 1968); E. Boorstein, *The Economic Transformation of Cuba* (New York, 1969) and L. Huberman and P. Sweezy, *Socialism in Cuba* (New York, 1969). The works of R. Dumont represent the views of a French adviser of the Cuban Government who has become increasingly critical of the Revolution's economic policy – *La réforme agraire en Cuba* (Paris, 1964); *Cuba, socialisme et développement* (Paris, 1964) and *Cuba est-il socialiste?* (Paris, 1970).

Relations between Cuba and the United States are discussed in R. F. Smith, *The United States and Cuba: business and diplomacy, 1917–1960* (New York, 1960); R. Scheer and M. Zeitlin, *Cuba: an American tragedy* (London, 1964); W. A. Williams, *The United States, Cuba and Castro* (New York, 1962) and J. Plank (ed.), *Cuba and the United States: long term perspectives* (Washington, 1967).

On the missile crisis see H. Pachter, *Collision Course: the Cuban missile crisis and co-existence* (London, 1963) and E. Abel, *The Missiles of October* for a day-by-day account. A version of the Bay of Pigs fiasco by one of its leaders is H. Johnson, *The Bay of Pigs* (New York, 1964) but more perceptive is Tad Szulc and K. E. Meyer, *The Cuban Invasion* (New York, 1962).

Guevara is best studied through his own writings which have been collected by J. Gerassi in *Venceremos: speeches* and writings of *Che Guevara* (London, 1968). There are selections by J. Mallin, *Che Guevara on Revolution* (Miami, 1969) and R. E. Bonachea and N. P. Valdes, *Che Guevara: selected works* (Cambridge, Mass., 1969). Particular works, separately printed, include *Reminiscences of the Revolutionary War* (London, 1968); *Guerrilla Warfare* (London, 1968). The account of his last campaign in Bolivia is in his *Bolivian Diary* (London, 1968) and the fuller edition by D. James, *The Complete Bolivian Diaries of Che Guevara and other captured documents* (London, 1968) (including three accounts by others in the group). L. I. González and G. A. Sánchez Salazar, *The Great Rebel: Che Guevara in Bolivia* (New York, 1969) is a sympathetic Bolivian account. The fullest biography is D. James, *Guevara: a biography* (New York, 1970); and on his early life R. Rojo, *My Friend Che* (New York, 1968). A good biography in Spanish is H. Gambini, *El Che Guevara* (Buenos Aires, 1968). A Sinclair, *Guevara* (London, 1970) is a laudatory account of his ideas and significance. See also M. Ebon, *Che: the making of a legend* (New York, 1969). For Jose Marti, the nineteenth century inspiration for the Revolution see R. B. Gray, *Jose Marti: Cuban patriot* (Gainesville, 1962).

Dominican Republic

The difficult task of writing on the Trujillo regime has been attempted by R. D. Crassweller in *Trujillo: the life and times of a Caribbean dictator* (New York, 1966), G. E. Ornes, *Trujillo: little Caesar of the Caribbean* (New York, 1948) and A. Espaillat, *Trujillo: the last Caesar* (Chicago, 1963). The democratic-Left view of the post-Trujillo period is represented by J. Bosch in *The Unfinished Experiment* (New York, 1965). The events of 1965 are detailed in D. Kuzman, *Santo Domingo: revolt of the damned* (New York, 1965) and J. B. Martin, *Overtaken by Events: the Dominican crisis from the fall of Trujillo to the civil war* (New York, 1966). T. Szulc, *Dominican Diary* (New York, 1965) is a day-by-day account of the intervention. The most detailed analyses are by H. J. Wiarda, *Dictatorship and Development: the methods of* control in the Dominican Republic (Gainesville, 1968) and *Dominican Republic: nation in transition* (New York, 1969).

Ecuador

A good short introduction is L. Linke, *Ecuador* (3rd ed., London, 1960). G. Blanksten, *Ecuador: constitutions and caudillos* (Berkeley, 1951), is the only available analysis of Ecuadorian politics apart from M. Needler's specific *Anatomy of a Coup d'état: Ecuador, 1963* (Washington, 1964). The boundary dispute with Peru is covered in D. H. Zook, *Zaramilla-Marañon: the Ecuadorian-Peruvian dispute* (New York, 1964).

Haiti

R. W. Logan, *Haiti and the Dominican Republic* (London, 1960) is a useful introduction. J. G. Leyburn, *The Haitian People* (New Haven, 1941) is crucial for an understanding of Haitian society. The difficult problem of writing on Duvalier has been attempted by B. Diedrich and A. Burt in *Papa Doc: the truth about Haiti today* (New York, 1969). See also L. F. Manigot, *Haiti of the Sixties: object of international concern* (Washington, 1964). On the economy see W. S. Gates, *Essays on Aspects of the Economic Development of Haiti* (Williamstown, 1959).

Mexico

The detailed coverage of the Revolution from 1910–17 is in marked contrast to the paucity of works on the later period. C. Cumberland, *Mexico: the struggle for modernity* (New York, 1968), is a standard general history, stronger on social and economic than political aspects. H. F. Cline, *Mexico: from revolution to evolution, 1940–1960* (Oxford, 1962), and his *The United States and Mexico* (Harvard, 1953) are factually useful. S. Ross (ed.), *Is the Mexican Revolution Dead?* (New York, 1966) is a useful introduction to the debate about the nature of the Revolution. An important interpretative

167

work by an economist with a historical slant is R. Vernon, *The Dilemma of Mexico's Development* (Harvard, 1963). An attempt to estimate the extent of social change by quantitative means is J. W. Wilkie, *The Mexican Revolution: federal expenditure and social change since 1910* (2nd revised ed., Berkeley, 1970). The same author's *Mexico visto en el siglo XX* (Mexico, 1969) is an interesting example of oral history techniques applied to prominent politicians in contrast to Oscar Lewis's analyses in depth of marginal groups in *The Children of Sanchez* (Harmondsworth, 1964) and *Pedro Martinez* (London, 1964). González Casanova, *Democracy in Mexico* (New York, 1970) is the best analysis of society. O. Lewis's chapter on Mexico in L. Bryson (ed.), *Social Change in Latin America Today* (New York, 1960) is useful.

Politics

A useful overview is F. Brandenburg, *The Making of Modern Mexico* (New York, 1964). General political science accounts are R. E. Scott, *Mexican Government in Transition* (Urbana, 1964). See also the chapter on Mexico in Verba and Almond, *The Civic Culture* (Boston, 1963). W. P. Tucker, *The Mexican Government Today* (Minnesota, 1957). is detailed and factual. L. V. Padgett, *The Mexican Political System* (Boston, 1966), is a useful introduction. L. S. Graham, *Politics in a Mexican Community* (Gainesville, 1968), studies politics at the local level.

For the Left see K. Schmitt, *Communism in Mexico* (Austin, 1964), and R. P. Millon, *Mexican Marxist: Vicente Lombardo Toledano* (Berkeley, 1960). For the Castroist MLN see D. T. Garza, 'Factionalism in the Mexican Left: the frustration of the MLN', in *Western Political Quarterly, 17(3)* September 1964, and for the 1968 student disturbances the collection of documents in R. Ramirez (ed.), *El movimiento estudiantil de Mexico: julio – diciembre de 1968* (Mexico, 1969).

Economy

Considerable attention has been paid to Mexico's complex mixed economy. R. Vernon (ed.), *Public Policy and Private*

Enterprise in Mexico (Cambridge, Mass., 1964) and W. P. Glade and C. W. Anderson, *The Political Economy of Mexico* (Madison, 1963), examine the interplay of the public and private sectors. Mexican economists discuss the economy in E. Pérez López *et al., Mexico's Recent Economic Growth: the Mexican view,* tr. M. Urquidi (Austin, 1967). M. Singer, *Growth, Equality and the Mexican Experience* (Austin, 1970) explores the relationship between development and equality. For the political implications of development see R. D. Honsen, *The Politics of Mexican Development* (Baltimore, 1970). The process of import-substitution industrialisation is examined by T. King in *Mexico: industrialization and trade policies since 1940* (Cambridge, 1970). The key oil industry is examined in A. J. Bermudez, *The Mexican National Petroleum Industry* (Stanford, 1963), and the steel industry in W. E. Cole, *Steel and Economic Growth in Mexico* (Austin, 1967).

There is no detailed study in depth of the striking advances made in agriculture. On agrarian reform and the land problem the standard works, now dated, are N. Whetten, *Rural Mexico* (Chicago, 1948), and E. N. Simpson, *The Ejido: Mexico's way out* (New York, 1937). Crucial for the agrarian myth is J. Womack's superb *Zapata and the Mexican Revolution* (London, 1970).

Paraguay

G. Pendle, *Paraguay* (3rd ed., London, 1967), is a short introduction. H. G. Warren, *Paraguay: an informal history* (Norman, 1949), is the only history in English. P. H. Lewis, *The Politics of Exile: Paraguay's Febrerista Party* (Chapel Hill, 1968) is the only detailed political analysis. On the economy see J. Pincus, *The Economy of Paraguay* (New York, 1968).

Peru

The only history in English is F. B. Pike, *The Modern History of Peru* (London, 1967). An introductory survey is R. J. Owens, *Peru* (London, 1963). More detailed is R. Marrett, *Peru* (London, 1969). F. Bourricaud, *Power and*

Society in Contemporary Peru (London, 1970) is an authoritative and perceptive analysis. See also M. S. Larson, *Social Stratification in Peru* (Berkeley, 1969) and R. Gomez, *The Peruvian Administrative System* (New York, 1969). J. L. Payne, *Labor and Politics in Peru: the system of political bargaining* (New Haven, 1965) breaks new ground. E. Dew, *Politics in the Altiplano* (Austin, 1969) is a regional study of politics in the Puno area. A useful political analysis is C. A. Astiz, *Pressure Groups and Power Elites* (Ithaca, 1969). There is no good study of Haya de la Torre and Apra – H. Kantor, *Ideology and Programme of the Peruvian Aprista Party* (Berkeley, 1953) is limited to ideas. G. Hilliker, *The politics of reform in Peru* (Baltimore 1970) deals with APRA. For relations with the United States see J. C. Cary, *Peru and the United States, 1900–1962* (Notre Dame, 1964). The land problem is discussed in T. R. Ford, *Man and Land in Peru* (Gainesville, 1955) and A. J. Coutu and R. A. King, *The Agricultural Development of Peru* (New York, 1969). An interesting analysis of the 1968 Revolution is J. Cotler, 'Crisis política y populismo en el Peru', in *Estudios Internacionales* (Santiago de Chile, no. 12, Jan. 1970).

Puerto Rico

The standard work is G. K. Lewis, *Puerto Rico: freedom and power in the Caribbean* (London, 1963). Short introductions are E. B. Lockett, *The Puerto Rican Problem* (New York, 1964) and E. P. Hanson, *Puerto Rico: ally for progress* (New York, 1962). On politics see R. W. Anderson, *Party Politics in Puerto Rico* (Stanford, 1965) and more specific, A. Liebman, *The Politics of Puerto Rican Students* (Austin, 1970). For society see M. M. Tumin with A. S. Feldman, *Social Class and Social Change in Puerto Rico* (Princeton, 1961), and H. Wells, *The Modernisation of Puerto Rico: a political study of changing values and institutions* (Cambridge, Mass., 1969).

Uruguay

General introductions are G. Pendle, *Uruguay* (London,

1965); R. H. Fitzgibbon, *Uruguay: portrait of a democracy* (New Brunswick, 1954); M. Alisky, *Uruguay: a contemporary survey* (New York, 1969). Detailed examinations of the complex political system are P. Taylor, *The Government and politics of Uruguay* (New Orleans, 1960), and H. Pühle, *Politik in Uruguay* (Hannover, 1969).

Venezuela

A general history is G. Moron, *A History of Venezuela,* tr. J. Street (London, 1964). A short but useful introduction is E. Liewen, *Venezuela* (London, 1961). Politics since 1958 are sympathetically discussed in R. J. Alexander, *The Venezuelan Democratic Revolution* (New Brunswick, 1964), whilst J. D. Martz has written the most detailed analysis of a Latin American party in English in his *Acción Democrática: the evolution of a modern political party in Venezuela* (Princeton, 1966). The Left has been studied in R. J. Alexander, *The Communist Party of Venezuela* (Stanford, 1969). A fundamental account of the pre-1958 period, still untranslated is R. Betancourt, *Política y petroleo* (Mexico, 1956). F. Bonilla and J. Silva Michelena (eds), *A Strategy for Research in Social Policy (The politics of change in Venezuela)* (Boston, 1967) is an important political-science analysis. The economy is discussed in IRBD, *The Economic Development of Venezuela* (Baltimore, 1961) and the development of the Venezuelan Oriente is treated in J. Friedmann, *Regional Development: a case study of Venezuela* (Boston, 1966).

On petroleum see E. Liewen, *Petroleum in Venezuela* (Berkeley, 1954).

The Non-Spanish Caribbean

J. Parry and P. M. Sherlock, *A Short History of the West Indies* (London, 1956), is a useful overall introduction to Caribbean history as is E. Williams, D. A. G. Waddell, *The West Indies and the Guianas* (New York, 1967), short. Two comprehensive surveys are Sir H. Mitchell

Caribbean Patterns: a political and economic study of the contemporary Caribbean (London, 1967), and G. K. Lewis, *The Growth of the Modern West Indies* (London, 1968). A series of publications covering various aspects of the Caribbean have been edited by A. Curtis Wilgus and published by the University of Florida, one of which may be noted here – *The Caribbean: British, Dutch, French, United States* (Gainsville, 1963). For US and British interest see M. Proudfoot, *Britain and the United States in the Caribbean* (London, 1954).

The West Indies Federation is covered in D. Lowenthal (ed.), *The West Indies Federation* (New York, 1961) and J. Mordecai, *The West Indies: the federal negotiations* (London, 1968). For the social structure see M. G. Smith, *The Plural Society in the British West Indies* (Berkeley, 1965). Racial problems are discussed in H. Hoetink, *The Two Variants in Caribbean Race Relations* (London, 1967), and R. G. Coulthard, *Race and Colour in Caribbean Literature* (New York, 1962).

Coverage of contemporary Jamaica is not as good as for earlier periods. See W. Bell, *Jamaican Leaders: political attitude in a new nation* (Berkeley, 1964), and K. Norris, *Jamaica, the search for an identity* (London, 1962).

For Trinidad and Tobago see E. Williams, *History of the People of Trinidad and Tobago* (London, 1964), as well as his autobiography *Inward Hunger: the education of a prime minister* (London, 1969). I. Oxaal, *Black Intellectuals come to Power: the rise of creole nationalism in Trinidad and Tobago* (Cambridge, Mass., 1968).

For migration problems see R. B. Davison, *West Indian Migrants: social and economic facts of migration from the West Indies* (New York, 1962).

For Guyana see R. T. Smith, *British Guiana* (London, 1962). L. A. Despres, *Cultural Pluralism and Nationalist Politics in British Guiana* (Chicago, 1967), is relevant to wider Caribbean issues. For a leftist view see P. Reno, *The Ordeal of British Guiana* (New York, 1964). For Jagan's views see Cheddi Jagan, *The West on Trial* (London, 1966), and for Burnham, Forbes Burnham, *A Destiny to Mould: selected discourses by the Prime Minister of Guyana* (London, 1970). There are few good studies of the smaller islands but see C. O'Loughlin, *Economic and Political Change in the Leeward and Windward Islands* (New Haven, 1968), and for politics in Grenada, A. W. Singham, *The Hero and the Crowd in a Colonial Polity* (New Haven, 1968).

For Surinam see A. L. Gastmann, *The Politics of Surinam and the Netherlands Antilles* (Rio Pedras, 1968). For the French Antilles and French Guiana see J. Pouquet, *Les Antilles françaises* (Paris, 1952); D. Guerin, *The West Indies and their Future* (London, 1961), and S. T. McCloy, *The Negro in the French West Indies* (Lexington, 1966).

General

Some of the problems mentioned in the Introduction to this section are discussed in C. Wagley (ed.), *Social Science Research in Latin America* (New York, 1964) and M. Diegues and Bryce Wood, *Social Science in Latin America* (New York, 1967). For a leftist critique see J. Petras, 'U.S.-Latin American Studies: a critical assessment' in *Science and Society,* vol. 32, 1968.

Journals

The most useful journal in English consisting mainly of bibliographical essays is the *Latin American Research Review* (University of Texas, 1965–). *The Hispanic American Report* (Stanford University, 1948–64) is invaluable for the period covered. A number of journals specialising in Latin American affairs contain useful articles on contemporary history – *Inter-American Economic Affairs* (Washington, 1947–); *Journal of Inter-American Studies* (University of Miami, 1959–); the *Hispanic American Historical Review* (Duke University, 1918–); *Journal of Latin American Studies* (Cambridge University, 1969–). A good bibliography of works in English is R. A. Humphreys, *Latin American History: a guide to the literature in English* (London, 1958). *The Handbook of Latin American Studies*

(Harvard UP, 1936–51; Univ. of Florida, 1951–) is invaluable. Among journals in Spanish the following are important – *Aportes* (Paris, 1966–); *America Latina* (Rio, 1957– , published by UNESCO, articles in Portuguese, Spanish and English); *Revista Latinoamericana de Sociología* (Buenos Aires, 1965–); *Foro Internacional* (Mexico, 1960–) and *Cuadernos Americanos* (Mexico, 1941–); *Estudios Internacionales* (Santiago de Chile, 1967–).

Among newspapers the following should be noted: *Le Monde, New York Times, Financial Times*. For Cuba the weekly edition of the official *Granma* in English is dull but crucial.

The mimeographed publications of the UN agency, the Economic Commission for Latin America (Santiago de Chile), are invaluable. Also useful are those of the Organization of American States (Washington).

An invaluable guide to article literature is the *International Political Science Abstracts* (Oxford, 1951–).

There is an enormous unpublished dissertation literature in the United States.

8

South East Asia

Ruth T. McVey

As a geopolitical region, South East Asia is something of an artificial construct. Its debut as a unit was largely the result of its designation as a theatre of operations during the second world war, and for some time thereafter there was little agreement as to whether it was a useful concept for scholarly purposes and, if so, just which countries it should be considered to include. In the end, political events seem to have determined its general acceptance even as they did its origination: the post-war substitution of American for European influence east of India and south of China, the rise of Communist Chinese power, and the fact that all of the South East Asian states have been weak and/or unstable meant that considerable attention was paid to the region as a 'trouble spot', particularly by American writers. This, however, has not meant that it has become a more coherent unit, and efforts to discuss its problems on an across-the-board basis have seldom been entirely successful. The considerable linguistic and historical differences separating most countries of the area means that knowledge of one South East Asian state is of restricted use in dealing with another; as a result, the 'country expert' who attempts to deal with the whole area is likely to produce an unbalanced work. Nor are there as yet enough comparable studies of individual countries to make it easy for the generalist to synthesise on the basis of secondary materials.

A few subjects thought to be particularly 'topical' have been the subject of studies for nearly all countries of the area.

Others have been treated according to the accessibility of the country, the interests of the one or two senior scholars specialising in its affairs, and its involvement in foreign-aid efforts. Thus Malaysia, Thailand, Burma and the Philippines of the 1950s have been the subject of numerous studies of public administration, but there has been scarcely any treatment of that topic for Indonesia or for post-1962 Burma. The steadily expanding number of scholars working on South East Asia, the diversification of their interests, the gradual development of persons with expert knowledge of the language, culture, and history of more than one South East Asian country, and most importantly the emergence of highly trained local scholars who direct their work to an international audience will undoubtedly lead to an improvement in this situation, but for the time being the reader will have to pick his way through studies of rather uneven quality and frequently limited scope.

General

The most important survey of South East Asian history is D. G. E. Hall's *A History of South East Asia* (3rd ed., London, 1968), which is particularly good for pre-colonial and early colonial periods. For the nineteenth and early twentieth centuries, John Cady's *Southeast Asia: Its Historical Development* (New York, 1964) is sometimes more useful. Both of these are massive conventional histories, and both fade in their coverage as they approach the middle of the present century. The reader who wishes an introduction limited to the presentation of basic themes may prefer Brian Harrison, *South-East Asia, a Short History* (3rd ed., New York, 1966); it is a small but very compact and well-written work, and provides a very good interpretative outline. Two other works, intended primarily for university students following a course in South East Asian history, are John Bastin and Harry Benda, *A History of Modern Southeast Asia* (Englewood Cliffs, 1968), which is concerned with the establishment, effect and decline of the European presence; and Harry Benda and John Larkin, *The World of Southeast Asia* (New York, 1967), which provides a good selection of documents illustrating South East Asian life and events from earliest times to the present.

Of the more specialised works on South East Asian history, we should mention J. S. Furnivall's *Colonial Policy and Practice* (2nd ed., New York, 1956), which contrasts Dutch techniques of rule in Indonesia with those employed by the British in Burma; it is a classic investigation which remains valuable for its discussion of the consequences which the styles of domination had for the social structure of the subject countries. The economic course and consequences of colonialism have been treated in C. D. Cowan (ed.), *Economic Development of South East Asia* (London, 1964), which contains essays on the economic history of Thailand, Indonesia, and Malaya, in addition to general articles on Britain's South East Asian role. Some of the individual papers are rather specialised for introductory reading, but the whole adds up to a cogent portrayal of the lasting effects of the colonial experience. Finally, attempts by the major South East Asian countries to change their situation since independence are dealt with individually in Frank Golay (ed.), *Underdevelopment and Economic Nationalism in Southeast Asia* (Ithaca, 1969).

The 1942–5 Japanese occupation of South East Asia was influential in the development of ideology and political institutions in most countries there, as well as for breaking the back of colonial rule. The reader looking for a general background on Japanese policies can refer to F. C. Jones, *Japan's New Order in East Asia, 1937–1945* (London, 1954) and Willard H. Elsbree, *Japan's Role in Southeast Asian Nationalist Movements, 1940–1945* (Cambridge, Mass., 1953). As both of these were written when the study of noncolonial South East Asian history was in its early days, their treatment of local reactions to Japanese rule is fairly unsophisticated. A much better idea of this aspect can be gained from Josef Silverstein (ed.), *Southeast Asia in World War II: Four Essays* (New Haven, 1967), which provides studies by country specialists on Burma (the origins and role of the Burma Independence Army), Indonesia (the relationship of the Japanese style to Javanese traditions and youthful revolutionary sentiments), and the Philippines (collaboration by the Filipino oligarchic elite), plus a general essay on Japan's role by the editor.

Of considerable value as an introduction to the problems facing South East Asia after the second world war is Cora Dubois, *Social Forces in Southeast Asia* (2nd ed., Cambridge, Mass., 1959). It is a brief and cogent essay, dating from the immediate post-war years but delineating problems that have been of continuing importance for South East Asian development. The best general source for South East Asian history since 1945 remains George McT. Kahin (ed.), *Government and Politics of Southeast Asia* (2nd ed., Ithaca, 1964). This provides a survey of the historical background, post-colonial history, and political problems of the nations of the area; each was done by a country specialist, and the imposition of a standard format has meant that common themes receive treatment in a comparable manner. The essays are written to a solid standard, and they provide useful bibliographies. However, the essays do not go beyond the early 1960s, and for more recent information on the rapidly changing politics of the region the reader should make use of journal material, which can be conveniently located via the annual bibliographies put out by the American *Journal of Asian Studies*; in these, a section is devoted to South East Asia, and this is then treated country-by-country. A very useful bibliography is Kennedy Tregonning, *South East Asia. A Critical Bibliography* (Tucson: University of Arizona Press, 1969); this is general in scope, but has a preference for history and the social sciences. It also lists other, more specialised bibliographies on South East Asia and its countries. For annual reviews of political events in South East Asia, see *Asian Survey,* which usually carries such articles early in the year; *Current History* also includes reviews of events, but not so regularly. *Far Eastern Economic Review* is perhaps the best source for generally good coverage of current developments.

Certain specialised topics which have been deemed important from the viewpoint of South East Asia's stability and development have received particular attention from post-war scholarship. One of these is the position of the Chinese minority, on which a number of country studies have been written. For the region as a whole, the most complete study is Victor Purcell, *The Chinese in Southeast Asia* (London, 1965), a historical survey that provides a good overall discussion but is best in its treatment of Malaysia.

Communism has been another favoured topic; an early study is Frank N. Trager (ed.), *Marxism in Southeast Asia* (London, 1960). The essays on Burma, Thailand, and Vietnam remain of interest, especially for the early history of left-wing movements. J. H. Brimmel, *Communism in South-East Asia* (London, 1959), has a good account of the communist movement in Malaya, but otherwise the discussion is weak. The most up-to-date collection, which provides essays of good standard for Burma, Malaysia, the Philippines, Indonesia, Laos, and Vietnam, is Robert Scalapino (ed.), *The Communist Revolution in Asia* (Englewood Cliffs, 1965).

The international relations of South East Asia is a subject Western writers have naturally found of concern. So far the best general study is Peter Lyon, *War and Peace in South-East Asia* (London, 1969). It attempts to provide a general background on the South East Asian countries, to describe the relationship of major outside powers to them, and then to analyse their position with regard to the great-power struggle. So much ground cannot be covered in a short work without loss of depth, but it is a very useful introduction to the problems of the area's diplomacy, and its judgment is always cool and considered. Charles McLane's *Soviet Strategies in Southeast Asia* (Princeton, 1966) is an excellent treatment of its subject; it limits itself, however, to the period before Stalin's death in 1953. Studies of the American role include Russell Fifield's *The United States and Southeast Asia* (New York, 1963), a detailed but unenquiring account; John Montgomery, *The Politics of Foreign Aid: American Experience in Southeast Asia* (New York, 1962), a critical discussion of the effect of US economic assistance programs in Burma, Thailand, and South Vietnam; and Melvin Gurtov, *Southeast Asia Tomorrow* (Baltimore, 1970), a study debat-

179

ing the 'domino theory' basis on which the United States justified its military role in South East Asia.

Burma

There are a number of good histories of Burma and several
useful accounts of the parliamentary period which comprised
the first decade of its independence; but there is almost no
monographic material on developments since General Ne
Win's seizure of power in 1962. The army's attempt to radically restructure Burmese society and economy makes this
period of Ne Win's rule in many ways the most interesting
of all, and one can only hope that it will soon be possible
for a proper study of its effects to be made.

For historical background there are two good studies:
D. G. E. Hall's brief *Burma* (3rd ed., London, 1960), and
John Cady's detailed *A History of Modern Burma* (Ithaca,
1958). Frank Trager, *Burma – From Kingdom to Republic*
(New York, 1966), places more emphasis on developments
following independence in 1948 and is particularly concerned
with Burma's 'neutralist' foreign policy. Richard Butwell has
written a study of Burmese parliamentary democracy in the
form of a biography of its most prominent leader: *U Nu of
Burma* (Stanford, 1963), while Hugh Tinker, *The Union of
Burma: a Study of the First Years of Independence* (3rd ed.,
London, 1961) surveys social and economic as well as political features of the country. A very different approach to
these rather staid studies of post-independence Burma is to
be found in Lucian Pye, *Politics, Personality and Nation
Building: Burma's Search for Identity* (New York, 1958), a
psychological investigation of the attitudes of members of
the Burmese ruling elite in the tradition of the American
behaviourist school of political science. Its conclusions do
not seem to be firmly based on evidence, but its arguments
are stimulating and it is one of the more notable products of
its genre.

The 'neutralist' foreign policy which Burma has pursued
since independence has attracted the attention of a number of
students; in addition to the above-mentioned work by Trager,

the reader should consult William C. Johnstone, *Burma's Foreign Policy: a Study in Neutralism* (Cambridge, Mass., 1963), which deals primarily with the late 1950s.

The post-independence Burmese economy has been treated in Louis J. Walinsky, *Economic Development in Burma, 1951–1960* (New York, 1962), written by a former American economic adviser and primarily concerned with planning and foreign aid. In addition, Everett E. Hagen, *The Economic Development of Burma* (Washington, 1956) provides a brief, stimulating analysis of the social and cultural problems affecting Burma's failure to achieve economic 'take-off'. Finally, those interested in the dynamics of Burma's economy should refer to Cheng Siok-hwa, *The Rice Industry of Burma: 1852–1940* (London, 1968), a very solid study of the development of the country's major industry, the expansion of which had a profound impact on the country's social structure.

Buddhism has played a major role in Burmese national development, and a very readable account of its role may be found in D. Smith, *Religion and Politics in Burma* (Princeton, 1965). This provides a historical survey of the political role of the monkhood but is primarily interested in the utilisation of the religious issue by U Nu's government. Those interested in a discussion of the role of Buddhism among the common people should turn to Manning Nash, *The Golden Road to Modernity: Village Life in Contemporary Burma* (New York, 1965), an anthropological study of two Upper Burma villages which stresses religious and other factors affecting government efforts to introduce new institutions. For the contrasting lifestyle and political structure of Burma's hill peoples, whose resistance to control by the Burman majority has been a major theme of post-independence Burmese history, see Edmund R. Leach, *Political Systems of Highland Burma: A Study of Kachin Social Structure* (London, 1954), which is an anthropological classic. The immigrant Indian minority, which played an economic role analogous to that of the Chinese in other South East Asian countries and which was subjected to severe harassment in the post-colonial period, is treated in Usha Mahajani, *The Role of Indian Minorities in Burma and Malaya* (Bombay, 1960).

Unlike other South East Asian leaders, Burma's have produced a number of valuable memoirs and biographies. They include Ba U, *My Burma: The Autobiography of a President* (New York, 1958); Ba Maw, *Breakthrough in Burma: Memoires of a Revolutionary 1939–1946* (New Haven, 1968); Thakin Nu (U Nu), *Burma Under the Japanese* (New York, 1954). In addition the Burmese jurist Maung Maung has edited a collection of remembrances of *Aung San of Burma* (The Hague, 1962), which brings that leader of the independence struggle vividly to life.

Indochina

For historical background, a solid study is provided by John Cady, *The Roots of French Imperialism in Eastern Asia* (Ithaca, 1954); it carries the discussion of colonial activities to the 1870s. Even more valuable is Milton Osborne, *The French Presence in Cochinchina and Cambodia: Rule and Response* (*1859–1905*) (Ithaca, 1970), which contrasts the styles of colonial domination in the two countries and their effect on local social structures. For a general introduction to the condition of the region at the end of the colonial period, see Virginia Thompson, *Indo-China* (London, 1937). Its economics have been described in two substantial works, Pierre Gourou, *Land Utilization in French Indochina* (New York, 1945), and Charles Robequain, *The Economic Development of French Indo-China* (London, 1944). Of the numerous works dealing with the decolonisation process, the best discussions of the area as a whole are to be found in Donald Lancaster, *The Emancipation of French Indochina* (London, 1961), and Ellen Hammer, *The Struggle for Indochina 1940–1955* (2nd ed., Stanford, 1966).

Laos

For Laos and Cambodia we can, unfortunately for those who wish to really find out something about them, be brief indeed.

182

The reader should look first of all to the treatment of these states in the works on Indochina cited above. The best history of Laos is Paul le Boulanger, *Histoire du Laos français* (Paris, 1930, reprinted 1969), which does not take the country's history beyond the establishment of French control in the nineteenth century. Other works have been overwhelmingly concerned with the recent war, and in their accounts the Laotians play a minor role in the struggle of international giants: Sissouk Na Champassak, *Storm Over Laos* (New York, 1961), is an anti-Communist Laotian version; while Arthur Dommen, *Conflict in Laos* (New York, 1964) is perhaps the best Western journalistic investigation. Bernard Fall, *Anatomy of a Crisis* (New York, 1969) provides a detailed and balanced discussion of the critical 1960–1 period of the Laotian struggle. For a general introduction to the non-military aspects of Laos, see Frank Lebar *et al., Laos: Its Peoples, Its Society, Its Culture* (New York, 1960), a 'handbook' which provides a useful general description and bibliography. Almost the only English-language writer on Laotian non-military affairs is Joel M. Halpern, who has produced a number of studies of Laotian society; of these, the most useful for contemporary history is *Government, Politics and Social Structure in Laos* (New Haven, 1964).

Cambodia

A survey of Cambodia's history may be found in Jean Imbert, *Histoire des Institutions Khmers* (Phnom Penh, Annales de la Faculté de Droit dc Phnom Penh, 1961, 2 vols.). The important period of 1945–60 has been treated in Philippe Preschez, *Essai sur la démocratie du Cambodge* (Paris, 1961); it is principally concerned with the emergence of parliamentary institutions and their subsequent eclipse by a revived royal absolutism. The former Cambodian ruler Prince Norodom Sihanouk has provided a highly personal history of the royal institution emphasising the pre-colonial period and decolonisation: *La monarchie cambodgienne et la croisade royale pour l'indépendance* (Phnom Penh, 1961). Sihanouk's ideas and personality are also vividly revealed in

John Armstrong's collection of his speeches, *Sihanouk Speaks* (New York, 1964).

In the post-colonial period, and prior to the overthrow of Sihanouk in 1970, Western scholarly attention was largely focused on that ruler's attempts to keep his country from entanglement in the Vietnamese and Laotian wars; his efforts have been discussed in two good books: Michael Leifer, *Cambodia, the Search for Security* (New York, 1967), and Roger Smith, *Cambodia's Foreign Policy* (Ithaca, 1965). Almost nothing of importance has been done on contemporary Cambodian internal affairs; an exception is W. E. Willmott, *The Chinese in Cambodia* (Vancouver, 1967), a sociological study of that important immigrant minority which also provides substantial information of the character and recent history of the Khmer ethnic majority.

Vietnam

In contrast to the other Indochina states, a great deal has been written about contemporary Vietnam. But if we look beyond mere quantity the contrast is less striking. Most of the writings concern the details of war; it is not so easy to discover in them the society that produced the fighting. The study which provides perhaps the best historical introduction to the problems of contemporary Vietnam is Ralph Smith, *Viet-nam and the West* (London, 1968); it is a well-written, compact, and balanced discussion of the reaction of Vietnamese society to the European (and later American) presence. For the history of Vietnam in the crucial years between the fall of France and the end of the first Indochina War, see John McAlister, *Vietnam: The Origins of Revolution* (New York, 1969). Jean Lacouture, *Vietnam Between Two Truces* (New York, 1966), explores the period of the Ngo Dinh Diem regime in South Vietnam in the 1950s; another good brief account of this regime is Robert Scigliano, *South Vietnam – Nation Under Stress* (Boston, 1963). Bernard Fall, *The Two Vietnams* (New York, 1963), is a detailed and impartial survey of the northern and southern regimes of the 1950s.

To date, the southern regimes since Diem have been less well described. Bernard Fall's *Vietnam Witness* (New York, 1967), is a moving account of South Vietnamese history to 1966 as experienced by the closest student of the Vietnam War. Fall's work is particularly good on aspects of military history, and his sceptical vision is a welcome contrast to the quick enthusiasms and ideological certainties of many of the other commentators. Dennis Duncanson, *Government and Revolution in Vietnam* (London, 1968), considers the development of the South Vietnamese regimes primarily from the security angle, attempting to delineate the reasons for the government's failure to achieve firm control of the populace.

Of the numerous books on the nature of the war in Vietnam, one of the very best is still Paul Mus, *Vietnam, Sociologie d'une guerre* (Paris, 1952); both its language and its argumentation are extremely complex, however, and the reader whose French is not fluent may prefer to use John McAlister and Paul Mus, *The Vietnamese and Their Revolution* (New York, 1970), a very much abridged and rearranged translation. The ideas which have inspired the revolutionists have been published in various editions, of which one of the most useful is Bernard Fall (ed.), *Ho Chi Minh on Revolution* (New York, 1967), a collection of Ho's writings from 1920 to 1966. An account of that leader's career may be found in Jean Lacouture, *Ho Chi Minh, a Political Biography* (New York, 1968). The reader should also consult Vo Nguyen Giap, *People's War, People's Army* (Hanoi, 1961), and Truong Chinh, *The Resistance Will Win* (Hanoi, 1960), key theoretical contributions on the nature of the Vietnamese struggle. Douglas Pike, *Viet Cong* (Cambridge, Mass., 1966) is a detailed study of the organisation of the National Liberation Front; its argument is often unconvincing, but it provides invaluable documentation. Robert Sansom's *The Economics of Insurgency in the Mekong Delta of Vietnam* (Cambridge, Mass., 1970) is the best study of the social dynamics of the war to appear so far; it is particularly interesting for its discussion of the relation of the land question to insurrection.

The American military involvement to 1966 is recounted in detail in George McT. Kahin and John Lewis, *The United*

States in Vietnam (New York, 1967). A very useful collection of writings on the same subject, seeing it in the broader context of American foreign policy, is Marcus Raskin and Bernard Fall (eds), *The Viet-Nam Reader* (New York, 1965).

For the other half of Vietnam, Bernard Fall described the first years of Communist government in *The Viet-Minh Regime: Government and Administration in the Democratic Republic of Vietnam* (Ithaca, 1956); there is a fuller and more recent account in French: *Le Viet Minh: République Démocratique du Viet-Nam, 1945–1960* (Paris, 1960). A political and economic survey is provided by P. J. Honey (ed.), *North Vietnam Today: Profile of a Communist Satellite* (New York, 1962); the articles are not all as strongly unsympathetic as the title indicates. The Democratic Republic's view of the war is presented in Patrick J. McGarvey (ed.), *Visions of Victory* (Stanford, 1969), which translates and analyses North Vietnamese military writings of the 1960s. North Vietnam's foreign policy has been discussed at length only in connection with the Sino-Soviet dispute, and the best study of this is Donald Zagoria, *The Vietnam Triangle: Moscow, Peking, Hanoi* (New York, 1967).

Indonesia

Indonesia differs from the rest of South East Asia in having a fairly substantial body of writings dealing with the contemporary period. It is understandable that the country has attracted more students: it is far the largest nation in the area, it has been relatively open to academic investigators, and it has more or less constantly been a 'trouble spot' and thus an object of international attention. A very good general introduction is John Legge's *Indonesia* (Englewood Cliffs, 1964), which is especially useful for its discussion of the basic assumptions of the major Western studies of Indonesian history and politics. For a more detailed survey, see Ruth McVey (ed.), *Indonesia* (New Haven, 1964), which contains essays by specialists on history, politics, economics, culture, and the arts. Probably the best brief narrative of Indonesian history before 1945 is to be found in the opening sections of

George McT. Kahin, *Nationalism and Revolution* (2nd ed., Ithaca, 1961); the main concern of this work is the revolution of 1945–1948, of which it is the standard account, but its discussion of the environment which produced the independence movement is very compact and of excellent analytical quality. The political development of Indonesian Islam is best followed through Harry J. Benda, *The Crescent and the Rising Sun* (The Hague, 1958), which is particularly devoted to the Japanese occupation of 1942–5 but also provides a useful history of the development of Indonesian Islam in the colonial period.

The parliamentary period of 1950–57 has been dealt with in Herbert Feith, *The Decline of Indonesian Constitutional Democracy* (Ithaca, 1962), a massive study which profoundly affected subsequent analyses of Indonesian affairs. Nothing approaching its stature has yet been written on subsequent periods. However, the excellent selection of speeches and articles by Indonesians translated in Herbert Feith and Lance Castles, *Indonesian Political Thinking* (Ithaca, 1970) includes material covering the Guided Democracy regime of 1959–65. A good specialised study which includes a treatment of the initial Guided Democracy years is Donald Hindley, *The Communist Party of Indonesia* (Los Angeles, 1964); it is particularly valuable for its discussion of the party's strategy and organisational base. Daniel Lev, *The Transition to Guided Democracy* (Ithaca, 1966) provides a detailed chronicle of the crucial period of 1957–9, when regional rebellion and the paralysis of the parliamentary regime brought Sukarno to pre-eminent power. P. F. Tan (ed.), *Sukarno's Guided Indonesia* (Melbourne, 1967) contains useful essays by Australian specialists on various aspects of the Guided Democracy period of 1959–1965; and J. M. Pluvier's essay on Malaysian-Indonesian relations, *Confrontations* (Kuala Lumpur, 1965), presents an interesting if overdrawn reinterpretation of Sukarno's role, which he sees as a fundamentally conservative one. A sociological analysis of the traditionalist aspects prominent in Guided Democracy politics can be found in Ann Willner, *The Neotraditional Accommodation: the Indonesian Case* (Princeton, 1966). The

187

traditional aspects of Sukarno's style have also been explored, to brilliant effect, in Clifford Geertz, *Islam Observed* (New Haven, 1968). So far, there has been no full-length study of the New Order regime established by General Suharto following Sukarno's overthrow in 1965.

In contrast to other areas of South East Asia, a fair amount has been done on contemporary Indonesian social history. One of the earliest post-independence studies was W. F. Wertheim, *Indonesian Society in Transition* (2nd ed., The Hague, 1964); the essays contained in this work were originally published in the early 1950s, but they still retain much of their usefulness. An excellent account of the transformation of a highly traditional area under the pressures of revolution is Selosoemardjan, *Social Change in Jogjakarta* (Ithaca, 1962). Another part of Java is explored anthropologically by Robert Jay in *Javanese Villagers* (Cambridge, Mass., 1968); this work is particularly important for its discussion of the relationship between religious and political conflict in Javanese society. A view of Javanese society as a whole is given by D. H. Burger, in *Structural Changes in Javanese Society: The Village Sphere and the Supra-Village Sphere* (Ithaca, 1957), which outlines broad changes taking place since the nineteenth century which have profoundly altered the substance if not the form of Javanese life.

For North Sumatra, William Liddle, *The Politics of Ethnicity* (New Haven, 1970) provides an excellent study of the links between provincial and local politics and of the role of cultural and linguistic divisions in political life. Donald Willmott, *The Chinese of Semarang* (Ithaca, 1960) is a good case study of the economically important but politically precarious role of Indonesia's Chinese minority.

Easily the most important writer on Indonesia's recent social history is, however, Clifford Geertz, who in his *The Religion of Java* (Glencoe, 1960) established a typology of socio-religious conflict that has profoundly affected subsequent analyses of that dominant ethnic group and its role in Indonesian social and political affairs. A second major work was *Agricultural Involution: the Process of Ecological*

Change in Indonesia (Glencoe, 1963), in which Geertz considered the effect of the colonial experience on Javanese peasant farming and more generally on Indonesian economic and social structure; he discussed this in more concrete terms in *The Social History of an Indonesian Town* (Cambridge, Mass., 1965), which also includes a very useful case study of early post-independence elections. Both Geertz and Jay did their work in the early 1950s and in the same locale; it is unfortunate, given the great influence of their writings on subsequent analyses of post-independence Indonesia, that no parallel studies have been undertaken elsewhere in Java and also that no more recent investigation has been made of the original site to determine the extent and direction of change.

For Indonesian economic history, the reader should turn first to *Indonesian Economics* (The Hague, 1961), which presents the arguments of (and major arguments against) the Dutch economist J. H. Boeke, who developed the 'dual economy' thesis describing the relationship between the dynamic, highly developed 'modern' economic sector organised around plantations and mines and the stagnant 'native' subsistence economy in Indonesia in the late colonial period. No study of this scope by an economist has been made since independence though Geertz' above-mentioned *Agricultural Involution* and some of Wertheim's essays deal sociologically with the problem. The main works on economic development of independent Indonesia have been concerned with central planning and finance in the period of liberal democracy: Benjamin Higgins, *Indonesia's Economic Stabilization and Development* (New York, 1957) and Douglas Paauw, *Financing Indonesia's Economic Development* (Glencoe, 1960). However, G. C. Allen and A. Donnithorne, *Western Enterprise in Indonesia and Malaysia* (London, 1957), includes a discussion of the relationship between the Indonesian government and foreign concerns in the early 1950s in their history. J. A. C. Mackie's *The Politics of the Indonesian Inflation* (Ithaca, 1968) provides the only monographic study of Guided Democracy economics thus far available. It considers its subject primarily from a social viewpoint, and although its observations are highly interesting they are not buttressed by statistics.

Malaysia and Singapore

The most complete general introduction to Malaysia is Wang Gungwu (ed.), *Malaysia* (New York, 1964), a massive work dealing with the country's history, society, politics, and economics. Its essays are rather too detailed to be satisfactory as surveys and too general to be interesting as studies in depth, so that the work does not quite come off as a whole, though it is valuable as a reference. There are, however, other, less extensive works, of which Victor Purcell, *Malaysia* (London, 1965) is perhaps the most succinct, providing a general history, particularly of the period since 1945, and including a useful 'who's who' of Malaysian leaders in its appendix. J. M. Gullick, *Malaysia* (London, 1969) gives a more detailed description of the country and its history since 1945. There are a number of colonial histories, and one of the quickest ways to be introduced to them is to peruse the selections in John Bastin and Robin Winks (ed.), *Malaysia: Selected Historical Readings* (London, 1966), which provides extracts from secondary sources as well as from original documents. The country's economic development is surveyed from a conservative viewpoint by Lennox Mills, *Malaya: A Political and Economic Appraisal* (London, 1958) and from a radical one by James Puthucheary, *Ownership and Control in the Malayan Economy* (Singapore, 1960).

The most important development in Malaya's post-war history prior to the formation of Malaysia itself was the communist insurrection that began in 1948. A great deal has been written about the 'Emergency' by military and police officers, journalists, and counter-insurgency specialists, but little of it is of first quality. In fact, the best portrayal of the experience is given in a novel: Han Suyin, *And the Rain My Drink* (London, 1956). A very interesting study of the psychology of those who engaged in the rebellion can be found in Lucian Pye, *Guerrilla Communism in Malaya* (Princeton, 1956); it is based on a sample of internees which one suspects may not be completely typical of the movement, however. Another attempt to analyse the inner nature of the insurrection is M. R. Stenson, *Industrial Conflict in Malaya* (London, 1970), which investigates its sources in the developing labour movement. For a general history of the Communist Party and the ideological sources of the revolt, see Justus M. van der Kroef, *Communism in Malaysia and Singapore* (The Hague, 1967), which provides a detailed if rather 'cold war' -ish account.

For the formation of the Federation of Malaysia in 1963 perhaps the most useful source is J. M. Gullick, *Malaysia and Its Neighbours* (London, 1967), which includes a selection of documents and an excellent discussion of the international turbulence surrounding the creation of the new state. Its loss of the component city-state of Singapore in 1965 is described circumstantially in Nancy Fletcher, *The Separation of Singapore from Malaysia* (Ithaca, 1969). Very little has been written on the contemporary history of the eastern half of Malaysia. K. G. Tregonning, *A History of Modern Sabah 1881–1963* (Singapore, 1964) provides an account of colonial rule in former British North Borneo; however, its emphasis lies on the period before 1946.

R. S. Milne, *Government and Politics in Malaysia* (London, 1967) is a solid if unexciting introduction to the political institutions of the federation. More specialised studies include James Scott, *Political Ideology in Malaysia* (New Haven, 1968). Subtitled 'Reality and the Beliefs of an Elite', it is an attempt to explore the world view of higher Malayan civil servants to discover the effect of economic security and communal rivalry on the behaviour of the administrative class. The book relies on too small and carelessly-chosen a sample to be sound on the 'scientific' basis to which it aspires, however. A less controversial, if also less stimulating, account of Malaysian administrative practice may be found in Robert Tilman, *Bureaucratic Transition in Malaya* (Durham, NC, 1964), which is concerned with efforts to change traditional ideas and colonial habits into modern managerial behaviour.

For the effect of Malaya-Chinese ethnic rivalries on political behaviour, see K. J. Ratnam, *Communalism and the Political*

191

Process in Malaya (2nd ed., Kuala Lumpur, 1965). Written when communal tensions seemed relatively manageable and by a scholar-politician committed to the 'Alliance' government, it now appears overly optimistic in its analysis, but it remains of value as a guide to the reasoning behind the formation of the rather elaborate system of racial checks and balances on which the parliamentary government rested. For those who wish to explore the development of the two major ethnic communities on which Malaysian government uneasily rests, J. M. Gullick, *Indigenous Political Systems of Western Malaya* (London, 1958) provides an excellent reconstruction of traditional Malay government and society. William Roff's fine account of *The Origins of Malay Nationalism* (New Haven, 1967) takes its tale only to 1941, but it is indispensable for understanding the subsequent political behaviour of that community. A discussion of the government's efforts to improve the largely peasant Malay population's living standards and economic role is provided by Gayl Ness, *Bureaucracy and Rural Development in Malaysia* (Berkeley, 1967). For the Chinese population, the classical study is Victor Purcell, *The Chinese in Malaya* (London, 1948); it is a historical work concentrating mostly on the period before the second world war. Another important and very detailed work is W. Blythe, *The Impact of Chinese Secret Societies in Malaya* (London, 1969). A detailed history of the smaller but important Indian community is provided by Kernial Singh Sandhu, *Indians in Malaya, 1786–1957* (London, 1969).

The Philippines

The Philippines has been readily accessible to foreign researchers and poses fewer language difficulties than any other South East Asian country; it is therefore surprising that very few studies have been made of its contemporary history. One suspects that, having absorbed so much of the American style, the Philippines has not been 'different' enough to attract the attention of post-war South East Asian scholars, many of whom were Americans attracted to Asian studies in the first place by a desire to study a region culturally different from their own. This is beginning to change, as the Philippines emerges again as a potential 'trouble spot' and therefore a centre of American academic and governmental attention, and also as an increasing number of Filipino scholars produce studies of their country aimed at an international scholarly audience.

The Philippines was under Spanish domination from the sixteenth through the nineteenth centuries, a period which shaped much of Filipino social structure and attitudes. There is an excellent study of this important experience, John Phelan's *The Hispanization of the Philippines* (Madison, 1967). Another good source is Onofre Corpuz, *The Bureaucracy in the Philippines* (Manila, 1957); it is really concerned with the development of that institution under the Spanish, though it takes its account into the subsequent period of American domination. The best study of the Chinese minority also concerns the Spanish period: Edgar Wickberg, *The Chinese in Philippine Life 1850–1898* (New Haven, 1965).

The war for independence from Spain at the end of the nineteenth century played a major role in shaping the Filipinos' view of themselves, and has received added attention in recent years with the new rise of nationalist sentiment. The nationalist martyr José Rizal has become the object of a cult; there are numerous biographies and memorials of him, but probably the best way to gain acquaintance is through reading one of his political novels, the most famous of which, *Noli Me Tangere*, has been translated as *The Lost Eden* by Rizal's biographer Leon Ma Guerrero (Bloomington, Indiana, 1961). Two good Filipino studies of the revolution, useful for revealing current nationalist intellectual attitudes as well as for understanding the insurrection itself, are Teodor Agoncillo, *The Revolt of the Masses* (Quezon City, 1956) and Cesar Majul, *Mabini and the Philippine Revolution* (Quezon City, 1960).

We still need a good study of the process by which the nationalists who led the revolution against Spain were persuaded to endorse the colonial domination of the United

States. However, there is one on the last phase of American domination which also provides valuable background for the post-colonial relationship between the Philippines and the United States; this is Theodore Friend, *Between Two Empires: The Ordeal of the Philippines* (New Haven, 1965). Of the various studies of the continuing US–Philippine tie, Frank Golay (ed.), *The United States and the Philippines* (Englewood Cliffs, 1968) provides specialist essays on a wide range of aspects; George E. Taylor, *The Philippines and the United States: Problems of Partnership* (New York, 1964) includes both the colonial and post-colonial periods in a detailed investigation conducted from a conservative American view-point; and William Pomeroy, *American Neo-Colonialism; its Emergence in the Philippines and Asia* (New York, 1970), provides a rather heated radical critique. Much of the argument centres on the economic aspects of the Philippine-American relationship, and for a broader discussion of this the reader should turn to Frank Golay, *The Philippines: Public Policy and Economic Development* (Ithaca, 1961), which provides a detailed account of the country's economy both before and after independence.

The first years following Philippine independence in 1946 were taken up with the Hukbalahap peasant rebellion, which was destroyed as a major movement in the mid-1950s but not as tradition of rural unrest. None of the available accounts of the rebellion can be accused of impartiality, but the most balanced and analytically sophisticated is Francis Starner, *Magsaysay and the Philippine Peasantry* (Berkeley, 1961), the first part of which contains a good portrayal of the social sources of Philippines rural restiveness. The rebel leader Luis Taruc has authored a biography, *Born of the People* (New York, 1953), which provides a useful critique of the insurrectionists' early strategy. Finally, the socio-economic basis from which the movement arose and which still is the source of severe tensions within the republic is investigated by Akira Takahashi, *Land and Peasants in Central Luzon* (Honolulu, 1970).

The best discussion of the post-independence Philippine

political system is Carl H. Lande, *Leaders, Factions and Parties: The Structure of Philippine Politics* (New Haven, 1965), which investigates, with some use of anthropological concepts, the sources of the stability which Philippine government exhibited in the decade following the defeat of the Huks. The relationships which it describes can be followed more concretely in Mary Hollnsteiner, *The Dynamics of Power in a Philippine Municipality* (Quezon City, 1963).

Thailand

Scholarly investigations of modern Thailand have tended to centre around four topics: the modernising kings of the later nineteenth century, the effect of Thai culture on peasant behaviour, problems of governmental administration, and national security. By far the best studies concern the nineteenth century or before, and there are few recommendable works for contemporary Thai history.

For those interested in a historical background to modern Thailand, the best single work is Walter Vella, *The Impact of the West on Government in Thailand* (Berkeley, 1955), a very good discussion of the changes that took place in the Thai governmental system and ideology in the late nineteenth and twentieth centuries. The Revolution of 1932, which followed these transformations, has not yet received the historiographic attention it deserves, but three works provide useful accounts: Kenneth Landon, *Siam in Transition* (Chicago, 1939, repr. 1969); Josiah Crosby, *Siam at the Crossroads* (London, 1945), written by a former British ambassador to the country; and Virginia Thompson, *Thailand, the New Siam* (New York, 1941), which includes a general survey of geography, society, and economics as well as the politics of the time. For the immediate post-war years, a rare and turbulent period of civilian government, see John Coast, *Some Aspects of Siamese Politics* (New York, 1953). There is also a good economic history, James Ingram, *Economic Change in Thailand Since 1850* (Stanford, 1955), which carries its account up to the 1950s; it is particularly concerned with the way in which Thailand became a major producer of rice for the world market without overtly changing its rural pattern of life.

The best general description of Thai political life in the period since the second world war is given in David Wilson, *Politics in Thailand* (Ithaca, 1962). It is at its best describing the nature of clique formation in the military-dominated Thai politics of the 1950s; it is, however, wholly devoted to elite politics and, exhibiting little sense of historical flow, treats the political style it describes as if it were immutable. Unfortunately no analytically better discussion has appeared since. There is, however, a fine study of Thai bureaucratic behaviour in Fred Riggs, *Thailand: The Modernization of a Bureaucratic Polity* (Honolulu, 1966); this analysis of the character of Thai society and its effect on efforts to create a modern bureaucracy has had considerable influence on American behavioural analyses of non-Western politics. For those who find it too devoted to model-building and not enough to the details of Thai administrative structure, the best of the more conventional studies is William Siffin, *The Thai Bureaucracy: Institutional Change and Development* (Honolulu, 1966).

Thailand's relations to the outside world have been discussed in Frank Darling, *Thailand and the United States* (Washington, 1963) and Donald Nuechterlein, *Thailand and the Struggle for Southeast Asia* (Ithaca, 1967). Both view Thailand from an American 'cold war' standpoint and are concerned with the threat to Thai security posed by the existence of the Chinese Peoples' Republic.

In the matter of Thai contemporary domestic conditions we are somewhat better off, for the literature on Thai peasant traditions and behaviour has produced a useful study of rural social change: Michael Moerman, *Agricultural Change and Peasant Choice in a Thai Village* (Berkeley, 1968). There is also a well-considered work on rural political attitudes in North-Eastern Thailand, an area which in recent years has been the subject of much speculation regarding its potential for secession or insurrection: Charles Keyes, *Isan, Regionalism in Northeastern Thailand* (Ithaca, 1967). Finally, there is an excellent and exhaustive study of the Thai Chinese minority by G. William Skinner, which is of great aid in understanding the recent history of the Thai ethnic majority as well as the Chinese who live among them; it has appeared in two volumes whose titles are self-explanatory: *Chinese Society in Thailand, an Analytical History* (Ithaca, 1957), and *Leadership and Power in the Chinese Community of Thailand* (Ithaca, 1958).

9

China

William Brugger and Stuart Schram

Introduction

The study of contemporary China has undergone considerable change in the past twenty years, and this change has
been substantially influenced by changes in the nature of
source materials. Much primary material for the early 1950s
found its way into Western libraries, and by about 1956
detailed studies began to appear on the Chinese polity and
economy. The comparative reliability of statistics for the
middle 1950s has meant that political and sociological studies
relating to that period have been heavily influenced by
economists.

The Great Leap Forward of 1958 saw a vast flow of
material from the Chinese People's Republic; the subsequent
retrenchment led to severe restrictions on the export of news-
paper and periodical material. Researchers in the 1960s
tended to rely more on refugee interviews. This situation was
somewhat eased by 1964, when a significant number of
journals were again exported.

Just as changes in the nature of source materials affected
studies of contemporary China, so the growth of social
science disciplines affected the perspectives of researchers.
The various political science theories that were developed
in the 1960s were all applied to China in differing measure.
Refugee-interviewing became a science which on the one hand
promoted clarity and on the other, restricted scope.[1]

From the mid 1950s many translation series appeared.[2]
The quality of translations is on the whole poor, but they are

invaluable to any researcher. They also offer the only recourse for the general reader who wishes to inform himself about one of the many problems about which there is as yet no adequate synthetic account.

Several bibliographies have appeared of which perhaps the most useful is *Contemporary China, A Research Guide.* Michel Oksenberg's extensive list of Western-language materials by topic is also helpful.[3]

The present essay deals exclusively with English language material. The English language periodicals produced in the People's Republic of China also contain useful documentation.[4] The principal serious journal dealing exclusively with China published in the West is *The China Quarterly* (hereafter *CQ*). A number of other periodicals, such as *Asian Survey, The Journal of Asian Studies,* the *Journal of Contemporary Asia* and *Modern Asian Studies,* devote considerable space to China. These journals vary widely in their political outlook and level of scholarship.[5]

The following essay attempts to give a sample of the literature available on contemporary China. The quality of the items varies considerably. It was felt, however, that it would be better to adopt a representative approach, since a stress on quality would reflect too much the present writers' subjective judgement, and would inevitably leave some fields uncovered.

General Studies

It is regrettable that no scholarly history of the Chinese People's Republic exists. Works which follow a standard chronological approach often switch to a topical approach once they get to 1949.[6] This often denies us a feel for the various policy shifts that occurred, and a sense of the relative importance of each of the hundred-odd political movements that took place.

There are some very good journalistic accounts and semi-scholarly works that cover significant portions of contemporary history.[7] There are many more bad ones that are

H

often so caught up in the Cold War perspectives that their findings are extremely suspect.[8]

General works that attempt to put the past twenty years into some kind of historical perspective would include those of Clubb, Chalmers Johnson, Fitzgerald and North.[9] Various collections of articles exist which attempt to examine particular periods of contemporary history from a variety of perspectives but which often lack internal unity.[10] There are also several compendia of translations which provide useful sources for the general student of contemporary history.[11]

One major comprehensive work deserves special mention. This is Schurmann's *Ideology and Organization in Communist China*, perhaps the most significant work on contemporary China to date.[12] It examines the period from the perspective of an organisational sociologist, and attempts to relate to contemporary developments a world-view that sees society in terms of contradiction.

Another study of a general character is Audrey Donnithorne's *China's Economic System*.[13] This is fundamentally a work on economic institutions rather than quantitative economics and as such it has met with severe criticism on the part of quantitative economists. Though not of the same stature as Schurmann's book, it can serve as a useful introductory account.

Detailed analyses of central government political and economic institutions are quite rare, though a few monographs exist on topics such as the People's Procuratorate, the trade unions, the relationship between central and local economic institutions, the Academy of Sciences etc.[14] Writers tend to be more interested in the functioning of the bureaucracy as a whole and the role of the cadre, manager and bureaucrat within it.[15] Several books and articles have been written on this subject. Most of them appeared before the Cultural Revolution and lack, therefore, the invaluable perspective on bureaucracy that these past years have given us.

There are also several good general geographical works

that are essential background reading for the student of contemporary history.[16]

Historiography

There has been considerable debate within China, especially during the last ten years, on exactly how to interpret China's long history. James Harrison sees three main strains in contemporary Chinese historiography: the traditional, the Marxian and the Maoist. He interprets the various criticisms of the contemporary historians according to how closely they adhere to one or other of these trends.[17] In China it has always been impossible to separate history from contemporary political reality. Some will argue that this is true of all societies. In China, however, it is more explicit.[18]

Biographies

Given the dearth of accurate and readable histories of the Chinese communist movement, biographies of leading figures are useful as a first approach to the subject. The first seriously-documented biography of Mao Tse-tung was completed in 1963, though publication was delayed until 1965. This was Jerome Ch'ên's *Mao and the Chinese Revolution.*[19] Ch'ên made extensive use of Li Jui's semi-official biography of the young Mao (now disavowed in Peking because it also gives considerable credit to Liu Shao-ch'i), which is at long last to be translated into English.[20] Ch'ên's biography ends with the establishment of the Chinese People's Republic in 1949. That of Stuart Schram[21] carries the story down to the beginning of the cultural revolution; a revised edition, scheduled for publication in 1973, will endeavour to place the events of the past decade in better perspective.

Biographies of other Chinese leaders tend to be disappointing. They are either fragmentary, owing to lack of source material and inadequate research, or resort to scurrilous gossip, and as such are in the Chinese biographical tradition.[22] On the whole, the best sources are therefore biographical dictionaries.[23] The last few years have produced a number of unofficial or semi-official biographical essays. They often give us a picture of leading personnel very different from that current in the past, and may perhaps be inspired more by the desire to fill a symbolic function than by a concern with historical accuracy. Thus they run the risk of becoming rapidly outdated.[24]

Political Science Studies

Many of the political science theories and conceptual frameworks developed during the 1960s have been applied to China. At the same time research on China is still considerably influenced by classical sinology, which tends to see China as a society that defies comparison. The field of 'comparative communism' is still dominated by sovietologists.[25] There are few serious studies placing China in a context which is perhaps more meaningful – that of the developing nations. Political-science journals have long debated the exact meaning of the term 'political development'. Two indicators, commonly used, are those of participation and institutionalisation and it is along these lines that James Townsend examines participation in China.[26]

Another contemporary trend in political science is elite studies. The value of these studies has been attacked quite convincingly in theoretical journals, and they are now somewhat less popular than they once were. Those attempted in the China field have not been very revealing due to inadequate data, and the fact that very little work has been done on the relation between elite position and actual behaviour. The release of the Hong Kong United States Consulate General biographical file has given new impetus to work on the distribution of leading personalities, and this promises to be of greater use than previous studies.[27]

There is a great amount of literature on leadership style, distinctions being made between traditional and modern styles and the Yenan guerilla style, as opposed to that of the modern bureaucrat.[28]

Developing sophistication in refugee interviewing has

furthered the work pioneered by Robert Jay Lifton in the psycho-analysis of people who have left the mainland.[29] His latest work, *Revolutionary Immortality,* is an attempt to relate Mao's alleged survival paranoia and search for symbolic immortality to the mass movement of the Cultural Revolution. Lifton's thesis, however, although stimulating, is constructed on very little evidence and on rather questionable methodological foundations.[30]

The work of Lifton, who is a practising psycho-analyst, is perhaps more convincing than that of those political scientists who have tried to use the political culture approach to examine the Chinese political process. Lucian Pye has attempted to relate the traditional Chinese socialisation pattern to what he defines as the current authority crisis in China. His observation that increasing Chinese hostility to Western influence is not so much a reaction against the realities of imperialism as a situation determined by the moral masochism and narcissistic needs of the Chinese personality, is questionable to say the least.[31]

Richard Solomon's approach is similar to that of Pye, but his work is better documented. Thus, whatever doubts one may have regarding his conceptual framework, his recent large-scale study stands out as an important contribution to knowledge.[32]

Ideology and the Thought of Mao Tse-tung

Perhaps the most important general work which examines the political ideas of recent decades from a historical viewpoint is Joseph Levenson's trilogy *Confucian China and its Modern Fate.*[33] Of the founding fathers of the Chinese Communist Party, Li Ta-chao's intellectual development has been the subject of a work interesting in itself, and also valuable for the light it throws on the formative years of Mao Tse-tung, who came under Li's influence in Peking in 1918–19.[34]

The pioneering work of Benjamin Schwartz, which first

dealt seriously with the thought of Mao Tse-tung as it emerged from the matrix of his experience, stressed his originality and heterodoxy as compared to the Leninist tradition.[35] The *Documentary History* of Brandt, Schwartz and Fairbank took a similar line.[36] This position was violently attacked by Karl A. Wittfogel in his polemic of 1960 with Benjamin Schwartz.[37] Arthur A. Cohen, in his book on Mao Tse-tung[38] and in his controversy with Stuart Schram,[39] likewise upheld the view that Mao was on the whole a faithful disciple of Stalin who had contributed nothing really fundamental to the theory and practice of communism. Schram, while recognising that Mao owed a great deal to Lenin and to Stalin, felt that he had made significant original contributions.[40] At the same time, unlike Vsevolod Holubnychy,[41] he held that Mao could scarcely be taken seriously as a philosopher in the strict sense.

During the past decade, in the context of the increasing involvement of Western governments in combating guerilla warfare in Asia and elsewhere, greater attention has also been devoted to Mao's military thinking.[42]

As in so many other fields, the cultural revolution forced students of Mao's thought to re-examine their whole perspective. In the revised version of his book on the subject, Schram concluded that Mao's belief that revolutionary virtue was imminent in the Chinese peasantry was, in the last analysis, incompatible with the logic of Leninism.[43] In the past four years, a vast amount of material attributed to Mao, and almost certainly authentic, has appeared, including many speeches and writings from earlier periods, and this can be expected to result in further reappraisals and self-criticisms by writers in this field.[44]

There are only a limited number of useful studies of recent political and economic thinking by writers other than Mao.[45] In most cases, the student would do better to go to the source material.[46]

Literary Policy

It is very difficult to separate literature from politics. In the

1950s and 1960s a number of campaigns were inaugurated in the domain of literature, art and culture, such as the criticisms of the film on the life of Wu Hsün, the anti-Hu Feng campaign, the Hundred Flowers and anti-rightist campaigns, and the reform of the Peking Opera.[47] All of these had important political overtones. The greatest of these campaigns, the Cultural Revolution, will be dealt with below.

A number of writers and literary bureaucrats have been singled out for special praise or blame, such as Lu Hsün, Mao Tun, Hsia Yen, Chou Yang etc. Monographs exist on most of these.[48] What is regrettable, however, is that though certain studies have been carried out on the political aspects of literary policy, very little research has been done into the literary quality of works produced in the last twenty years.[49] We regret that few of the major contemporary novels have been read by many people in the West; for surely the novel is one of the best means of giving the potential researcher background information on various fields.[50]

General Economic Studies

Scholars have differed considerably in their estimates of China's economic growth both from the official statistics published up to 1959 and amongst themselves.[51] Most detailed information is available for the First Five Year Plan (1953–57) though many works exist showing economic trends over the whole period since 1949 and before.[52] Most works are aggregative studies, though during recent years more and more scholars have concentrated on a sectoral approach, and more attention has been paid to economic institutions and the operation of economic sub-systems.[53] Very little attempt has been made, however, to combine some of the more sophisticated trends of political analysis with economic studies.[54]

Rural Policy and Agriculture

There exists considerable background material on agriculture and the Chinese peasant.[55] Some of the items previously mentioned under the historiography section deal with the problem of how the historical role of the peasant is seen today, though very few works consider the exact role of the peasant in the Anti-Japanese and Civil Wars.[56]

As yet, no comprehensive survey of land reform has been written, though a few monographs have appeared on the political aspects of land reform in certain areas.[57] One of the most fascinating books to have been written on contemporary China is William Hinton's *Fanshen*.[58] This is the author's eye-witness account of land-reform in a particular village of North China.[59] Hinton describes the various fluctuations in the land-reform campaigns in the period just prior to 'liberation' and the peasants' response to them. During the Cultural Revolution, Hinton made a reappraisal of his interpretation, feeling that he had underestimated the different approach to land-reform on the part of Liu Shao-ch'i and its effect on the village in question.[60] The validity of these subsequent observations has been a matter of dispute.

Bernstein has written on changes in the character of village leadership following land-reform and compares Chinese collectivisation with its Soviet counterpart in the years 1929–30.[61] Material on collectivisation is comparatively detailed, and consequently the period 1955–7 has been treated very thoroughly both from an economic and politico-economic point of view.[62] Walker's *Planning in Chinese Agriculture* deals with the private sector during the middle and late 1950s.[63] Both the role of a private sector in agriculture and the problem of collectivisation before mechanisation have been at the heart of the Cultural Revolution debates on agricultural policy.[64]

Many economic, sociological and political studies on the People's Communes have been produced, and have been written from every conceivable point of view.[65] Of these, William G. Skinner's articles stand out as works of great methodological importance.[66] Skinner seeks to relate the scope of the various forms of rural organisation to traditional social structures and marketing areas and later attempts to fit the various rural campaigns into an overall conceptual framework.[67]

Whereas work on rural organisation in the period after 1959 has been very sparse, there are a number of works that deal with food production and agriculture during this period.[68] Due to the non-availability of agricultural statistics since the Great Leap Forward, a considerable amount of guesswork has been practised (both informed and otherwise) as to China's current food-grain output. The present writers do not feel competent to judge which of the many estimates is most reliable.[69]

Throughout the early 1960s, China produced a substantial amount of technical information on agriculture.[70] Much of this exists in translation and has been the subject of various studies.[71]

Urban Development and Industry

The role of the city in the Chinese polity and society has been consistently underrated. No work exists on the functioning of the urban Communist Party branches in the pre-1949 period, and this prevents a full understanding of the social origins of the clash between the two developmental models that became prominent during the Cultural Revolution. At the micro-societal level far more attention has been paid to the rural sector than the urban; indeed, only one comprehensive study of any city has been produced.[72] Various writers have dealt with certain social, political and economic aspects of some other major cities but their scope is narrower, being confined to such topics as urban housing, rationing etc.[73]

Industrial society in general has also been treated very scantily. The mammoth work of Barry Richman was an attempt to rectify this.[74] *Industrial Society in Communist China*, however, is a trifle rambling and the reader would do well to confine himself to Richman's smaller volume based on valuable personal observations of industrial management.[75] Useful information on industrial society can be gleaned from various travelogues, from English-language pamphlets published in Peking and periodicals such as

Peking Review, China Reconstructs, the US Consulate General translation series and JPRS.[76]

Studies have been carried out on urban political movements, urban communes, trade unions, individual large corporations, workers' wages and welfare and these have touched on the relationship between the urban and rural sectors.[77]

Studies on China's industrial development are particularly detailed for the early 1950s when adequate statistical material was available.[78] As in the agricultural sphere, non-availability of statistical material for the 1960s has meant that work on this period is less reliable.

Population and Manpower

Ho Ping-ti's valuable background work on population takes us up to the 1953 census.[79] Since then no nation-wide census has been carried out, though there have been rumours of local census figures having been compiled. The few works listed here evaluate the scanty evidence we have on population growth and examine the little data we have on birth control.[80]

Education

Though there have been a few useful works on the background to the problems faced by education in modern China, and a number of documentary collections on educational policy, very little has been done on the structure of the educational system.[81]

Two introductory works on education in contemporary China are those of Chiu-Sam Tsang and Ronald Price. The former provides much information on political background, the basic issues facing education and the main political movements affecting the structure of the educational system and the content of courses. Tsang does not, however, give great detail on educational institutions.[82] Ronald Price relates Mao's thought and the Chinese cultural tradition to contemporary education spelling out the obstacles to the development of a successful education system.[83]

Orleans' attention is directed to education and the provision of technical manpower; he provides us with a certain amount of statistical material.[84]

Closely allied to the question of education is the role of the intellectual in the new society and his response to various political movements especially the Hundred Flowers movement and the Cultural Revolution.[85] These studies often tend to reflect all too clearly the fact that they are written by intellectuals, about intellectuals and for intellectuals.

Law

Though many important legal documents have been translated into English by Peking Foreign Languages Press, Joint Publications Research Service, and individual scholars, there has been comparatively little work done on the application of these laws. Perhaps the most important source material on Chinese law is to be found in the *Compendium of Laws and Regulations of the People's Republic of China*, a series of fourteen volumes published in Chinese from 1954–62, most of which have been translated by JPRS.[86]

Introductory studies have been carried out on pre-1949 law in the liberated areas and the operation of Criminal Law in the Chinese People's Republic, research on the latter being very largely dependent on refugee interview.[87] Useful bibliographies exist of both contemporary and earlier laws and their implementation.[88]

National Minorities

Because of the international implications of the Tibetan rebellion, central government policy towards Tibet and the life of the Tibetan nationality has been the subject of much study.[89] There has, however, been a complete lack of detailed information as to exactly what has been going on in Tibet. Sources are Tibetan refugees in India who can hardly be expected to give a balanced account, and travellers to Tibet who are sympathetic to Peking's Tibetan policy.[90] Certain documents exist, such as the enquiry conducted by The International Commission of Jurists which, because of the nature of its sources, does not perhaps reflect an entirely balanced point of view.[91]

George Moseley has written prolifically on national minority policy and a few other writers have touched on Inner Mongolia and Sinkiang with particular reference to their implication in the Sino-Soviet conflict.[92] A few impressionistic accounts exist on the life of other national minorities and these give brief accounts of the implementation of national minority policy.[93]

Military Development and the Role of the People's Liberation Army

In view of the paucity of source material on the size and distribution of China's armed forces, the number of 'hardware' studies and prognostications about military strategy is truly remarkable.[94] Since China's first detonation of a nuclear device in October 1964, the press has given China's nuclear policy considerable priority, and this has led scholars to attempt to evaluate her nuclear strategy.[95]

The military and political performance of the People's Liberation Army (henceforth PLA) in the 1950s has been the subject of some studies, but perhaps the most valuable contribution is an estimation of the changing military organisation and the role of the PLA in Chinese society in the 1960s as a result of Lin Piao's policy.[96]

In contrast to almost every other sector of society, our knowledge of the PLA for the 1960s is far richer than for the 1950s. This is in part due to the release of the *Kung-tso t'ung-hsün*, a classified military journal issued to officers of regimental (brigade or brigade-group) level or above.[97] More generally, it reflects the increasingly important role of the Army in this period.

Before the Cultural Revolution a number of studies were carried out on Party-Army relations.[98] Though some of the guesses made were intelligent ones, scholars perhaps underestimated the national significance not only of policies carried out within the PLA but also of the role of the PLA General Political Department.

During the Cultural Revolution, the Army's involvement in all aspects of political and economic activity reached an unprecedented peak.[99] It is probably too early to draw any lasting conclusions as to what the Army's future role will be.

Foreign Policy and Attitudes Toward China

A vast quantity of literature exists on US-China relations. Tang Tsou's background study, *America's Failure in China,* helps to give us some kind of historical perspective, and Felix Greene's *Curtain of Ignorance* shrilly denounces the lack of information resulting from the prevalence of cold war attitudes in the United States.[100] The hearings before the Senate Committee on Foreign Relations showed that, to some groups in America, China at that time remained a bugbear.[101]

The most popular area of research on China's foreign relations has been the Sino-Soviet dispute. Many books of widely varying quality have been written on this during the past decade, but Zagoria's study remains one of the best. The most useful compilations of materials are Gittings' *Survey of the Sino-Soviet Dispute* and the various collections of documents made by Griffith.[102]

China's relations with Africa have been poorly covered. One of the best accounts is by Colin Legum in *Policy Towards China* but the reader might also consider Emmanuel Hevi's account of China's activities in Africa.[103]

Accounts of China's relations with Asian countries range from the ecstatic to the hysterical. In the latter category we would put much of the work done in India with regard to Sino-Indian relations.[104] Certain significant periods in China's relations with Asian countries, such as the Bandung period and the 1961 Geneva Conference, have been the subject of detailed studies and relations with Indonesia, Pakistan and other Asian countries also are covered.[105]

China's relations with European countries include works on Sino-British relations and Sino-French relations which are interesting but not really the central concern in China's foreign policy.[106] We can only regret that China's attitude towards Latin America has been poorly covered.[107] There are a number of general works on China's foreign policy which attempt to deal with China's place in the contemporary world.[108] Some of them have very interesting insights into the future of world diplomacy and others still talk about a diplomatic world which is now in the process of disintegration.

The Cultural Revolution

The Cultural Revolution of 1966–9 took everyone by surprise, causing scholars of all sympathies radically to re-examine their own perspectives in the light of the mass of new data that appeared. We have already mentioned some of the revisions in basic works that have so far been made.[109]

The first journalistic analyses tended to follow a power-struggle approach as did Philip Bridgham's serialised account.[110] After a while, however, though the power struggle was seen to be central to any analysis, researchers turned more to examination of socio-economic, psychological and ideological determinants.[111]

Neuhauser attempted to examine the background to the events of 1966–9 in terms of the role of the Party, and Baum and Teiwes' excellent monograph on the 'Four Clean-up Movements' helped our understanding of the period immediately prior to the revolution.[112]

A number of eyewitness accounts exist, some fanciful, others naive and still others which offer an insight into the dynamics of the revolution.[113]

A vast number of Red Guard publications that found their way into Western libraries, and the various policy editorials for 1966–8 have provided the bulk of many documentary collections,[114] but it will probably take many years before we begin to have anything like an adequate perspective on all this material.

The effect of the Cultural Revolution on various institutions and social groups has been examined.[115] It is still too early

212

to say how it has affected China, and it is likewise too early to say how it has affected social scientists and contemporary historians. After its outbreak, it made all previous attempts at prediction look somewhat silly; it made Western observers humble. One wonders how long this humility will last.

If China scholars are now somewhat wary of short term prediction, long term predictions continue to be made.[116] What will China really look like in 2001?

References

Introduction
1 For a discussion of methodological problems see:
OKSENBERG, Michel, 'Sources and Methodological Problems in the Study of Contemporary China' in BARNETT, *Chinese Communist Politics in Action* (Seattle & London, 1969).
2 Translation series include:
Hong Kong: US Consulate General, *Extracts from China Mainland Magazines* (1955–60), weekly (hereafter ECMM).
Hong Kong: US Consulate General, *Selections from China Mainland Magazines* (commenced August 1960; succeeded ECMM; hereafter SCMM).
Hong Kong: US Consulate General, *Survey of China Mainland Press* (commenced 1 November 1950), daily (hereafter SCMP).
Hong Kong: US Consulate General, *Current Background* (commenced June 1950), weekly (hereafter CB).
Hong Kong: US Consulate General, *Index to SCMP, SCMM & CB* (commenced 10 March 1956), bi-monthly.
BBC Monitoring Service, *Summary of World Broadcasts* (commenced 28 August 1939), 6 times per week.
Hong Kong, Union News Agency: Union Research Service (commenced 16 September 1955), approx. 9 times per month (hereafter URS).
Peking Hsin-hua News Agency, *Hsin-hua News Agency Release* (commenced 21 April 1949), daily (also known as NCNA).

A number of English language editions have been published. Perhaps the most easily available is the London edition published by S. CHINQUE.

Washington Joint Publications Research Service (hereafter JPRS). A number of series is published by this agency. See: SORICH, Richard, *A Bibliography of Reports on China Published by the United States Joint Publications Research Service, New York*. Prepared for the Joint Committee on Contemporary China of the American Council of Learned Societies and the Social Science Research Council, 1961. (This gives some idea of the fields covered though of late this scope has been considerably restricted.)

Hong Kong, *China News Analysis*, weekly.

3 Bibliographies:

BERTON & WU, *Contemporary China: A Research Guide* (Stanford, California: Hoover Institution on War, Revolution and Peace, 1967).

OKSENBERG, Michel C., *A Bibliography of Secondary English Language Literatures on Contemporary Chinese Politics* (New York, A Research Aid of the East Asian Institute, Columbia University [1967]).

See also:

Journal of Asian Studies: Bibliography of Asian Studies (an annual compilation).

4 Peking Foreign Languages Press: English Language Periodicals:

Peking Review (commenced 1958);
People's China (1950–57);
China Reconstructs (commenced 1952);
China Pictorial (commenced 1951);
The Chinese Trade Unions (1951–66);
Women of China (1952–66);
China's Sports (1957–66);
Chinese Literature (commenced 1951);
Evergreen (1957–66);
Science Record (1957–66);
Scientia Sinica (1952–66).

5 For a list of current Western Periodicals dealing with China see:

References

HARRIS & BRUGGER, 'A Reader's Guide to Publications from and on China', *Bulletin of the Atomic Scientists*, February 1969, vol. xxv, No. 2. (The list is not included in the Random House volume *China After the Cultural Revolution.*)

Also: BERTON & WU, *Contemporary China: A Research Guide* (Stanford, California, 1967).

General Studies

6 A good example of a switch in approach would be:

HOUN, Franklin W., *A Short History of Chinese Communism* (Englewood Cliffs, NJ, 1967).

7 WILSON, Dick, *A Quarter of Mankind: An Anatomy of China Today* (London, 1966).

SNOW, Edgar, *The Other Side of the River: Red China Today* (New York, 1962).

BARNETT, Doak, *China on the Eve of Communist Takeover* (New York, 1963).

BARNETT, Doak, *Communist China: The Early Years 1949–1955* (New York, 1964).

KAROL, K.S., *China: The Other Communism*, trans. from French by Tom Baistow (London, 1967).

8 Examples of the 'cold war' approach:

WALKER, R., *China under Communism: the First Five Years* (London, 1956).

TANG, Peter S.H., *Communist China Today: Domestic and Foreign Policies* (London, 1957; revised and enlarged volume, 1961). The domestic policy section has been further revised and updated in:

TANG & MALONEY, *Communist China: the Domestic Scene 1949–1967* (South Orange, New Jersey, 1967).

9 CLUBB, O. Edmund, *Twentieth Century China* (New York & London, 1964).

JOHNSON, Chalmers A., *Peasant Nationalism & Communist Power: the Emergence of Revolutionary China 1937–1945* (Stanford, 1964).

Johnson's work stresses perhaps to excess the role of the nationalist appeal in the Communists' success. For a study which interprets the same period in a different light, see:

SELDEN, Mark, *The Yenan Way in Revolutionary China* (Cambridge, Mass., 1971).

FITZGERALD, C.P., *The Birth of Communist China* (Harmondsworth, 1964.) (First published 1952 as *Revolution in China* – much revised.)

NORTH, Robert C., *Chinese Communism* (London, 1966).

10 Collections of articles:

HO PING-TI & TSOU TANG (ed.), *China In Crisis*, 3 vols (Chicago, 1968).

GRAY, J., *Modern China's Search for a Political Form* (London, 1969).

LEWIS, J. (ed.), *Party Leadership and Revolutionary Power in China* (Contemporary China Institute Publications, London, 1970).

11 For example:

SCHURMANN, H.F. & SCHELL, Orville, *China Readings 3: Communist China* (Harmondsworth, 1968). (Part of a three volume series covering also Imperial China and Republican China.)

12 SCHURMANN, H.F., *Ideology and Organisation in Communist China* (Berkeley & Los Angeles, 1966; revised edition, 1968).

13 DONNITHORNE, Audrey, *China's Economic System* (London, 1967).

14 GINSBURGS & STAHNKE, 'The People's Procuratorate in Communist China', *CQ*, **20, 24, 34;** 1964, 1965, 1968.

HARPER, Paul, 'The Party and the Unions in Communist China', *CQ*, **37**, 1969.

PFEFFER, Richard M., 'The Institution of Contracts in the Chinese People's Republic', *CQ*, **14 & 15**, 1963.

LINDBECK, John M.H., 'The Organisation and Development of Science', *CQ*, **6**, 1961.

15 See:

VOGEL, Ezra F., 'From Revolutionary to Semi-Bureaucrat: the Regularisation of Cadres', *CQ*, **29**, 1967.

BARNETT, A. Doak, *Cadres, Bureaucracy & Political Power in Communist China* (New York, 1967).

16 Geographical works include:

BUCHANAN, Keith, *The Transformation of the Chinese Earth* (London, 1970). A sympathetic account of China's path to development and its geographical and economic determinants.

TREGEAR, T.R., *A Geography of China* (London, 1965).
TREGEAR, T.R., *An Economic Geography of China* (London, 1970).

Historiography

17 HARRISON, James P., *The Communists and Chinese Peasant Rebellions: A Study in the Rewriting of Chinese History* (London, 1970).

18 A broad survey of the problem is:
FEUERWERKER, Albert (ed.), *History in Communist China* (Cambridge, Mass., 1968). (A collection of articles reprinted from *CQ* and other journals.)

See also the extensive bibliography by FEUERWERKER, Albert & CHENG, S., *Chinese Communist Studies of Modern Chinese History* (Cambridge, Mass., 1961).

Biographies

19 CH'EN, Jerome, *Mao and the Chinese Revolution* (London, 1965).

20 LI JUI, *Mao Tse-tung t'ung-chih ti ch'u-ch'i ko-ming huo-tung* (The Early Period of Comrade Mao Tse-tung's Revolutionary Activity) (Peking, 1957; a translation will be published in 1972 by Praeger Publishers).

21 SCHRAM, Stuart R., *Mao Tse-tung* (Harmondsworth, 1966; revised edition 1967).

22 Examples of 'traditional' Chinese biographies:
HSU KAI-YU, *Chou En-lai: China's Gray Eminence* (Garden City, NY, 1968).

CHUNG HUA-MIN & MILLER, Arthur C., *Madame Mao: A Profile of Chiang Ch'ing* (Hong Kong, Union Research Institute, 1968).

23 KLEIN & CLARK, *Biographic Dictionary of Chinese Communism 1921–1965* (Cambridge, Mass., 3 vols, 1971).

See also:
Who's Who in Communist China (Hong Kong, Union Research Institute, 1969 & 1970).

Hong Kong Union Research Service Biographical Service, commenced July 1956.

BOORMAN, Howard L., *A Biographical Dictionary of Republican China* (New York & London, 1967–70). (The first three of four volumes have been published. The criterion for inclusion in this dictionary is eminence during the Republican period; thus many of the older generation of Chinese leaders, still active today, are covered.)

See also articles by BOORMAN in *CQ*, **19** & **21** on Tung Pi-wu and Teng Hsiao-p'ing.

WALES, N., *Red Dust: Autobiographies of Chinese Communists as Told to Nym Wales* (Stanford, 1952). (Contains interesting data collected in 1937 regarding the early careers of many figures who later achieved prominence.)

24 *Current Background*, 894, October 1969 (translation) 'Chairman Mao's Successor—Deputy Supreme Commander Lin Piao'.

The Case of P'eng Teh-huai 1959–1968 (Hong Kong, Union Research Institute, 1969). (A useful collection of documents only partly of a biographical nature.)

Political Science Studies

25 On comparative studies see:

MEYER, Alfred G., 'The Comparative Study of Communist Political Systems', *Slavic Review*, March 1967.

SCHAPIRO & LEWIS, 'The Roles of the Monolithic Party Under the Totalitarian Leader', *CQ*, **40**, 1969.

26 TOWNSEND, James, *Political Participation in Communist China* (Berkeley, 1967).

27 NORTH & POOL article in:

LASSWELL & LERNER, *World Revolutionary Elites: Studies in Coercive Ideological Movements* (Cambridge, Mass., 1965).

TEIWES, Frederick, *Provincial Party Personnel in Mainland China* (New York, Occasional Papers of the East Asian Institute, Columbia University, 1967).

KAU YING-MAO, 'The Urban Bureaucratic Elite in Communist China: A Case Study of Wuhan, 1949–65', in BARNETT, *Chinese Communist Politics in Action* (Seattle & London, 1969). The first example of a more sophisticated approach is: OKSENBERG, Michel, 'Local Leaders in Rural China, 1962–65: Individual Attributes, Bureaucratic Positions and Political Recruitment', in BARNETT, *Chinese Communist Politics In Action*.

References

28 LEWIS, John Wilson, *Leadership in Communist China* (London, 1963, and Ithaca, 1962).
See also:
SCHURMANN, *Ideology and Organisation in Communist China* (Berkeley & Los Angeles, 1966; rev. ed. 1968).

29 LIFTON, Robert Jay, *Thought Reform and the Psychology of Totalism: A Study of Brainwashing in China* (New York, 1961).

30 LIFTON, Robert Jay, *Revolutionary Immortality: Mao Tse-tung and the Chinese Cultural Revolution* (London, 1969).
For a discussion of Townsend & Lifton's contribution to political science, see:
TANG TSOU, 'Western Concepts & China's Historical Experiences', *World Politics* (vol. XXI, no. 4, July 1969).

31 PYE, Lucian, *The Spirit of Chinese Politics: a Psychocultural Study of the Authority Crisis in Political Development* (Cambridge, Mass., & London, 1968).

32 SOLOMON, Richard H., *Mao's Revolution and the Chinese Political Culture* (Berkeley, 1971).
SOLOMON, Richard H., 'Mao's Effort to Reintegrate the Chinese Polity. Problems of Authority. Conflict in Chinese Social Processes', in BARNETT, *Chinese Communist Politics in Action* (Seattle & London, 1969).
SOLOMON, Richard H., 'Communications Patterns and the Chinese Revolution', *CQ*, **32**, 1967.

Ideology and the Thought of Mao Tse-tung

33 LEVENSON, Joseph, *Confucian China and Its Modern Fate,* vol. I, 'The Problem of Intellectual Continuity', vol. II, 'The Problem of Monarchical Decay', vol. III, 'The Problem of Historical Significance' (London, 1958–65).

34 MEISNER, Maurice, *Li Ta-chao and the Origins of Chinese Marxism* (Cambridge, Mass., 1967).

35 SCHWARTZ, Benjamin, *Chinese Communism and the Rise of Mao* (3rd ed., Cambridge, Mass., 1958).

36 BRANDT, SCHWARTZ & FAIRBANK, *A Documentary History of Chinese Communism* (Cambridge, Mass., 1959).

37 WITTFOGEL, Karl A., 'The Legend of Maoism', *CQ*, **1** & **2**, 1960.

219

SCHWARTZ, Benjamin, '*The Legend of "The Legend of Maoism*" ', *CQ*, **2**, 1960.

38 COHEN, Arthur A., *The Communism of Mao Tse-tung* (London & Chicago, 1964).

39 COHEN, SCHRAM and others, 'Maoism: a Symposium', *Problems of Communism*, vol. 15, no. 5, September-October 1966).

40 SCHRAM, Stuart R., *The Political Thought of Mao Tse-tung* (London & Dunmow, New York, 1963).

41 HOLUBNYCHY, Vsevlod, 'Mao Tse-tung's Materialist Dialectics', *CQ*, **19**.

42 ELLIOTT-BATEMAN, M., *Defeat in the East: the Mark of Mao Tse-tung on War* (London, 1967).

GRIFFITH, Samuel B., *Mao Tse-tung on Guerilla Warfare* (New York, 1961). (Translation of a manual published in 1937.)

MAO TSE-TUNG, *Basic Tactics*, translated and with an introduction by Stuart R. Schram (New York, 1966; London, 1967). In recognition of Mao's contribution to the theory of People's War, PFLP has published *Selected Military Writings of Mao Tse-tung* (1963). This consists of extracts from MAO TSE-TUNG, *Selected Works* (4 vols., PFLP, 1964). (A revised selection of Mao's works up to 1949.)

See also *Selected Readings from the Works of Mao Tse-tung* (PFLP, 1967).

43 SCHRAM, S. R., *The Political Thought of Mao Tse-tung* (Harmondsworth, 1969).

44 For example:

JPRS: Washington, *Selections from Chairman Mao*, Translations on Communist China Nos. 90 and 109, 1970.

Current Background, 891, *Long Live Mao Tse-tung Thought* (a collection of statements by Mao Tse-tung), 1969.

Current Background, 892, *Selections of Statements by Mao Tse-tung (1956–1967)*, 1969. (Contains *The Ten Great Relationships*, translated by Jerome Ch'en in CH'EN, J., *Mao* (Englewood Cliffs, 1969).

CHEN, Jerome, *Mao Papers: Anthology and Bibliography* (London, 1970).

References

45 JOHNSON, Chalmers A., 'An Intellectual Weed in the Socialist Garden: The Case of Ch'ien Tuan-sheng', *CQ*, **6**, 1961.

HSIA, Ronald, 'The Intellectual & Public Life of Ma Yin-ch'u', *CQ*, **6**, 1961.

MUNRO, Donald, 'The Yang Hsien-chen Affair', *CQ*, **22**, 1965.

46 Source material includes:

LIU SHAO-CH'I, *How to be a Good Communist*, PFLP, 1951.

LIU SHAO-CH'I, *On the Party*, PFLP, 1951.

Collected Works of Liu Shao-ch'i (Hong Kong, URI, 1968–9, 3 vols).

CHOU EN-LAI, *The Collected Works of Chou En-lai* (Hong Kong, URI, 2 vols, awaiting publication.)

Literary Policy
47 BUTTERFIELD, Fox, *The Legend of Sung Ching-shih. An Episode in Communist Historiography*. Harvard Papers on China, No. 18, 1964, pp. 129–54.

GOLDMAN, Merle, 'Hu Feng's Conflict with the Communist Literary Authorities', *CQ*, **12**, 1962.

YANG I-FAN, *The Case of Hu Feng* (Hong Kong, URI, 1956). For references to the Hundred Flowers and Anti-Rightist Campaigns see section on Education and the Intellectuals.

'Mao Tse-tung's Thought Victorious in the Theatre', *Chinese Literature*, **3**, 1967, pp. 1–23.

48 'In Commemoration of Lu Hsün', *Chinese Literature*, **1**, 1967, pp. 1–98.

CHI HUNG-HSU, 'Liu Shao-ch'i Is the Ringleader in the Attack on Lu Hsün', *Chinese Literature*, **2**, 1969, pp. 87–98. (For other criticisms made during the Cultural Revolution see *Chinese Literature*, section on 'Literary Criticism and Repudiation' appearing in each issue.)

PFLP, *Commemorating Lu Hsün Our Forerunner in the Cultural Revolution* (Peking, PFLP, 1967).

GOLDMAN, Merle, 'The Fall of Chou Yang', *CQ*, **27**, 1966.

SHIH, Vincent, 'Mao Tun: the Critic', *CQ*, **19** & **20**, 1964.

49 General works on literary policy include:

FOKKEMA, D. W., *Literary Doctrine in China and Soviet Influence 1956–60* (The Hague, 1965).

CHAO, CHUNG, *The Communist Program for Literature & Art in China* (Hong Kong, URI, 1955).

GOLDMAN, Merle, *Literary Dissent in Communist China* (Cambridge, Mass., 1967). (Contains a general survey of writers' criticism of Party control since the Yenan days.)

50 LIU CH'ING, *The Builders*, trs. Sidney Shapiro (PFLP, 1964).

CHOU LI-PO, *The Hurricane*, trs. Hsü Mêng-hsiung (PFLP, 1955).

AI WU, *Steeled and Tempered* (PFLP, 1961).

KUO KUO-FU, *Among the Ominans* (PFLP, 1961).

General Economic Studies

51 For a sample of different estimates see:

ADLER, Solomon, *The Chinese Economy* (New York, 1957).

ECKSTEIN, Alexander, *The National Income of Communist China* (Glencoe, Illinois, 1961).

HOLLISTER, W. W., *China's Gross National Product and Social Accounts (1950–57)* (New York, 1958).

LIU & YEH, *The Economy of the Chinese Mainland: National Income and Economic Development 1933–1959* (Princeton, 1963, 2 vols).

WU, Y.L., *Economic Development and the Use of Energy Resources in Communist China* (New York, 1963).

CHENG CHU-YÜAN, *Communist China's Economy 1949–1957: Structural Changes and Crisis* (South Orange, New Jersey, 1963).

KANG CHAO, *The Rate and Pattern of Industrial Growth in Communist China* (Ann Arbor, Michigan, 1965).

Ten Great Years (PFLP, 1960).

CH'EN NAI-RUENN, *Chinese Economic Statistics: a Handbook for Mainland China* (Edinburgh, 1967).

For a general background on statistical work see:

LI CHOH-MING, *The Statistical System of Communist China* (Berkeley and Los Angeles, 1962).

52 For an introduction see:

FEUERWERKER, Albert, *The Chinese Economy c.1870–1911* (Michigan Papers, No. 5, 1969).

FEUERWERKER, Albert, *The Chinese Economy 1912–1949* (Michigan Papers, No. 1, 1968).

References

ROSTOW, W.W., *Prospects for Communist China* (Cambridge, Mass., 1954).

LI CHOH-MING (ed.), *Economic Development of Communist China* (New York, 1964).

US Congress, Joint Economic Committee, *An Economic Profile of Mainland China* (Washington, US GPO, 1967).

ECKSTEIN, GALENSON & LIU, *Economic Trends in Communist China* (Chicago, 1968).

WU, LING & WU, *The Spatial Economy of Communist China: a Study on Industrial Location & Transportation* (New York, London, 1967).

WU YÜAN-LI, *An Economic Survey of Communist China* (New York, 1956).

US Congress, Joint Economic Committee, *Mainland China in the World Economy: Hearings before the Joint Economic Committee* (Washington US GPO, 1967).

53 WU YUAN-LI, *The Steel Industry in Communist China* (New York & London, 1965).

LEWIN, Pauline, *The Foreign Trade of Communist China: Its Impact in the Free World* (London & New York, 1964).

ECKSTEIN, A., *Communist China's Growth and Foreign Trade* (New York, 1966).

CHENG CHU-YÜAN, 'Growth and Structural Change in the Chinese Machine Building Industry 1952–66', *CQ*, **41**, 1970.

LIPPIT, Victor D., 'Development of Transportation in Communist China', *CQ*, **27**, 1966.

KANG CHAO, *The Construction Industry in Communist China* (Chicago, 1968).

TADA, Myashita, *The Currency and Financial System of Mainland China*, trs. by J.R. McEwan (Tokyo: Institute of Asian Economic Affairs, 1966).

PERKINS, D., *Market Control and Planning in Communist China* (Cambridge, Mass., 1966).

DONNITHORNE, A., *China's Economic System* (London, 1967).

54 For example see:

RICHMAN, B., *Industrial Society in Communist China* (New York, 1969).

54 For a critique of narrow analyses see:

223

BUCHANAN, *The Transformation of the Chinese Earth* (London, 1970).

RISKIN, Carl, 'China's Economic Growth, Leap or Creep?: Comments on Some Recent Pekinological Revisionism', *Bulletin of Concerned Asian Scholars*, January, 1970.

A useful bibliography is provided by:

CH'EN NAI-RUENN, *The Economy of Mainland China 1949–1963. A Bibliography of Materials in English* (Berkeley, 1963).

Rural Policy and Agriculture

55 CARIN, Robert, *China's Land Problem Series* (Hong Kong, 1960–62, 5 vols).

CARIN, Robert, *State Farms in Communist China* (*1947–61*) (Hong Kong, 1962).

(Both provide useful bibliographical material.)

PERKINS, D.H., *Agricultural Development in China 1368–1968* (Chicago, 1969).

BUCK, J.L., *Land Utilisation in China* (New York, 1968). (First published 1937.)

BUCK, DAWSON & WU, *Food and Agriculture in Communist China* (New York & London, 1966).

BUCK, J.L., *Chinese Farm Economy: a Study of 2866 Farms in 17 Localities and 7 Provinces in China* (Chicago, 1930).

BARRINGTON MOORE Jnr, *Social Origins of Dictatorship and Democracy: Lord and Peasant in the Making of the Modern World* (chapter on China) (Boston, 1966).

56 JOHNSON, Chalmers, *Peasant Nationalism and Communist Power* (Stanford, 1962).

HOFHEINZ, Roy, 'The Autumn Harvest Insurrection', *CQ*, **32**, 1967.

SELDEN, Mark, 'The Guerilla Movement in Northwest China: the Origins of the Shensi-Kansu-Ninghsia Border Region', *CQ*, **29**, **30**, 1967.

HOFHEINZ, Roy, 'The Ecology of Chinese Communist Success: Rural Influence Patterns, 1923–45', in BARNETT, *Chinese Communist Politics in Action* (Seattle & London, 1969).

57 VOGEL, Ezra, 'Land Reform in Kwangtung 1951–53: Central Control and Localism', *CQ*, **38**, 1969.

References

BAYS, Daniel, *Agrarian Reform in Kwangtung 1950–53* (Michigan Papers in Chinese Studies, No. 4, 1969).

58 HINTON, William, *Fanshen: a Documentary of Revolution in a Chinese Village* (New York, 1966).

59 A number of other works exist dealing with social, political and economic developments in particular villages during various periods; for example:

YANG, C.K., *Chinese Communist Society: the Family and the Village* (Cambridge, Mass., 1965). (Originally published 1959.)

CROOK, Isobel & David, *Revolution in a Chinese Village, Ten Mile Inn* (London, 1959).

CROOK, Isobel & David, *The First Years of the Yangi Commune* (London, 1966). (A description of the same area ten years later.)

60 HINTON, William, *China's Continuing Revolution* (London, 1969).

61 BERNSTEIN, Thomas P., 'Problems of Village Leadership After Land Reform', *CQ*, 36, 1968.

BERNSTEIN, Thomas P., 'Leadership and Mass Mobilisation in the Soviet and Chinese Collectivisation Campaign of 1929–30 and 1955–56: a Comparison', *CQ*, 31, 1967.

62 BERNSTEIN, Thomas P., 'Cadre and Peasant Behaviour under Conditions of Insecurity and Deprivation: the Grain Supply Crisis of the Spring of 1955', in BARNETT, *Chinese Communist Politics in Action* (Seattle & London, 1969).

WALKER, Kenneth, 'Collectivisation in Retrospect: the "Socialist High Tide" of Autumn 1955 – Spring 1956', *CQ*, 26, 1966.

WALKER, Kenneth, 'Organisation of Agricultural Production', in ECKSTEIN, GALENSON & LIU, *Economic Trends in Communist China* (Edinburgh, 1968). (An economic survey of collectivisation focusing on the period 1955–58.)

63 WALKER, Kenneth, *Planning in Chinese Agriculture: Socialisation and the Private Sector 1956–1962* (London, 1965).

64 For a typical discussion of these problems in Cultural Revolution context, see *SCMM* 633, 4 Nov. 1968.

65 STRONG, Anna-Louise, *The Rise of the Chinese People's Communes* (Peking, 1959).

TANG, Peter S.H., *The Commune System in Mainland China* (Washington, 1961).

HUGHES, Richard, *The Chinese Communes* (London, 1960).

DUTT, Gargi, *Rural Communes of China* (London, 1967).

Peoples Communes in China (PFLP, 1958).

66 SKINNER, G. William, 'Marketing and Social Structure in Rural China', in *Journal of Asian Studies*, vol. XXIV, nos 1, 2, 3 (1964-5).

See also:

PFEFFER, Richard M., 'Contracts in China Revisited. With A Focus on Agriculture 1949-63', *CQ*, **28**, 1966. (On operation of supply and marketing co-operatives.)

67 SKINNER & WINCKLER, 'Compliance Succession in Rural Communist China', in ETZIONI, Amitai (ed.), *Complex Organisations: a Sociological Reader* (2nd ed., New York, 1969, pp. 410-38).

68 Notable exceptions to this are:

BIRRELL, R.J., 'The Centralised Control of the Communes in the Post "Great Leap" Period', in BARNETT, *Chinese Communist Politics in Action* (Seattle & London, 1969).

CHEN, C.S. (ed.), *Rural People's Communes in Lien-chiang*, trs. Ridley, C.R. (Stanford, 1969). (A documentary collection seized during a Kuomintang raid on the Fukien coast.)

BUCHANAN, K., *The Transformation of the Chinese Earth* (London, 1970), ch. 6.

ROBINSON, Joan, 'A British Economist on the Chinese Communes', *Eastern Horizon*, May, 1964.

69 SWAMI & BURKI, 'Food Grains Output of the Peoples Republic of China 1958-65', *CQ*, **41**, 1970. (A survey of some of the conflicting estimates.)

FIELD, Robert M., 'How much grain does Communist China produce?', *CQ*, **33**, 1968. See also his comments on the Swami and Burki figures in *CQ*, **46**, 1971.

70 See:

US Joint Publications Research Service, *Translations on Communist China's Agriculture, Animal Husbandry and Materials*.

References

71 LIU JUNG-CHAO, 'Fertilizer Application in Communist China', *CQ*, **24**, 1965.

RICHARDSON, S., *Forestry in Communist China* (Baltimore, Maryland, 1966). (Based on personal observations.)

The following books and pamphlets published by PFLP offer source material on rural development in the 1950s and 1960s.

Co-operative Farming in China, 1954.

Decisions on Agricultural Co-operation, 1956.

Draft Programme for Agricultural Development in the People's Republic of China (1956–1967), 1956.

Model Regulations for an Agricultural Producers' Co-operative, March 1956.

Model Regulations for Advanced Agricultural Producers' Co-operatives, June, 1956.

National Programme for Agricultural Development, 1956–1967, 1960.

Socialist Upsurge in China's Countryside, 1956, 1957.

TUNG, TA-LIN, *Agricultural Co-operation in China*, 1959.

LIAO, LU-YEN, *The Whole Party and the Whole People Go in for Agriculture in a Big Way*, 1960.

PO I-PO and LIAO LU-YEN, *Socialist Industrialisation and Agricultural Collectivisation in China*, 1964.

Urban Development and Industry

72 VOGEL, Ezra, *Canton under Communism. Programs and Politics in a Provincial Capital 1949–1968* (Cambridge, Mass., 1969).

73 LEWIS, John W. (ed.), *The City in Communist China* (Stanford, 1971). See also LEWIS, John W., 'Political Aspects of Mobility in China's Urban Development', *American Political Science Review*, December 1966.

HOWE, C., 'The Supply and Administration of Urban Housing in Mainland China: the Case of Shanghai', *CQ*, **33**, 1968.

HOWE, C., *Employment and Economic Growth in Urban China, 1949–1957* (Cambridge, 1971).

KAU YING-MAO, 'The Urban Bureaucratic Elite in Communist China: A Case Study of Wuhan 1949–65', in BARNETT, *Chinese Communist Politics in Action* (Seattle & London, 1969).

74 RICHMAN, Barry, *Industrial Society in Communist China* (New York, 1969).

75 RICHMAN, Barry, *A Firsthand Study of Industrial Management in Communist China* (Los Angeles, 1967).

76 See for example the following JPRS series:
Wages in Communist China
Wages, Manpower and Standard of Living in Communist China.

77 GARDNER, John, 'The Wu-fan Campaign in Shanghai: a Study in the Consolidation of Urban Control', in BARNETT, *Chinese Communist Politics in Action* (Seattle & London, 1969).

SALAFF, Janet, 'The Urban Communes and Anti-City Experiment in Communist China', *CQ*, **29**, 1967.

SHIH CH'ENG-CHIH, *Urban Commune Experiments in Communist China* (Hong Kong, URI, 1962).

See Paul Harper, 'The Party and the Unions in Communist China', *CQ*, **37**, 1969.

PRIESTLEY, K.E., *Workers of China* (London, 1965).

SHENG CHU-YUAN, *Anshan Steel Factory in Communist China* (Hong Kong, URI, 1955).

HOFFMANN, Charles, 'Work Incentive Policy in Communist China', *CQ*, **17**, 1964.

KALLGREN, Joyce, 'Social Welfare and China's Industrial Workers', in BARNETT, *Chinese Communist Politics in Action* (Seattle & London, 1969).

78 See for example:
LI CHOH-MING (ed.), *Industrial Development in Communist China* (New York, 1964).
See also section on 'General Economic Studies'.

Population and Manpower

79 HO PING-TI, *Studies on the Population of China 1368–1953* (Cambridge, Mass., 1959).

80 For two conflicting views of birth control campaigns see:
HAN SUYIN, 'Birth Control in China: Recent Aspects', *The Eugenics Review*, vol. 52, no. 1, 1960.
ORLEANS, Leo A., 'Birth Control: Reversal or Postponement', *CQ*, **3**, 1960.

References

See also:

ORLEANS, Leo A., 'A New Birth Control Campaign?', *CQ*, **12**, 1962.

ORLEANS, Leo A., 'Evidence from China's Medical Journals on Current Population Policy', *CQ*, **40**, 1969.

WERTHEIM, 'Recent Trends in China's Population Policy', *Science and Society*, spring 1966. New York.

BUCHANAN, *The Transformation of the Chinese Earth* (London, 1970), ch. 13.

AIRD, John S., 'Population Growth', in ECKSTEIN, GALENSON & LIU, *Economic Trends in Communist China* (Edinburgh, 1968).

CHANDRASEKHAR, Sripati, *China's Population, Census and Vital Statistics* (revised 2nd ed. Hong Kong, 1960).

EMERSON, John Philip, *Non-Agricultural Employment in Mainland China, 1949–1958* (Washington, 1965).

ULLMAN, M.B., *Cities of Mainland China, 1953 and 1958* (Washington, 1961). (A discussion of urban population statistics.) For a bibliographical survey of earlier articles see: US Dept of Commerce, Bureau of the Census, *The Population and Manpower of China: an Annotated Bibliography* (Washington, US GPO, 1958).

Education

81 For example:

WANG, Y.C., *Chinese Intellectuals and the West, 1872–1947* (Chapel Hill, NC, 1966). (A background study.)

Documentary collections include:

FRASER, Stewart, *Chinese Communist Education: Records of the First Decade* (Nashville, Tennessee, 1965).

FRASER, Stewart F., *Education and Communism in China – An Anthology of Commentary and Documents* (Hong Kong, 1969). (Foreigners' accounts covering general education and primary and secondary level teachers, including a section on the Cultural Revolution. There is very little on part-work, part-study schools.) HU CHANG-TU, *Chinese Education under Communism* (New York, 1962). (A collection of documents by Mao, Liu Shao-ch'i and Lu Ting-i, with a useful bibliography and introduction.)

82 TSANG CHIU-SAM, *Society, Schools and Progress in China* (Oxford, 1968).
83 PRICE, Ronald F., *Education in Communist China* (London, 1970).
See also:
KUN, Joseph E., 'Higher Education: Some Problems of Selection and Enrolment', *CQ*, **8**, 1961.
HSÜ, Immanuel C.Y., 'The Reorganisation of Higher Education in Communist China, 1949–61', *CQ*, **19**, 1964.
BARENDSEN, Robert D., 'The Agricultural Middle School in Communist China', *CQ*, **8**, 1961.
See also:
BASTID, Marianne, 'Economic Necessity and Political Ideals in Educational Reform During the Cultural Revolution', *CQ*, **42**, 1970.
ABE, Munemitsu, 'Spare Time Education in Communist China', *CQ*, **8**, 1961.
BARENDSEN, Robert D., *Half Work, Half Study Schools in Communist China* (US Office of Education, 1964 [OE 14100]).
HARPER, Paul, *Spare Time Education for Workers in Communist China* (US Office of Education, 1964 [OE 14102]).
LEE, Rennsalaer W., 'The Hsia Fang System: Marxism and Modernisation', *CQ*, **28**, 1966.
For a bibliographical survey of articles on education see US State Department, *Education in Communist China: A Selective List of Books, Pamphlets and Periodical Articles on the State of Education in Mainland China 1953–1963* (External research paper), 1964.
84 ORLEANS, *Professional Manpower and Education in Communist China* (Washington, 1961).
85 CH'EN, Theodore H.E., *Thought Reform of the Chinese Intellectuals* (Hong Kong, 1960). (An account of policy towards intellectuals, 1949–57.)
GOLDMAN, Merle, 'The Unique "Blooming and Contending" of 1961–62', *CQ*, **37**, 1969.
DOOLIN, Dennis J., *Communist China: the Politics of Student Opposition* (Stanford, 1964).
JOHNSON, Chalmers, *Communist Policies Toward the Intellectual Class* (Hong Kong, 1959).

References

OLIVER, Adam, 'Rectification of Mainland China Intellectuals 1964–65', *Asian Survey*, October 1965.

MU FU-SHENG, *The Wilting of the Hundred Flowers* (London 1962).

ISRAEL, John, 'The Red Guards in Historical Perspective: Continuity and Change in the Chinese Youth Movement', *CQ*, **30**, 1967.

NEE, Victor, *The Cultural Revolution in Peking University* (New York, 1969).

GOLDMAN, René, 'Peking University Today', *CQ*, **7**, 1961.

GOLDMAN, René, 'The Rectification Campaign at Peking University May–June 1957', *CQ*, **12**, 1962.

MACFARQUHAR, Roderick, *The Hundred Flowers Campaign and the Chinese Intellectuals* (New York, 1960). (A translation of various types of criticisms with comment.)

Law

86 Examples of translations include:

Compendium of Laws and Regulations of the People's Republic of China. 14 volumes since 1954–62. In Chinese, mostly translated into English by JPRS.

RICKETT, W. Allyn, *Legal Thought and Institutions of the People's Republic of China: Selected Documents* (Preliminary draft) (Philadelphia, 1963).

COHEN, Jerome A., *Preliminary Materials on the Law of Communist China* (Berkeley, California, 1961).

BLAUSTEIN, Albert P., *Fundamental Legal Documents of Communist China* (South Hackensack, New Jersey, 1962).

Agrarian Reform Law of the People's Republic of China and Other Relevant Documents (PFLP, 1959).

Important Labour Laws and Regulations of the People's Republic of China (PFLP, 1961).

The Trade Union Law of the People's Republic of China (PFLP, 1951).

The Marriage Law of the People's Republic of China – with explanatory materials by Teng Ying-ch'ao (Mme. Chou En-lai) (PFLP, 1959).

Policy Towards Nationalities of the People's Republic of China (PFLP, 1953).

I

The Electoral Law of the People's Republic of China (PFLP, 1953).

87 MICHAEL, Franz, 'The Role of Law in Traditional, Nationalist and Communist China', *CQ*, 9, 1962.

LENG SHAO-CHUAN, 'Pre-1949 Development of the Communist Chinese System of Justice', *CQ*, 30, 1967.

COHEN, Jerome Alan, *The Criminal Process in the People's Republic of China, 1949–1963, An Introduction* (Cambridge, Mass., 1968).

88 BODDE & CLARK, *Chinese Law: a Selected Bibliography with a Bibliography of the Communist Period* (Cambridge, Mass., 1961).

LIN FU-SHUN, *Chinese Law Past and Present* (New York, 1966) (a bibliography).

For a comparison of Soviet and Chinese legal practice see TREADGOLD, *Soviet and Chinese Communism* (Seattle and London, 1967: part III, 'Communist Law and Social Change').

National Minorities

89 GINSBURGS & MATHOS, *Communist China and Tibet, the First Dozen Years* (The Hague, 1964). *Concerning the Question of Tibet* (PFLP, 1959).

Tibet 1950–1967 (Hong Kong, URI, 1968). (Contains a useful selected bibliography.)

MORAES, Frank, *The Revolt in Tibet* (New York, 1960).

PATTERSON, George, *Tibet in Revolt* (London, 1960).

RAJA HUTHEESING (ed.), *Tibet Fights for Freedom, A White Book* (Bombay, 1960).

90 For examples of two opposing views see:

HOWARTH, David (ed.), *My Land and My People: the Auto-biography of His Holiness the Dalai Lama* (London, 1962).

GELDER, Stuart and Roma, *The Timely Rain, Travels in New Tibet* (London, 1964).

91 *Tibet and the Chinese People's Republic: a Report to the International Commission of Jurists by Its Legal Inquiry Committee on Tibet* (Geneva, 1960).

92 MOSELEY, George, 'China's Fresh Approach to the National Minority Question', *CQ*, 24, 1965.

References

MOSELEY, George, *A Sino-Soviet Cultural Frontier – the Ili Kazakh Autonomous Chou* (Cambridge, Mass.; London, 1967).

MOSELEY (ed.), *The Party and the National Question in China* (Cambridge, Mass. & London, 1966).

SCHWARTZ, Henry G. ,'Chinese Migration to North West China and Inner Mongolia 1949–59', *CQ*, **16**, 1963.

WHEELER, Geoffrey, 'Sinkiang and the Soviet Union', *CQ*, **16**, 1963. LO, J.P., 'Five Years of the Sinkiang-Uighur Autonomous Region 1955–60', *CQ*, **8**, 1961.

93 WINNINGTON, Alan, *The Slaves of the Cool Mountains* (London, 1959).

Military Development and the Role of the People's Liberation Army

94 HALPERIN & PERKINS, *Communist China and Arms Control* (New York, 1965).

FORD, Harold P., 'Modern Weapons and the Sino-Soviet Estrangement', *CQ*, **18**, 1964. (*CQ*, **18** was a special issue devoted to military affairs. There are some useful articles not quoted here.)

BUESCHEL, R. M., *Communist Chinese Air Power* (New York, 1968).

GARTHOFF, Raymond, *Sino-Soviet Military Relations* (New York, 1966; London, 1967).

95 HSIEH, Alice Langley, *Communist China's Strategy in the Nuclear Era* (Englewood Cliffs, NJ, 1962).

HALPERIN, Morton H., *China and the Bomb* (London, 1965).

YOUNG, Oran R., 'Chinese Views on the Spread of Nuclear Weapons', *CQ*, **26**, 1966.

CLEMENS, Walter C. Jnr, 'Chinese Nuclear Tests: Trends & Portents', *CQ*, **32**, 1967.

96 On the military and political performance of the PLA in the late 1940s and early 1950s see:

CHASSIN, Lionel Max, *The Communist Conquest of China: a History of the Civil War 1945–49* (Cambridge, Mass., 1965; London, 1966). (Translated from the French by Timothy Osalo and Louis Gelas; originally published in French, Paris, 1952.)

GEORGE, Alexander L., *The Chinese Communist Army in Action* (New York, 1967). (A far ranging work of military sociology.)
GRIFFITH, Samuel B., II, *The Chinese Peoples Liberation Army* (London, 1968; New York, 1967).
For a good general introduction to the role of the PLA in society see:
GITTINGS, John, *The Role of the Chinese Army* (London, 1967).
See also:
GITTINGS, John, 'Military Control and Leadership 1949–64', *CQ*, **26**, 1966. (A study of top level military organisation.)
WHITSON, William, 'The Field Army in Chinese Communist Military Politics', *CQ*, **37**, 1969. (An analysis of how the old field army organisation affects current military organisation. This will be amplified in a forthcoming book.)
JOFFE, Ellis, 'The Conflict Between Old and New in the Chinese Army', *CQ*, **18**, 1964.
97 CHENG, J. Chester (ed.), *The Politics of the Chinese Red Army*, a translation of the Bulletin of activities of the People's Liberation Army (Hoover Institution, 1966).
See also:
LEWIS, John Wilson, 'China's Secret Military Papers: "Continuities" and "Revelations"', *CQ*, **18**, 1964.
HSIEH, Alice Langley, 'China's Secret Military Papers: Military Doctrine and Strategy', *CQ*, **18**, 1964.
98 JOFFE, *Party and Army: Professionalism and Political Control in the Chinese Officer Corps, 1949–1964* (Cambridge, Mass., 1965).
HALPERIN AND LEWIS, 'New Tensions in Army-Party Relations in China 1965–66', *CQ*, **26**, 1966.
POWELL, Ralph L., *Politico Military Relationships in Communist China, 1963* (US Dept of State, Bureau of Intelligence and Research. External Research Staff, 1963).
99 CHIEN YU-SHEN, *China's Fading Revolution: Army Dissent and Military Division 1967–68* (Hong Kong, 1969). (A mass of semi-digested material.)

Foreign Policy and Attitudes Towards China

100 TSOU TANG, *America's Failure in China 1941–1950* (London & Chicago, 1963).

References

For a very different view of the same topic see:
KOLKO, Gabriel, *The Politics of War* (London, 1968). (Relevant chapters on US–China relations.)

See also:

MORGENTHAU, Hans J., 'The Roots of America's China Policy', *CQ*, **10**, 1962.

FAIRBANK, John K., *China: the People's Middle Kingdom and the U.S.A.* (Cambridge, Mass., 1967).

APPLETON, Sheldon, *The Eternal Triangle? Communist China, the United States and the United Nations* (Mich., 1961).

WHITING, Allen S., *China Crosses the Yalu: the Decision to Enter the Korean War* (New York, 1960).

REES, David, *Korea: the Limited War* (London, 1964).

GREENE, Felix, *Curtain of Ignorance* (NY Garden City, 1964).

See also:

UNIVERSITY OF MICHIGAN: SURVEY RESEARCH CENTER, *The American Public's View of U.S. Policy Toward China* (New York, 1964).

HENSMAN, C.R., *China: Yellow Peril? Red Hope?* (London, 1968).

101 *U.S. Policy with Respect to Mainland China.* Hearings before the Committee on Foreign Relations. (US Senate, Washington US GPO, 1966.)

102 ZAGORIA, Donald, *The Sino-Soviet Conflict 1956–61* (Princeton NJ, 1962).

GITTINGS, John, *Survey of the Sino-Soviet Dispute 1963–1967* (London, 1968).

HUDSON, LOWENTHAL & MACFARQUHAR, *The Sino-Soviet Dispute* (London; published by *CQ*, 1961).

GRIFFITH, W.E., *The Sino-Soviet Rift* (Cambridge, Mass., 1964).

GRIFFITH, W.E., *Sino-Soviet Relations* (Cambridge, Mass. & London, 1967).

See also:

ZAGORIA, Donald, *Vietnam Triangle – Moscow/Peking/Hanoi* (New York, 1967).

The Polemic on the General Line of the International Communist Movement (PFLP, 1965).

For theoretical discussions of the Sino-Soviet dispute see:

235

SCHWARTZ, Benjamin, *Communism and China: Ideology in Flux* (Cambridge, Mass., 1968).

TUCKER, Robert, 'The Deradicalisation of Marxist Movements', *American Political Science Review*, June 1967.

CARRÈRE D'ENCAUSSE & SCHRAM, *Marxism and Asia* (London, 1969).

103 LEGUM, Colin, 'Africa and China: Symbolism and Substance', in HALPERN, A.M., *Policies Towards China: Views from Six Continents* (New York, 1965). (Other items in this collection are worthy of consideration.)

HEVI, Emmanuel J., *The Dragon's Embrace: the Chinese Communists and Africa* (London, 1967).

The Chinese People Resolutely Support the Just Struggle of the African People (Peking, PFLP, 1961).

104 The most recent and authoritative contribution to this problem is:

MAXWELL, Neville, *India's China War* (London, 1970).

See also:

VAN EEKELEN, W.F., *Indian Foreign Policy and the Border Dispute with China* (The Hague, 1964).

Documentary collections include:

The Sino-Soviet Boundary Question (Peking; PFLP, 1962).

Selected Documents on Sino-Indian Relations (December 1961–May 1962) (Peking: PFLP, 1962).

Indian Ministry of External Affairs: *Report of the Officials of the Governments of India and the People's Republic of China on the Boundary Question* (Delhi: Government of India, 1961).

105 WILSON, David, 'China, Thailand and the Spirit of Bandung', *CQ*, **30** & **31**, 1967.

LALL, *How Communist China Negotiates* (New York & London, 1968).

WILLIAMS, Lea E., 'Sino-Indonesian Diplomacy: a Study of Revolutionary International Politics', *CQ*, **11**, 1962.

VAN DER KROEF, 'The Sino-Indonesian Rupture', *CQ*, **33**, 1968.

SHARMA, B.L., *The Pakistan-China Axis* (London, 1968). (A highly impassioned defence of Indian foreign policy.)

MUSHTAQ AHMAD, *Pakistan's Foreign Policy* (Karachi, 1968).

KUN, Joseph C., 'North Korea: Between Moscow and Peking', *CQ*, **31**, 1967.

References

VAN DER KROEF, Justus M., 'Philippine Communism and the Chinese', *CQ*, **30**, 1967.

106 LUARD, *Britain and China* (London, 1962). (Provides useful background material though does not fit Sino-British relations into a wider world-context.)

ERASMUS, Stephen, 'General de Gaulle's Recognition of Peking', *CQ*, **18**, 1964.

107 See:

HALPERIN, Ernst, 'Peking and the Latin American Communists', *CQ*, **29**, 1967.

ALBA, Victor, 'The Chinese in Latin America', *CQ*, **5**, 1961.

108 YAHUDA, Michael B., 'Chinese Foreign Policy After 1963: the Maoist Phases', *CQ*, **36**, 1968.

HU SHENG, *Imperialism and Chinese Politics* (Peking: PFLP, 1955).

FITZGERALD, C.P., *The Chinese View of their Place in the World* (London, 1964). (An introductory essay for the non-expert.)

HINTON, Harold C., *Communist China in World Politics* (Boston, 1966).

DUTT, Vidya Prakash, *China's Foreign Policy* (London, 1964).

The Cultural Revolution

109 For a general discussion of source material see:

BENNETT, Gordon A. (notes), 'Hong Kong and Taiwan Sources for Research into the Cultural Revolution Period', *CQ*, **36**, 1968.

110 BRIDGHAM, Philip, 'Mao's Cultural Revolution', *CQ*, **29**, 1967; *CQ*, **34**, 1968; *CQ*, **41**, 1970.

See also:

JOFFE, Ellis, 'China in Mid-1966: Cultural Revolution or Struggle for Power', *CQ*, **27**, 1966.

111 GRAY & CAVENDISH, *Chinese Communism in Crisis, Maoism and the Cultural Revolution* (London, 1968).

LIFTON, R.J., *Revolutionary Immortality* (London, 1969).

UHALLEY, Stephen Jnr, 'The Cultural Revolution and the Attack on the Three Family Village', *CQ*, **27**, 1966.

ROBINSON, Joan, *The Cultural Revolution in China* (Harmondsworth, 1969).

112 NEUHAUSER, Charles, 'The Chinese Communist Party in the 1960s: Prelude to the Cultural Revolution', *CQ*, **32**, 1967.

BAUM & TEIWES, *Ssu Ch'ing: the Socialist Education Movement 1962–66* (Berkeley, California, University of California Research Monographs, No. 2, 1968).

See also:

BAUM, Richard, 'Revolution and Reaction in the Chinese Countryside: the Socialist Education Movement in Cultural Revolutionary Perspective', *CQ*, **38**, 1969.

113 HUNTER, Neale, *Shanghai Journal: an Eyewitness Account of the Cultural Revolution* (New York, 1969).

MORAVIA, Alberto, *The Red Book and the Great Wall: an Impression of Mao's China* (London, 1968).

BENNETT & MONTAPERTO, *Red Guard: The Political Biography of Dai Hsiao-ai* (New York and London, 1971).

MACKERRAS & HUNTER, *China Observed* (London, 1968).

114 *CCP Documents on the Great Proletarian Cultural Revolution 1966–67* (Kowloon: URI, 1968).

The Great Socialist Cultural Revolution in China (afterwards *The Great Proletarian Cultural Revolution in China*) (10 pamphlets) (Peking: PFLP, 1966–67).

FAN, K.H., *The Chinese Cultural Revolution: Selected Documents* (New York, 1968).

115 On the impact of the Cultural Revolution on institutions and social groups see:

GURTOV, Melvin, 'The Foreign Ministry and Foreign Affairs During the Cultural Revolution', *CQ*, **40**, 1969.

FITZGERALD, Stephen, 'Overseas Chinese Affairs and the Cultural Revolution', *CQ*, **40**, 1969.

WELCH, Holmes, 'Buddhism Since the Cultural Revolution', *CQ*, **40**, 1969.

DOMES, Jurgen, 'The role of the Military in the Formation of Revolutionary Committees 1967–68', *CQ*, **44**, 1970.

DREYER, June, 'China's Minority Nationalities in the Cultural Revolution', *CQ*, **35**, 1968.

OKSENBERG, RISKIN, SCALAPINO & VOGEL, *The Cultural Revolution, 1967 in Review* (Michigan Papers in Chinese Studies, No. 2, 1968).

References

HEYER & HEATO, 'The Cultural Revolution in Inner Mongolia', *CQ*, 36, 1968.

KLEIN, Donald W., 'The State Council and the Cultural Revolution', *CQ*, 35, 1968.

NEE, Victor, *The Cultural Revolution in Peking University* (New York, 1969).

TSOU TANG, 'The Cultural Revolution and the Chinese Political System', *CQ*, 38, 1969.

PERKINS, Dwight H., 'Economic Growth and the Cultural Revolution (1966 – April 1967)', *CQ*, 30, 1967.

116 See:

BARNETT, A. Doak, *China After Mao* (Princeton NJ, 1967).

HAN SUYIN, *China in the Year 2001* (London, 1967).

Africa

Dennis Austin and William Tordoff

The volume of literature on African government and politics is now so vast that one scarcely knows where to begin, and what follows must necessarily fall far short of a complete bibliography. Four trends are discernible. First, there is a shift in the focus of attention away from parties and interest groups towards a study of the instruments of control – the bureaucracy, army and police. Secondly, micro-political studies are now in vogue: more scholars are turning their attention to the rural areas and town-wards in order to test the validity of research hitherto conducted primarily (though not exclusively) at national and provincial levels. Thirdly, there is an increasing number of volumes pursuing Africa-wide themes, some looking at Africa in an international setting, others trying to understand what is meant by 'political development' in the continent as a whole. Fourthly, there is a continuing interest in the loose array of arguments and beliefs employed by a number of African leaders to explain and justify their politics.

The emergence of political parties in Africa after 1945 stimulated the growth of behavioural enquiries which found parties and the political process more interesting than constitutional structures. Gabriel A. Almond and James S. Coleman (eds), *The Politics of the Developing Areas* (Princeton, 1960) stressed the unifying function of parties. They were followed by Thomas Hodgkin, *African Political Parties* (Harmondsworth, 1961), Immanuel Wallerstein, *Africa: The Politics of Independence* (New York, 1961), and by Ruth Schachter Morgenthau who wrote a pioneer study, *Political Parties in*

French-Speaking West Africa (Oxford, 1964). Kenneth Robinson drew upon the manuscript of the latter in his electoral study of Senegal in the book, *Five Elections in Africa* (Oxford, 1960), which he edited with W. J. M. Mackenzie; his chapter served as a model for subsequent electoral studies, including K. W. J. Post's *The Nigerian Federal Election of 1959* (London, 1963). These early works were supplemented by more detailed studies of post-independence politics in individual countries.

Among studies of French-speaking Africa were Aristide R. Zolberg, *One-Party Government in the Ivory Coast* (Princeton, 1964), Frank G. Snyder, *One-Party Government in Mali* (New Haven and London, 1965), and Clement H. Moore, *Tunisia since Independence: The Dynamics of One-Party Government* (Berkeley and Los Angeles, 1965). On the English-speaking states, useful contributions include David E. Apter, *Ghana in Transition* (New York, 1963), Dennis Austin, *Politics in Ghana, 1946-60* (London, 1964), Richard L. Sklar, *Nigerian Political Parties* (Princeton, 1963), John P. Mackintosh (ed.), *Nigerian Government and Politics* (London, 1966), B. J. Dudley, *Parties and Politics in Northern Nigeria* (London, 1968), Martin Kilson, *Political Change in a West African State – Sierra Leone* (Cambridge, Mass., 1966), Catherine Hoskyns, *The Congo since Independence* (London, 1965), Crawford Young, *Politics in the Congo* (Princeton, 1965), William Tordoff, *Government and Politics in Tanzania* (Nairobi, 1967), Henry Bienen, *Tanzania* (Princeton, 1967), and David C. Mulford, *Zambia, 1957-64* (London, 1967). These country-by-country studies were supplemented by the autobiographies and collected speeches of the African leaders themselves – Awolowo, Azikiwe, Ahmadu Bello, Kaunda, Kenyatta, Mboya, Nkrumah, Nyerere, Oginga Odinga, Senghor and Sékou Touré. Among the more refreshing were those by Julius K. Nyerere, *Freedom and Unity* and *Freedom and Socialism*, published in Dar es Salaam in 1966 and 1968.

These early African studies showed that, while the new states faced many common problems, they often tackled them differently. Some of the differences are brought out in the volumes edited by Gwendolen Carter: *African One-Party*

States (1962), *Five African States* (1963), and *National Unity and Regionalism* (1966), Ithaca, New York. Competitive elections in the one-party state, as in Tanzania in 1965, prompted a full-scale study edited by Lionel Cliffe – *One Party Democracy: the 1965 Tanzania General Elections* (Nairobi, 1967); by contrast, there was little to prompt research interest in the corresponding elections in 1965 in Ghana. There were in fact such sharp contrasts between one single party system and another that it was very difficult to plot them typographically, as James S. Coleman and Carl G. Rosberg tried to do in their introduction to *Political Parties and National Integration in Tropical Africa* (Berkeley and Los Angeles, 1964). It was not clear, for example, whether Uganda and Zambia belonged to the group of uniparty or one-party-dominant states said to be following a 'pragmatic-pluralistic pattern' or to the other group marked by what was said to be a 'revolutionary-centralising trend'. Students of African politics were finding, with some dismay which may be the beginning of more cautious interpretations, that the self-projected image of the African leaders and their parties did not often correspond with the facts. Thus Henry Bienen in his *Tanzania: Party Transformation and Economic Development* (Princeton, 1967) showed that TANU was not at all the 'revolutionary, ideological and mobilising party' that the Coleman-Rosberg typology had led its readers to believe. Moreover, the number of military coups, riots and disturbances in Black Africa exploded the myth that the single party system was any more conducive to political stability than other forms of civilian rule. More cautionary accounts had already been voiced by W. Arthur Lewis in a challenging essay, *Politics in West Africa* (London, 1965), by Aristide Zolberg in a short perceptive study *Creating Political Order: The Party-States of West Africa* (Chicago, 1966), and by S. E. Finer in his contribution to the special African issue of *Government and Opposition* (London, July-October 1967) edited by Dennis Austin.

Despite a growing attention to the military, countrywide political studies continued to appear. Christopher Clapham wrote on *Haile Selassie's Government* (London, 1969); Cherry

Gertzel produced *The Politics of Independent Kenya* (London, 1970) and helped to edit a collection of documents on *Government and Politics in Kenya* (Nairobi, 1969). Guy de Lusignan provided useful information in *French-Speaking Africa since Independence* (London, 1969), though the need for a definitive study of the politics of Francophone Africa remains. Detailed studies of the constitutions and legal framework of the African states are relatively few in number, and such accounts that have appeared – for example, Leslie Rubin and Pauli Murray, *The Constitution and Government of Ghana* (London, 1961) – tend to be quickly outdated by events.

Some attention also continues to be given to interest groups, especially trade unions, though after independence they have tended to lose much of their former autonomy. Wallerstein followed up his discussion of voluntary associations in *The Road to Independence: Ghana and the Ivory Coast* (The Hague, 1965) with a chapter in Coleman and Rosberg (eds), *Political Parties and National Integration in Tropical Africa* (see above). That book also contained a chapter on 'Trade Unions' by Elliot J. Berg and Jeffrey Butler who challenged the accepted view that African unions were politically involved during the colonial period and pointed to their restricted role after independence. Evidence to support these conclusions was subsequently provided for Uganda by Roger Scott in *The Development of Trade Unions in Uganda* (Nairobi, 1966), for Zambia by David C. Mulford in his carefully documented *Zambia: The Politics of Independence, 1957–64* (London, 1967), and for Tanzania by William H. Friedland in *Vuta Kamba: The Development of Trade Unions in Tanganyika* (Stanford, 1969). Friedland had earlier contributed a chapter to Jeffrey Butler and A. A. Castagno (eds), *Boston University Papers on Africa: Transition in African Politics* (New York, 1967) which also contained a discussion on 'Pan-African Trade Union Organisation' by Dorothy Nelkin, and a study of the development of trade unionism in Ethiopia by Arnold Zack. We are indebted to Friedland for producing an extremely useful bibliography, *Unions, Labour and Industrial Relations in Africa* (Ithaca, 1965).

As to the military, early works by Samuel Huntington, Morris Janowitz and S. E. Finer set the scene for subsequent volumes more directly concerned with Africa. The analysis by James Coleman and Belmont Brice, 'The Role of the Military in Sub-Saharan Africa', in J. F. Johnson (ed.), *The Role of the Military in Underdeveloped Countries* (Princeton, 1962) was followed by the studies of W. F. Gutteridge, the most recent being *The Military in African Politics* (London, 1969); Henry Bienen edited *The Military Intervenes: Case Studies* (New York, 1968), J. M. Lee looked at *African Armies and Civil Order* (London, 1969) and Ruth First wrote *The Barrel of a Gun* (Harmondsworth, 1970) in which the colonial scapegoat is once again slaughtered in ritual manner. There is also a growing literature on the army in individual African countries. The pioneering work on Egypt by P. J. Vatikiotis, *The Egyptian Army in Politics* (Indiana, 1961) has been followed by A. Abdel Malik, *Egypt – Military Society* (New York, 1968). Ghana and especially Nigeria have attracted most attention. Participants in the Ghana coup have provided their own accounts – including A. A. Afrifa, *The Ghana Coup* (London, 1966) and A. K. Ocran, *The Myth is Broken*. For Nigeria, some works have already appeared, including S. K. Panter-Brick (ed.), *Nigerian Politics and Military Rule: Prelude to the Civil War* (London, 1970), while others – by Robin Luckham, Martin Dent and B. J. Dudley – are either already in the press or nearing completion. By contrast, much less has been written about the role of the police in African states. One of the first studies in this respect is C. Okonkwo, *The Police and the Public in Nigeria* (London, 1966). Other studies are likely to follow, while demilitarisation in Sudan, Ghana, Dahomey and Sierra Leone, and the prospect of a return to civilian rule elsewhere, give promise of a number of books dealing with the problem. One study, now nearing completion, is Dennis Austin and Robin Luckham (eds), *The Return to Military Rule in Ghana* to be published for the Royal Institute of International Affairs by Oxford University Press in 1972–3.

The disappearance from the political scene of what seemed to be strong political parties – for example, the CPP in Ghana and the US in Mali – and the transitional nature of military rule, have led scholars to turn to a study of the bureaucracy as perhaps the only constant element in the government of new African states. That this is overdue is reflected by the lack of substantial works to serve as a modern version of Lord Hailey's four volume study: *Native Administration in the British African Territories* (London, 1951) or of particular studies, such as Margery Perham's *Native Administration in Nigeria* (London, 1937). Kenneth Younger's pioneering study *The Public Service in New States* (London, 1960) went beyond Africa and was not, moreover, followed by full-scale studies of African bureaucracies in published form. The problem tended to be subsumed in wider enquiries, as for example, by Taylor Cole in his chapter on Nigeria in the book *The Nigerian Political Scene* (Durham, N. Carolina, 1962) which he edited with Robert O. Tilman; by I. Nicolson, 'The Machinery of the Federal and Regional Governments' in John P. Mackintosh (ed.), *Nigerian Government and Politics* (London, 1966); by A. H. M. Kirk-Greene, John Chick and other contributors to L. Franklin Blitz (ed.), *The Politics and Administration of Nigerian Government* (London, 1965); and by William Tordoff in *Government and Politics in Tanzania* (Nairobi, 1967). The administrative aspects of local government have been given some attention in (for example) L. Gray Cowan, *Local Government in West Africa* (London, 1958), Ronald E. Wraith, *Local Government in West Africa* (London, 1964) and in more particular studies such as Philip J. Harris, *Local Government in Southern Nigeria* (London, 1957), J. K. Nsarkoh, *Local Government in Ghana* (Accra, 1964), F. G. Burke, *Local Government and Politics in Uganda* (Syracuse, 1964), and Stanley Dryden, *Local Administration in Tanzania* (Nairobi, 1968). In addition, a large number of articles (often detailed) on aspects of administration appeared, and continue to appear, in periodicals such as the *Journal of Administration Overseas* (London).

The publication, in 1963, of a study in the Princeton series – *Bureaucracy and Political Development*, edited by Joseph La Palombara – was less of a pioneering study than might have been expected. Only one chapter (by J. Donald Kingsley) concerned Africa, and it dealt mainly with Nigeria. Even more worrying was the fact that in their own substantive works some of the American scholars who contributed to this volume – Joseph La Palombara, S. N. Eisenstadt and Fred W. Riggs – seemed determined to endow the new state bureaucracies with some of the virtues (for example, of unity and cohesion) that other writers had once given to political parties – a transfer of hope rather than a conclusion from conviction? The need for closer studies of African bureaucracies was still evident. A book that pointed the way to filling this gap appeared in 1965: A. L. Adu's *The Civil Service in New African States* (London, 1965), which examined the changing role of the civil service in the machinery of government in Africa and considered especially the need to establish and maintain service standards and traditions. Brian C. Smith's *Field Administration: An Aspect of Decentralisation* (London, 1967) carried further the earlier work of Henry Maddick; more recent studies, based on particular countries, include A. Adedeji, *Nigerian Administration and its Political Setting* (London, 1968) – a collection of seminar papers; and I. F. Nicolson, *The Administration of Nigeria, 1900–60 – Men, Methods and Myths* (Oxford, 1970) which concentrates on destroying the myth of Lugard. More exciting is the prospect of a full-scale study of the Zambian civil service, now being prepared by Dennis L. Dresang of the University of Wisconsin at Madison. Dresang is also one of the contributors to a forthcoming volume on *Government and Politics in Zambia,* being edited by William Tordoff, which will include a number of chapters dealing specifically with development and administration. The growing interest in development administration is also reflected in the work of the Institute of Development Studies in Sussex, and at Nairobi in Kenya. (See, for example, the comprehensive bibliography on 'Development in Africa: Planning and Implementation' prepared by Angela Molnos and published by the East African Academy Research Information Centre in April 1970.) The Nairobi Institute has attracted a number of students of administration, including Robert Chambers, to whom we are indebted for his studies of the administrative aspects of Ghana's Volta River Project and rural settlement in Kenya. The study of administration and politics in Tanzania by another 'East African', R. Cranford Pratt, is also awaited.

Micro-political studies are now being undertaken in many parts of the Continent, but nowhere with more vigour than in East Africa from the Universities of Makerere, Dar es Salaam and Nairobi. Early and valuable fruits of this work are: Colin Leys, *Policies and Politicians: An Essay on Politics in Acholi, Uganda, 1962–65* (Nairobi, 1967), Goran Hyden's *Tanu Yajenga Nchi: Political Development in Rural Tanzania* (Lund, Scandinavian University Books, 1968), and G. Andrew Maquire's study of the Wasukuma, *Toward 'Uhuru' in Tanzania: The Politics of Participation* (London, 1970).

By contrast, a number of scholars continue to explore broad themes across the Continent. For example, Ali Mazrui has produced yet another stimulating collection of essays, *Violence and Thought: Essays on Social Tensions in Africa* (London, 1969) and, with Robert Rotberg, has edited the monumental *Protest and Power in Black Africa* (New York, 1970). Irving L. Markovitz has edited *African Politics and Society* (New York, 1970), which attempts to focus on the dynamics of African societies in transition. Inter-African relations are investigated by Immanuel Wallerstein in *Africa: The Politics of Unity* (New York, 1967), an account of the major political developments in Africa between 1957 and 1965 written from the perspective of the movement, such as it is, towards African unity. Nominal success in reaching the goal of African unity was achieved in 1963 through the formation of the Organisation of African Unity, whose organisational problems are studied by Zdenek Cervenka, *The Organisation of African Unity, and its Charter* (New York, 1969). Catherine Hoskyns has drawn upon her extensive knowledge of Congo (Kinshasa) in writing *The Organisation of African Unity and the Congo Crisis, 1964–65* (London, 1969), while the OAU's attempt to arbitrate African boundary problems is one of the subjects studied in Carl Widstrand (ed.), *African Boundary Problems* (Uppsala, 1969). Studies of particular foreign policies of the African States are only now beginning to appear: a weighty contribution was the detailed examination of Ghana's foreign policy under Nkrumah by W. Scott Thompson (Princeton, 1969).

Consideration of Africa is also included in the growing volume of literature dealing with the Third World. Peter Worsley's book of that title (London, 1964) has been followed by a large number of volumes on conceptual problems and practical policies, as in David E. Apter, *The Politics of Modernization* (Chicago, 1965); James S. Coleman (ed.), *Education and Political Development* (Princeton, 1965) – one of a number of Princeton studies in political development; Claude Welch (ed.), *Political Modernization* (Belmont, 1967); and F. R. Van der Mehden, *Politics of the Developing Nations* (New York, 1969). Perhaps the best of these books – because one of the most specific in terms of the problems with which it deals – is Colin Leys (ed.), *Politics and Change in Developing Countries* (Cambridge, 1969).

Very few African states have an ideology in the sense of a systematic and coherent pattern of beliefs. On the other hand, clusters of ideas are expressed: on nationalism; negritude and the African personality; African socialism and one-party theories; neo-colonialism, pan-Africanism and non-alignment. These ideas can be studied in edited collections and commentaries, such as James Duffy and Robert A. Manners (eds), *Africa Speaks* (Princeton, 1961), Paul E. Sigmund (ed.), *The Ideologies of the Developing Nations* (New York, 1963), Claude Wauthier, *The Literature and Thought of Modern Africa* (London, 1966), and William H. Friedland and Carl G. Rosberg Jr (eds), *African Socialism* (London, 1964) as well as in the writings of the new state leaders with whom these ideas are usually associated. Thus, the neo-colonialist predicament is examined from different standpoints by Kwame Nkrumah, Frantz Fanon, Rene Dumont, Stanislav Andreski, John Saul and Giovanni Arrighi. Writings on African socialism abound, and this is inevitable perhaps given the looseness of the concept, as may be seen by comparing Kenya's White Paper on African Socialism, 1965, Tanzania's Arusha Declaration, 1967, and Uganda's *The Common Man's Charter*, 1969. The last publication, as well as Kaunda's speeches, point to the trend since 1966 of placing greater emphasis on the economic aspects of socialism, including forms of nationalisation.

When we turn to those large areas of the continent where European power is manifest, the literature is surprisingly thin. For South Africa, the most substantial book is still Gwendolen M. Carter, *The Politics of Inequality* (London, 1958), although an analytical study of *The Party System in South Africa* by A. Stadler is now being prepared for publication. See, too, the interesting account by Leo Kuper, *An African Bourgeoisie: Race, Class and Politics in South Africa* (New Haven, 1965), and by Mary Benson, *The African Patriots: the story of the African National Congress of South Africa* (London, 1963). In addition, there is the indispensable annual Survey of Race Relations, compiled by Muriel Horrell, published in Johannesburg by the South African Institute of Race Relations. Shorter studies include Govan Mbeki, *South Africa: The Peasant's Revolt* (Harmondsworth, 1964); L. M. Thompson, *Politics in the Republic of South Africa* (Boston, 1966); Brian Bunting, *The Rise of the South African Reich* (Harmondsworth, 1964); Mary Benson, *South Africa: The Struggle for a Birthright* (Harmondsworth, 1966); and Jordan Ngubane, *An African Explains Apartheid* (London, 1964). Nicholas Mansergh, *South Africa 1906–61: The Price of Magnanimity* (London, 1962) and Shula Marks, *Reluctant Rebellion: the 1906–8 Disturbances in Natal* (Oxford, 1970) are interesting studies in which the present is illuminated by enquiries into the past history of South Africa. An attempt to compare the rival nationalisms of the Republic was made by E. S. Munger, *Afrikaner and African Nationalism* (London, 1967). See, too, W. H. Vatcher, *White Laager: The Rise of Afrikaner Nationalism* (London, 1965) and – for the position of the Transkei and other 'homelands' – Christopher Hill, *Bantustans* (London, 1964) and Gwendolen Carter, Thomas Karis and Newell Stultz, *South Africa's Transkei* (Evanston, 1967). But perhaps the clearest expression of the conflicts in South African society is to be found in the biographies and autobiographies of the political leaders: Sir Keith Hancock, *Smuts: The Sanguine Years, 1870–1919*, vol. I and *Smuts:*

The Fields of Force, 1919–50, vol. II (London, 1962–68); Albert Luthuli, *Let My People Go* (London, 1962); Nelson Mandela, *No Easy Walk to Freedom* (London, 1965); Alexander Hepple, *Verwoerd* (Harmondsworth, 1967), and (an Afrikaner view) J. Botha, *Verwoerd is Dead* (Cape Town, 1967).

For South West Africa, there is Ruth First, *South West Africa* (Harmondsworth, 1963), which contains a useful bibliography.

Surveys of political developments in the former High Commission territories have recently appeared: Richard Stevens, *Lesotho, Botswana and Swaziland* (London, 1967) and Jack Halpern, *South Africa's Hostages* (Harmondsworth, 1965). Country-by-country studies include: E. S. Munger, *Bechuanaland* (London, 1965); J. E. Spence, *Lesotho: The Politics of Dependence* (London, 1968).

The standard book on Malawi, for the present, is John Pike, *Malawi: A Political and Economic History* (London, 1968), although the reader should also consult Lucy Mair's pioneering study, *The Nyasaland Elections of 1961* (London, 1962).

The involved politics of Rhodesia, and of what was once the Central African Federation, have been examined by several writers. But one should begin with Claire Palley's monumental study, *The Constitutional History and Law of Southern Rhodesia, 1888–1965* (Oxford, 1966). In addition, there are studies, differing in outlook and interpretation, which include: Patrick Keatley, *The Politics of Partnership* (Harmondsworth, 1963); James Barber, *Rhodesia: The Road to Rebellion* (London, 1967); David Murray, *The Governmental System in Southern Rhodesia* (Oxford, 1970) is a useful study stressing the conflict of economic interests within local society and something of a corrective therefore to Colin Leys' earlier book *European Politics in Southern Rhodesia* (Oxford, 1959); Kenneth Young, *Rhodesian Independence* (London, 1969); and the special number on Rhodesia of the *Journal of Commonwealth Political Studies* (Leicester: Leicester University Press, July, 1969), vol. 7, no. 2. There are useful autobiographies: Roy Welensky,

Welensky's 4,000 Days (London, 1964); Ndabaningi Sithole, *African Nationalism* (London, 1959); and Lord Alport, *The Sudden Assignment* (London, 1965).

Finally, there are the areas of Portuguese rule, which have yet to be subjected to the detailed enquiries which have sometimes illuminated, sometimes darkened, the rest of the continent. The standard authority is James Duffy, *Portuguese Africa* (Cambridge, Mass., 1959) and *Portugal in Africa* (Harmondsworth, 1962). One should also add *Angola, A Symposium: Views of a Revolt* (London, 1962); J. Marcum, *Angolan Revolution,* vol. I (Madison, Wisconsin, 1969); Basil Davidson, *Liberation of Guinea: Aspects of an African Revolution* (Harmondsworth, 1969); and Eduardo Mondlane, *The Struggle for Mozambique* (Harmondsworth, 1969).

Increasingly – and rightly so – political scientists are now turning for help to other disciplines in trying to reach some understanding of the politics of the African states: to the historian, the social anthropologist, and to economists. But to catalogue even in outline such studies would be to extend this brief bibliography far beyond its present bounds.

Index

Index

Index

'Cold War', the, 24, 146–7
Colombia, 161–2
Common Market, the European, 30–5: and rest of world, 32–3; and United Kingdom, 33–4; economic integration, 31; introductory books, 30–1; political questions, 33; specialised aspects, 31–2
Communism, 15, 72–3, 88–9, 98, 103, 105–11, 118–19, 158, 179, 186, 190–1
Congo, the, 241
Contemporary history: contact with living witnesses, 12; controversies over its writing, 6–7; meaning, 1–2; official material, 6–12; quality, 2–3
Costa Rica, 162–3
Council of Europe, 15, 29
Cuba, 146, 163–6: crisis (1962), 5, 89, 165; Revolution, 146, 164–5
Czechoslovakia, 85, 105–6

Democracy in USA, 45, 50–2
Dominican Republic, 166–7
Dominion home rule, 3

East Germany, 104–5
Eastern Europe, 98–111: general surveys, 99–102
See also under names of individual countries
Economic aid: by Soviet Union, 92; by USA, 15, 26; international, 4
Ecuador, 167
Egypt, 133–5, 244
El Salvador, 163
European Communities, 15, 29–35
See also Common Market
'European Idea', the, 28

Finland, 85
France, 15, 36–8: de Gaulle and the Fifth Republic, 37; general works, 36; surveys, 37–8

Germany, 38–41: Berlin, 40; East-West problems, 39–40; economic revival, 40; foreign policy, 40–1; general surveys and histories, 38; Nuremberg trials, 38–9; post-war military government, 39; relations with Soviet Union, 84–5; zoning, 38, 39
See also East Germany
Ghana, 241, 243–5
Government reports and blue books, 8–10, 16
Great Britain, see United Kingdom
Greece, 41, 111–12
Guatemala, 162, 163
Guyana, 172–3

Haiti, 167
Honduras, 162, 163
Hungary, 108–9

Iceland, 41
India: administration, 119–20; agriculture, 125; anthropology, 126; biographies, 121–2; economy, 122–5; education, 120; foreign policy, 120–1; government and politics, 115–19; independence and transfer of power, 114–15; industrialisation, 124–5; planning, 123–4; population problems, 125; relations with China, 121; relations with Pakistan, 121; relations with Soviet Union, 87; sociology, 125–6; urbanisation, 125
Indochina, 182
Indonesia, 186–90: economic history, 189–90; social history, 188–9

256

Index

Index